Your House, Your Garden

Your House, Your Garden

A Foolproof Approach to Garden Design

Gordon Hayward

ILLUSTRATIONS BY JANET FREDERICKS

WITH PHOTOGRAPHS BY RICHARD FELBER

W. W. NORTON & COMPANY

NEW YORK ■ LONDON

First Edition

For information about permission to reproduce selections from this book,
write to Permissions, W. W. Norton & Company, Inc.,
500 Fifth Avenue, New York, NY 10110

Manufacturing by R.R. Donnelley & Sons
Book design by Susan McClellan
Illustrations by Janet Fredericks
Production manager: Julia Druskin

Jacket photograph of Mary Azarian's
Vermont garden by Richard W. Brown

Library of Congress Cataloging-in-Publication Data

Hayward, Gordon.
Your house, your garden : a foolproof approach to garden design / by
Gordon Hayward ; illustrations by Janet Fredericks.—1st ed.
       p.   cm.
Includes bibliographical references (p.   ) and index.
ISBN 0-393-05770-4 (hardcover)
1. Gardens—Design. 2. Landscape gardening. I. Title.
SB473.H393 2003
712' .6—dc21   2002156442

W. W. Norton & Company, Inc., 500 Fifth Avenue, New York, NY 10110
www.wwnorton.com

W. W. Norton & Company Ltd., Castle House, 75/76 Wells Street, London W1T 3QT

1 2 3 4 5 6 7 8 9 0

CONTENTS

Dedication and Acknowledgments   11
Introduction   13

1.
THE ENTRANCE GARDEN   20
Practical Problems Solved   43

2.
SIDE GARDENS   50
Practical Problems Solved   68

3.
BACK GARDENS, PATIOS, AND TERRACES   74
Practical Problems Solved   93

4.
GARDENS IN AN ELL OR COURTYARD   102
Practical Problems Solved   119

5.
GARDENS BETWEEN BUILDINGS   126
Practical Problems Solved   146

6.
OUTBUILDINGS AND GARDENS   148
Practical Problems Solved   174

Visual Index to the Plans   178
Glossary   184
Selected Bibliography   186
Photography Credits   187
Index   189

1

2

3

4

5

6

DEDICATION AND ACKNOWLEDGMENTS

To my son, Nate, with love

Thanks to John Barstow, editor for this and two previous books; to Tom Cooper and Roger Swain, who have encouraged me to write about garden design these twenty-five years; to Nan Sinton at *Horticulture Magazine*. Thanks also to Sybile Kreutzberger and Pamela Schwerdt for their help on the subject of phototropic instinct in plants.

Many thanks to Ellis Derrig, excavator; Don Precourt, electrician; Raif Southworth of Anderson Excavating; Jon Jesup for assessment of small buildings; Debbie Wood, a field service associate with Green Mountain Power; and Francis Temple, plumber, for all their advice and information regarding all those troublesome problems that gather around utilities.

Also thanks to Allison and Adam Hubbard and Torben Larsen and their crew for all their hard work to see my designs planted in the ground, and to Mary McGrath for her hospitality.

Thank you to the many clients over these past twenty years who have trusted my eye as we developed designs for gardens around their homes, with special thanks to Peter and Theodora Berg, Stan and Cheri Fry, and John and Joyce Phelan.

And finally, thank you, Mary.

INTRODUCTION

YOUR HOUSE IS THE CENTER OF your garden. The moment you fully understand the implications of that statement, designing your garden will become a more manageable and rewarding task. Think of it this way: the doors of your house dictate starting points for paths out into your garden, physically and visually linking the two while launching the design process. Each window is, in varying degrees of importance, a vantage point from which to look into your garden; so those windows help determine the placement of other paths, as well as trees, shrubs, and garden structures such as fences to screen unsightly views.

The idea that your house is the center of your garden is not just an aesthetic notion but a practical tool. The shapes, proportions, and materials of your house give rise to the shapes, lines, proportions, and even materials of your gardens. Those initial design decisions, in concert with design decisions generated by outbuildings and other major elements of framework – stone walls, existing terraces or decks, the driveway, mature trees, even the shape of your property and the relationship of your house to the street – can result in a coherent, overall landscape plan that seamlessly links house to garden. English author Alfred Austin (1835–1913) summarizes the idea this way: "I am quite of the opinion that a garden should look as though it belonged to the house, and the house as though it were conscious of and approved the garden. In passing from one to the other, one should experience no sense of discord, but the sensations produced by the one should be continued, with a delicate difference, by the other."

BUILDINGS INSPIRE GARDEN DESIGN

Susan and Charles Boswell, a young couple with an infant son named Russell, came to me with architectural plans for their new home to be built on a 2-acre level clearing in a 20-acre apple orchard that slopes gently to the south (see figure Int.1). First I helped them site the house on a high but level part of the orchard to take advantage of the views to the east across the Connecticut River Valley and the hills and mountains of New Hampshire in the distance. Because they wanted as much after-noon sun as possible, we decided to locate the house about 200 feet east of a neighbor's mature woodland (and within 50 feet of the top of an east-facing slope) so that they would get direct sunlight through west-facing win-dows until early evening.

Being flat and open, the 2-acre building lot offered little indication as to what shape the garden should take. However, the house and two-car garage wing at a right angle off the north end of the house offered no end of clues. The design process through which I led Susan and Charles followed the sequence of the journey that arriving family and guests would take from driveway and parking area to the front door, through the house, and into the garden.

Once we chose the house site and the ori-entation of the house itself, we decided on the location and configuration of the 200-foot-long driveway. With vinyl landscaping flags, I helped the Boswells design a driveway that curved and flowed with the gentle south-facing slope of the land. I wanted the driveway to wind in and out among groups of apple trees,

THE GARDEN MUST BE STUDIED IN RELATION TO THE HOUSE, AND BOTH IN RELATION TO THE LANDSCAPE.

– EDITH WHARTON (1862–1937), U.S. writer, gardener, and aunt to Beatrix Farrand, eminent American landscape architect

FIGURE INT.1

The process I followed in designing the Boswells' garden is a good model for you to follow:

▓ Assess the house, its layout, location of doors and windows, its materials and proportions.

▓ Assess the existing landscape both near and at a distance from your house.

▓ Develop a list of uses to which you will put your garden – outdoor dining, flower and vegetable beds, sitting and children's play areas – as well as any structures you might want, such as an arbor, gazebo, fencing, or garden shed.

▓ Design the driveway (see figures 1.17, 1.18, and 1.19 for help).

▓ Design the area between parking area and front door, that is, the entrance garden.

▓ Design the side gardens so that they relate to front garden and side doors of the house.

▓ Design the back gardens so that they relate to front and side gardens.

▓ Review all design decisions to be certain all parts are integrated into a whole.

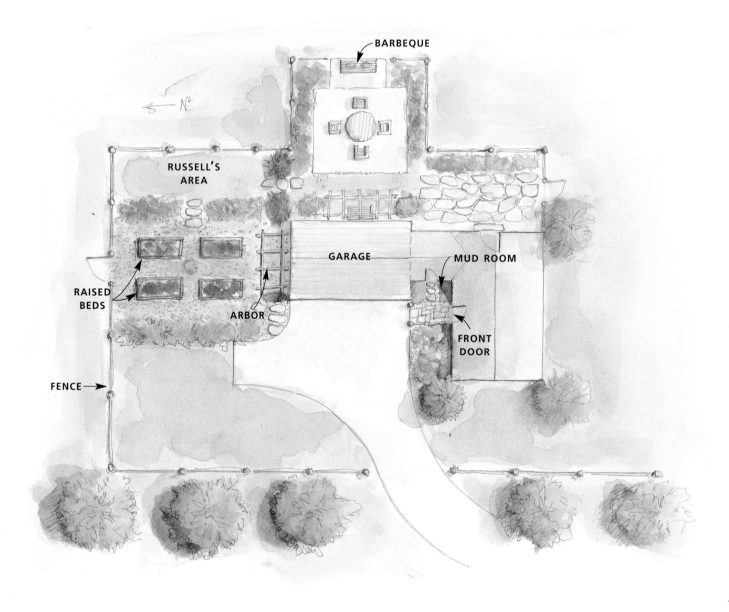

affording only teasing glimpses of the house. Furthermore, those same apple trees helped screen much of the driveway from the south-facing windows in the sitting room and master bedroom. Driveways are rarely attractive. The placement of the west-facing garage, of course, determined for the most part the location of the last 75 feet or so of the driveway, while the size of an automobile influenced the configuration and dimensions of the parking and turn-around areas. What was left between garage and house would become garden.

The next task was to direct guests from that parking area to the front door and not to the nearby mudroom door. I sketched out the generous 6-foot-wide, 15-foot-long primary walkway made of tightly fitting geometric bluestone from driveway edge to the steps up to the front door, framing the beginning of the path with a pair of traditional granite fenceposts set on either side of the path near the drive. I lessened the visual importance of the secondary path that the family would use to the mudroom – a turn to the left halfway down the primary path – by siting small shrubs which would hide most of it from the view of those walking along the main path. To further reduce the temptation to take a left-hand turn to the mudroom, I made that path narrower and used stepping-stones so that it would attract less attention.

Once in the house, guests would need to know how to get out into the garden. The French doors on the east side of the sitting room showed us where to locate stone steps down to a bluestone terrace, around which would be perennial borders. The 18-foot-high east wall adjacent to the proposed bluestone terrace suggested the width of the terrace; the 24-foot-long sitting room suggested its length. To enhance the feeling of enclosure and intimacy when sitting on the terrace,

especially given the expanse of featureless meadow around the house, we fenced in that and adjacent areas. The split two-rail fence, appropriate for this rural setting, went out some 22 feet from one corner of the house, turned north and ran parallel with the east side of the house, and then turned west back toward the far corner of the house. Gates in the fence opened to paths leading to the back of the house, as well as to mowed paths, invitations to explore the meadow.

But where, Susan asked, could we put the vegetable garden? The sunny area at the back of the garage beyond its shadow line seemed perfect; the length of the garage provided the width of the garden. I designed 5-foot-high blueberry bush hedges to screen the view of this practical area of the garden from the parking area and entrance garden. Because they had an infant, I suggested setting a sandbox in the middle of the vegetable garden with raised beds arranged around it. This would enable Susan and Charles to shell peas or shuck corn while Russell played in his sandbox. Once he outgrew the sandbox, it could become another raised bed. But where would they sit to shuck corn? I sketched in an arbor to be situated against the middle of the back, gable end of the garage, under which the Boswells could set a bench and chairs. The position of the arbor, in turn, gave me the idea for a central path leading north down the middle of the vegetable garden.

Charles then made two more requests: a spot for a mortared stone barbecue and nearby picnic table and a play space for his son. We had already designed the area off the north end of the garage, but not the area to its east. That was where we would put the barbecue section; the width of the garage provided us with its width. The area beyond the east hedge of the vegetable garden would become the play space. That's when it hit us: run the split-rail fence all the way along the east side of the house and garage, with a jog out as wide as the garage to provide more room for the barbecue, table and chairs, making certain that all fencing was either parallel or perpendicular to the nearby walls of house and attached garage. The fence would then run 15 feet out from the vegetable garden and then turn west to meet the back end of the 5-foot-high blueberry hedge. That, in turn, gave us the idea to repeat the fence on the other side of the vegetable garden to enclose the entrance to the parking area, thereby making the whole entry experience cozy without the feeling of being too firmly hemmed in with hedges.

That's how easily garden design can develop if you see the house and buildings as the center of your gardens – that is, if you consult the architecture. Follow this fundamental principle that house and garden should form a seamlessly designed whole in which to live, and it will be hard to go wrong.

PRACTICAL SOLUTIONS

I want this book to be a useful source of design ideas *and* a source of practical solutions to problems that crop up for virtually anyone who is creating a garden around a home.

Walk around your house looking closely at every corner, surface, and detail, and you will notice an air-conditioning condenser or heat pump that stands out in stark contrast to the 'Miss Kim' lilac you planted years ago to screen it. The perennial border along the south foundation reaches its conclusion in a collection of wires and meter boxes at the corner of your house. You sit on a bench at the back of the garden, and there stand two upright propane tanks in full view against the house. You walk by the garden along the side of the house to see that, once again, shrubs planted there were crushed by the snow

cascading off your roof last winter. Water is eroding soil along the driplines and under roof valleys.

The solution to these problems is initially one of seeing. We have become so inured to the distractions of power lines and meter boxes, propane tanks, and satellite dishes, mounded leachfields and their vent pipes that we often don't perceive them as visually unpleasant.

Once you do see the problem, you need to find a solution that is not as bad if not worse than the problem itself. Here in the Northeast, for example, thousands of homeowners follow a time-honored fall ritual. They haul 4-to-6-foot-high hinged wooden covers out of storage and set them up over shrubs (often yews and rhododendrons) along the eaves of the house to protect them from snow falling off the roof above. These wooden triangles stand in place for five months, nearly half the year; they are not attractive. The solution to crushed shrubs lies not in wooden triangles but in smarter plant choice or some other creative solution. But such remedies are predicated on information. Before you can solve the problem of screening air-conditioning condensers or the exposed black caps of buried propane tanks, you need to understand how the condenser works and what's under that black cap out in the lawn.

To address both the aesthetic and the practical in this book, then, I have divided each chapter into two parts. The first looks at inspiring design ideas; the second suggests answers to the ubiquitous problems. Be sure to work with the spirit, as well as the facts, of each of my solutions before deciding on your own. If what I offer doesn't quite fit the dilemma you're faced with, work creatively until you find just the right solution. And although this is a garden design book, don't expect all the answers to rely solely on plants;

many problems require architectural solutions. If, in the end, you do decide to solve the problem with plants, make certain that the design of new planting beds and the plants within them relate to existing shrubs and perennials. New beds or plants used for screening need to blend in with the overall design of your existing gardens.

That brings up one final point. Good garden design results when the lines of the house relate to the shapes of adjacent garden beds and lawn – that is, when all parts relate to the whole. As a writer who needed to give structure to this book, I had to separate the main areas of your garden and address each of them as a discrete area: the front, side, and back gardens, as well as gardens in an ell or courtyard, around outbuildings, or between them and the house. As garden designers, however, you and I need to establish the flow – the inevitable relationship and integration – of all six of these areas into one whole garden.

Your House, Your Garden

THE ENTRANCE
GARDEN

THE GARDENS AROUND YOUR FRONT door see you off every morning and welcome you home every evening. If you have children, you walk through your entrance garden time and again throughout the day on your way to this event or that, perhaps weeding as you go. When guests arrive, it's the first garden they see; for them, the garden by the front door is an introduction to you and to your style both in the house and out. As eminent landscape architect Thomas Church (1902–1978) wrote in his book *Gardens Are For People,* "We need to roll out the red carpet for our guests" – and for yourself. Because our back gardens get so much attention, we often take the entrance and front gardens for granted and revert to time-worn foundation plantings and a narrow path through the lawn to the front door. If you take the time to get the entrance garden right, however, you create a lively, engaging experience for you and your guests *and* you link

house to garden, initiate a style, and set a design process in motion that ripples out to all other parts of your design work around your home.

Nancy Waterhouse, a friend who lives here in Vermont, called me several years ago to ask for help in designing an entrance garden in the 50-foot-long area between her driveway and new two-story shingle-style house set at the east edge of a woodland clearing. Because the section from the parking area to the front door sloped down 4 feet, and because the land dipped gently down from her house to the east and rose softly to the west behind her house, it was important to create level areas near the house for entertaining, for gardening, and for play spaces for Nancy's child.

We began the design with a 48-inch-high 20-foot-long stone retaining wall that ran parallel with the north side of the house to create a 40-foot level area between driveway and wall. We used the remaining 10 feet for

steps down to a generous front door landing at the north end of her house (see figure 1.1).

Nancy – an accomplished gardener – and I then designed the garden itself. Because she didn't want to see parked cars from the north-facing second-story windows of her house or from the entrance garden itself, we designed a lilac hedge that would grow 10 to 12 feet high to screen cars and to provide a feeling of enclosure along the north side of the garden. This hedge, in turn, provided a line for the south edge of the parking area. She also didn't want to have a view of parked cars as she opened the front door to leave the house, so I curved the path to prevent a sight line between front door and cars.

With the now level entrance garden defined by a stone wall to the south, a lilac hedge to the north, a woodland to the west, and an access road to the east, and with a broad curving path running through the space, we knew the limits and structure of the entrance garden. Plant choice and layout was next. Nancy is a relaxed, easy-going person

FIGURE 1.1
The style of house and existing natural landscape should inform your design process. Here, an informal entrance garden is appropriate for an informal shingle-style home at a woodland edge in southern Vermont. All are integrated.

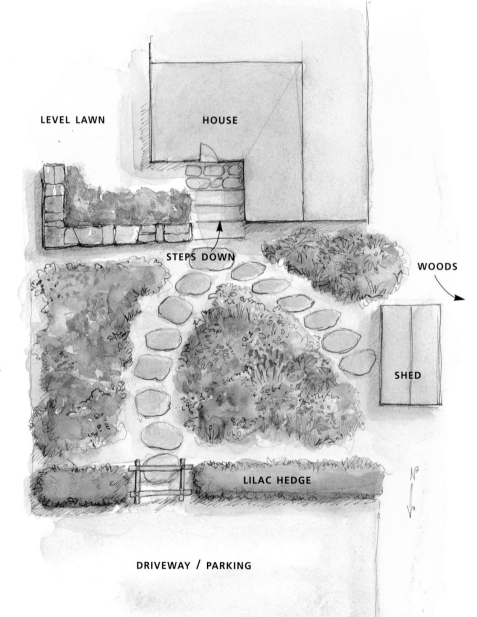

LEVEL LAWN

HOUSE

STEPS DOWN

WOODS

ACCESS ROAD

SHED

LILAC HEDGE

DRIVEWAY / PARKING

PROPORTION: THE MODULE

Proportion also plays an important part in any design decision, so I want to give you a clear example of how house, primary path, lawn, planted beds, and stone walls work together in one particularly fine example from a front garden in a Baltimore suburb I visited a few years ago. While your garden may not require such precision, this example will show you how math can help you establish a terrific garden plan.

Abby Siegel noticed that she needed a 5-foot-high retaining wall 20 feet out and parallel with the entire length of the front of her home to support a parking area, with stone steps at the far end of the wall leading down to her entrance garden. She designed the wall and a 6-foot-high evergreen hedge along the top of it so that cars would not loom above to dominate the view from her front door. She then turned her attention to the 20-foot-wide, 70-foot-long entrance garden. She discovered the portico to the front door came out 5 feet from the front wall of the house. Taking that dimension as a module, she designed 5-foot-wide beds on either side of the portico that ran the full length of the house. She then used that 5-foot module to determine the width of her blue-stone path to the front door, with a 5-foot-wide panel of lawn running between the path and a 5-foot-wide perennial bed planted in front of the 5-foot-high stone retaining wall. What resulted was a series of long, narrow shapes that shared a specific dimension and direction parallel with the façade of the house. All the parts related to the whole; that's the definition of design.

who had designed an informal house; I knew the plant selection and design would reflect her informal and approachable nature. Choosing plants was easy. The farther west we went toward thinned native woodland, the more shade-tolerant the plants became; the farther east and away from the woods, the more sun-tolerant they became. The closer plants got to the path, the lower they got; the farther from the path, the taller they got. And because she lived in her house year-round, we interplanted evergreens, grasses, and deciduous shrubs with interesting bark texture and color for winter interest.

When designing residential gardens, I begin by thinking about the entrance garden. It is in this space where decisions are made about style, materials, and plants not only for the entrance garden but also for the entire property. You want to create a theme, an overall mood and tone, to create a garden. A rose garden here and an island bed there do not a garden make. After all, when you prepare a meal for guests, you don't serve Thai soup for an appetizer followed by a Tuscan fish entrée and rhubarb pie for dessert. You choose a theme: Thai, Tuscan, or New England. Once you make that Big Decision, you know what to cook, in part by knowing what *not* to cook. Look to your house for help in determining this theme.

One of the most helpful passages I have read about the entrance garden is from *A Pattern Language* by Christopher Alexander, a city planner still at work in Berkeley, California. Back in the 1960s, he and his team traveled the world and discovered more than 250 patterns of residential design that hold true across nations, regions, and cultures. Here is what he wrote about the entrance to the home and the garden space around it:

Buildings, and especially houses, with a graceful transition between the street and the inside, are more tranquil than those that open directly off the street. The experience of entering a building influences the way you feel inside the build-

FIGURE 1.2

This entrance garden uses a strong panel of lawn and a broadly curving bluestone path to provide structure for a garden of birches, a dogwood, burgundy-leaved cutleaf maples, and evergreen trees and shrubs. This path, designed by Patrick Chassé, leads to figure 1.3.

ing. If the transition is too abrupt there is no feeling of arrival, and the inside of the building fails to be an inner sanctum. . . . Make a transition space between the street and the front door. Bring a path which connects street and entrance through this transition space, and mark it with a change of light, a change of sound, a change of direction, a change of surface, a change of level, perhaps by gateways which make a change of enclosure, and above all with a change of view.

That is, the FedEx driver can pull into your driveway just as you can because it's a semipublic space. But the surfaces and surroundings of the walk that he, you, and your guests take from the driveway to your front door should change the moment you step from the driveway surface onto the walkway. If the driveway is concrete or asphalt, then the walkway to the front door should shift to blue-

stone, sandstone, or limestone to mark a transition onto a new surface and into a new, more personal space. The very change of material acts as a subconscious indication that purpose, mood, and tone have changed. The beginning of the path from driveway to front door should be a generous 5 or 6 feet wide, with planted containers, lighting, perhaps even a gate or break in a hedge or fence at its beginning. If the land slopes gently up from driveway or sidewalk to front door, define that grade change with steps and level landings wherever possible, for each step is another zone change on the walk from semipublic to private space. Put lots of planted pots on either side of the landings.

Once that path is more personal, see it as the spine of a garden. Plant a pair of flowering trees on either side of the beginning of the path; plant shrubs or perennials along one or both sides so that people walk along or through a garden, not just on a path through lawn. Plants with fragrant leaves or flowers make the walkway feel all the more intimate and separate from the public world of cars and streets. Appeal to as many senses as possible so that your garden engages and draws people in.

As the path approaches the front door, be certain the garden and path are level. This might require a low retaining wall some 15 to 20 feet out from the foundation of the house. A house sitting on a flat plane, an extension of the interior floor, feels more settled than one sitting on ground that slopes down toward the driveway or street. Even if you level the area just by the front door, you resolve the problem. Look closely at figures 1.2 and 1.3; you will see an entrance garden that landscape architect Patrick Chassé designed for clients here in the Northeast. The garden gently rolls up from the driveway and then down; the area around the front door is welcoming, generous, and level. Place a bench near the front door or in its own generous space along the walkway as a visual center and as an invitation to sit for a moment.

Plant a tree in the entrance garden that is appropriate to the scale and style of your home, the branches of which will arch over the entrance landing to provide a welcoming, shady canopy or semitransparent ceiling over the beginning of the path to the front door (see figure 1.4) or over the landing by the front door. A tree that sheds filtered shade onto the ground – a honey locust or birch tree, for example – is the best; research shows that this is the kind of shade people prefer. By underplanting that tree and the space on either side of the entrance landing with flowering and fragrant perennials, shrubs, and groundcovers, you set your front door and related landing into a richly planted, intimate space. Within this entrance garden, set a sculpture or garden ornament that reflects the style of your home and its interior decoration.

Notice that the preceding few paragraphs are filled with prepositions. Satisfying entrance gardens provide lots of prepositions, for in each preposition lies another zone, another experience that subconsciously helps you make the emotional transition from the public highways, roads, and streets to the private inner sanctum of your home.

As guests get OUT of their cars and walk ACROSS the asphalt driveway, they step ONTO a sandstone walkway. There they walk BETWEEN potted plants or THROUGH a gate and UP a step or two and ACROSS a landing UNDER the branches of a tree and AROUND a corner of the path and INTO a garden and AMONG shrubs and perennials. Then they walk UNDER the portico or porch before stepping UP steps and THROUGH your front door INTO your home.

All of the design decisions gathered around each of these prepositions should be made in relation to the style and materials, proportions,

and dimensions of your home. There are as many styles for the entrance garden as there are architectural styles. An entrance garden for a home in the Florida Keys or on any of the Hawaiian Islands, such as the home of Bill Dodge, a floral designer and passionate gardener whose bed-and-breakfast I stayed at on Kauai, might include areca and fan palms underplanted with heleconias, anthuriums, crotons, black-foliage begonias, and mondo grass. At a home near the seashore, such as the Hamptons on Long Island, I have seen an entrance garden planted solely as a bamboo forest or as a cottagey Nantucket dooryard garden of 'New Dawn' roses interplanted with the hybrid musk rose 'Lavender Lassie,' all underplanted with 'Walker's Low' catmint and snapdragons. A formal stuccoed Georgian home on the Eastern Shore of Maryland calls for a symmetrical, restrained alignment of live oaks or sycamores set in lawn, whereas for an entrance garden leading to a shingle-style vacation

FIGURE 1.3
This generous bluestone landing by the front door is the destination for the path in figure 1.2. Birches and pines set the long light-shingled roof into the background. The birch by the front door will become a living roof over the landing. The house and the garden embrace visitors in an intimate space.

DIG SAFE

If you are going to dig into the ground with any piece of heavy equipment, such as a backhoe or excavator, for any major garden project, you run the risk of damaging underground utilities. And the list of utility lines that might be running underground through your property has grown immeasurably during the past two or three decades: fiber-optic or wire cables for electricity, telephone, television, computers, and satellite communications, alarms, and lighting; pipes for potable or reclaimed water, sewer, irrigation, natural gas, oil, or steam. In some new communities, as many as 15 different utility lines might serve a single home.

State statutes require that you, your excavator, or landscaper contact a national organization called Dig Safe at least a week before excavating with heavy equipment on your private property. You can get the appropriate number for your state by looking in the Yellow Pages of your phone book, by going to digsafe.com on the Internet, or, if you have a cellular phone, by calling #344, and you'll automatically be connected to your state Dig Safe center.

This company, supported by the utilities and acting as a liaison between homeowners, contractors, and utility companies, acts at no cost to you or the excavating company working for you. Given that the landscaper or excavating company you hire is more conversant with the nature of the work, the depth to which digging will be necessary, and the equipment required to do the job, it is best to ask them to make the call.

If you fail to call Dig Safe and the work you or your landscaper authorizes results in damaged utility lines or personal injury to the equipment operator, you or your contractor are liable for damages. Go to digsafe.com on the web, and you will be able to read state laws that govern your responsibilities and liabilities.

To give you an indication of the importance of this service, during the primary construction months from March through November, residents or contractors from five New England states (not counting Connecticut) make on average 15,000 requests a week to the regional Dig Safe center to mark out utility lines.

As you learn about the location of existing utility lines or have new ones installed, keep a record of their exact locations with sketches, photographs, or scaled drawings.

home set in Maine woodland, landscape architect Patrick Chassé designed a pine-needle path through birches and boulders, moss and ferns. Notice that none of these recommendations include yews and rhododendrons, junipers and hollies all lined up – and pruned to a fair-thee-well – along the foundation of a house. Foundation planting is not gardening; a landscape made up of paths and sitting areas among trees, shrubs, perennials, annuals in pots, furniture, and garden ornaments is.

THE AMBIGUOUS FRONT DOOR

A classic dilemma that can arise is that guests unfamiliar with your home arrive, park their car, see two or three doors, and not know which to approach. While this might appear to be a small problem, it in fact indicates a flaw in the design of your entrance garden. You are not rolling out Thomas Church's "red carpet" if you don't send clear signals. Guests caught in this confusing situation feel ill at ease as they approach your home, not knowing whether they are about to knock on the kitchen door, the mudroom door, or the front door.

To solve this problem, stand near the parking area in your driveway and size up all the paths leading from that point to the house. Can you see one path going to the kitchen door and another to the front door? Are they made of the same material and of similar width? Are they lit by lampposts or only by

FIGURE 1.4 (OPPOSITE)
This pathway forms a strong line to the front door of the designer's house. The stone wall, gate, and overarching branches of the Japanese maple increase the feeling of leaving the driveway and entering a sunny garden, while the steps, brick landing, and entry porch announce arrival at the front door.
(Designer: Armand Benedek)

wall lights by the front door? Are overgrown shrubs and trees hiding the appropriate front door from view? If by taking a new look at these paths you find you are not providing appropriate signals to your guests, here are a few principles that will help.

First, rank the paths you can see from the driveway in order of importance. The path to the front door is clearly the primary path. Which is secondary? Tertiary? By making the primary path 4 to 6 feet wide out of tightly laid cut stone (or widening the existing path with more of the same material), distinguishing it from other, narrower paths, you confirm for visitors that this is the walkway to the front door. Notice in figure 1.4, for example, how the front door of this suburban Connecticut home is visible from the beginning of the path, whereas the side door is obscured by rhododendrons. Also notice in that same figure how the broad stone path and granite steps meet a

broad brick landing by the front door. There's no mistaking where guests unfamiliar with the house are meant to go.

Next, consider adding further visual weight to the beginning of the primary path by creating a landing that is wider than the path itself. Use both sides of this broad stone or brick area as a surface on which to set beautifully planted pots and perhaps garden ornaments such as a few antique watering cans or an old wheelbarrow. A lamppost or other methods of drawing attention to the beginning of the primary path, such as the rustic arbor and stone landing under it in figure 1.5, also add visual weight. However, don't set any of these decorative elements at the beginning of secondary and tertiary paths; you don't want to draw attention to them.

Once guests are at the beginning of the primary path, it helps if they can see the front door. If the door does not have enough visual punch to be seen from a distance, paint it a different color from that of adjacent walls. Attach a portico over it or a railing to the set of steps that leads up to it. Add a lamppost of the same sort as at the beginning of the path (see figure 1.4), or repeat planted pots along as well as at the end of the primary path. If the landing near the front door is roomy enough, install a bench.

While you might widen the entrance to the primary path, make the beginning of other paths narrower or shift from cut stone to stepping-stones, a less formal material, as Oehme and Van Sweden did (see figure 1.6). Plant shrubs to hide as much of the secondary path's beginning as you can. A gate at the entrance of this path can also act as a subtle visual barrier. Light the secondary paths with low-voltage light fixtures, and don't place any planted pots or garden sculptures along them. In short, up the visual interest of the primary path; lower the visual emphasis on the lower-priority paths.

FIGURE 1.5

The rustic vine-covered arbor and profusion of color, form, and texture gathered around this front door only 20 feet from the arbor turn this narrow space between house and sidewalk into an effusive, relaxed garden. The colors of perennials and pots complement the colors of the house.

THE SMALL ENTRANCE GARDEN

Sometimes your front door is only a few feet from the edge of the driveway. The notion of broad landings, steps, and lots of prepositions just doesn't work or doesn't appear to apply. In fact, many of the same principles I've been discussing do apply; they just have to be applied differently and creatively. Such a garden is like needlework – you have to use every square inch wisely.

First, let's look at the path from the driveway edge to the front door. Make it as broad and generous as you can so that there is room on the stone path and landing by the front door for containers filled with annuals and perennials. This might mean removing some of the driveway or adjacent lawn and paving that new surface with the same stone you have used for the walkway to the front door. If there is a slope away from the front door, perhaps build a low retaining wall to create a more generous stone- or brick-paved landing.

Second, if you can, increase the feeling of enclosure around your entrance garden by installing a hedge or low fence a few feet beyond the side of the path. Then plant perennials, small shrubs, or annuals between fence and path. For example, Judy Davidson, who took a design workshop with me years

FIGURE 1.6
Using grasses, sedums, and stachys, among other plants, landscape architects Oehme and Van Sweden created this bold entrance garden. The path, which echoes the color of the roof and window trim, leads straight to the front door, contrasting with the wildness of the grasses and Russian sage. A fieldstone cross path invites guests to gardens at the front and sides of the house.

FIGURE 1.7

Take advantage of the smallest of spaces by your front door to create a welcoming entrance garden. A bench by the front door implies calm.

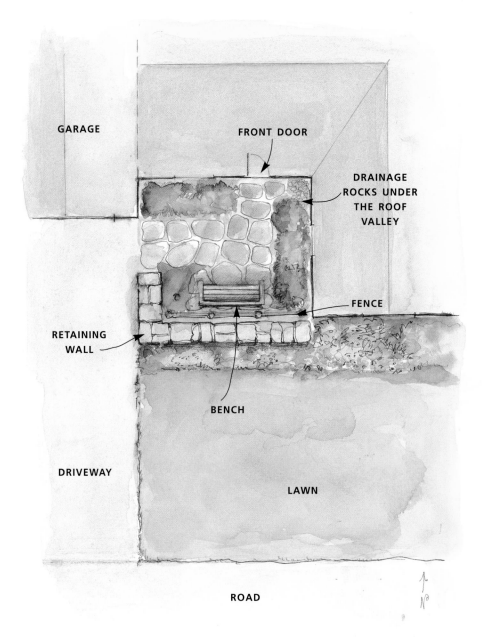

GARAGE

FRONT DOOR

DRAINAGE ROCKS UNDER THE ROOF VALLEY

FENCE

RETAINING WALL

BENCH

DRIVEWAY

LAWN

ROAD

ago, had a space 14 feet long and 16 feet wide for her entrance garden, but only the first 6 feet of it was level. Based on the design she developed in my workshop (see figure 1.7), she hired a dry stone waller to build a 14-foot-long, 18-inch-high retaining wall 2 feet wide, which increased the width of her entrance garden from 4 to 14 feet. She then installed a white picket fence atop the stone wall, paved an area for a teak bench against the fence, and planted perennials and small shrubs on either side of the bench to create an inviting entrance garden in a very small space.

A third alternative is to take advantage of vertical gardening. Install a trellis against a nearby wall or walls of the house or garage, and send flowering vines up that trellising. Plant a small- to medium-size tree near the entrance landing so that you form a semi-transparent ceiling over the entrance walkway.

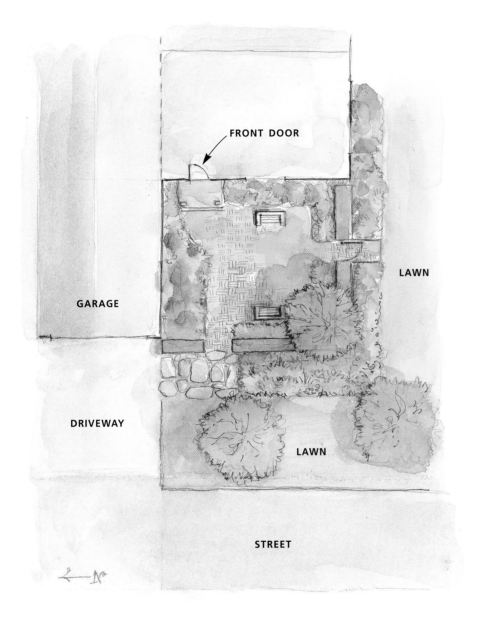

FRONT DOOR

GARAGE

LAWN

DRIVEWAY

LAWN

STREET

FIGURE 1.8
Squaring off the other
two sides of an ell in your
house with a wall, fence,
or hedge helps you design
a welcoming entrance
garden/sitting area.

Even if such a planting requires a jackhammer to remove some of the driveway, do it if at all possible.

Finally, there is one last option: create the entrance garden with built structures. Construct a generous portico or broad, finely crafted arbor over the front door, and then gather planted pots and garden ornaments on the stone-paved area that isn't essential as a walking surface. Send climbing vines up and over the arbor (see figure 1.5), even if only annual vines growing in 24-inch-diameter pots.

THE ENTRANCE GARDEN IN AN ELL

An ell is created when two sides of your house meet at a right angles. There is great potential for creating an enclosed entrance garden in the ell because two of the four sides are

FIGURE 1.9 (OPPOSITE)
In this entrance garden in the
Southwest, a broad path
winds through a garden to
the front door. A concrete
landing, tinted the same
color as the gravel to create a
seamless path, is covered
with a roof, which provides a
shaded gathering space by
the front door. The tree con-
trasts with the stark architecture, setting the house into
rather than on the landscape.

already enclosed, thereby adding great visual
emphasis around the front door.

By fencing or hedging the other two sides
of the space, you create either a rectangle or a
square, depending on where the two outer
corners of your home are positioned. A path
can then run from a gap in that fence or hedge
to your front door. The design for such a garden can be quite manageable for even the
beginning garden designer, because once
hedging or fence is in place, four edges of your
entrance garden are established and a path
runs through it to provide you with design
clues.

For example, let's say a 20-foot-long garage
meets a 20-foot-long wing of a house at right
angles, with the front door of the house being
near the point where the two meet. To create
an entrance garden in this ell, build two brick
walls (or a hedge, a fence, or perennial beds),
each 20 feet long, that start at the outer corner of the wing of the house and the garage
(see figure 1.8). They will meet at right angles,
thereby enclosing an entrance garden 20 feet
on all four sides. Set a delicate wrought-iron
gate in a gap in the wall or fence closest to the
driveway for access, and then create a brick or
cut-stone surface in the center, leaving room
for plantings between that paving and the four
sides of the square. Plant a broad-spreading
tree near the outer corner of the wall or fence,
and set a bench or two chairs and a table
under it. You and your guests will then walk
from the driveway and through an attractive,
expansive yet enclosed garden to the front
door.

When enclosing an ell in this way, look to
the material of your house for clues regarding
how to enclose the other two sides of the ell.
If you have an ell in a small white clapboard
home in New England, enclose the other two
sides with a white picket fence and design a
cottage or dooryard garden with a brick or

stepping-stone path through it to the front
door. Then fill the garden inside and outside
the fence with plants associated with a cottage
garden: delphiniums and hollyhocks, roses
and catmint, mock orange and clematis,
lamb's ears and lady's mantle, peonies and
Siberian iris. If you have a stone house in
Kentucky with an ell, enclose the other two
sides with a 24-inch-high coursed limestone
wall – just like the one out along the road, but
lower. Then plant perennials and low shrubs
on either side of the wall to settle it and your
home into the landscape. For an entrance garden in the Rockies that has split-rail fencing
in view from the front door, enclose the other
two sides of the ell with a split-rail fence, and
plant a garden on both sides. But you can see,
I'm sure, that such cozy gardens could not
compete with two walls of a two- or three-
story house; plant two or three upright trees in
such an entrance garden, underplanted with
low shrubs and perennials.

THE COURTYARD
ENTRANCE GARDEN

One of the most inviting spaces by the front
door is a courtyard formed by two wings
extending out from the main body of the
house. For example, a sitting room wing and a
dining room wing might both extend out the
same or a similar distance from the main part
of the house to form an enclosed three-sided
space, the fourth being open. The potential
for a welcoming entrance garden within such
an already-enclosed space is considerable.

If the three-sided space is sufficiently generous, all you need do is connect the dots to
enclose the entrance garden along its fourth
side. Run a 24-inch-high evergreen hedge, a
stone wall, or a picket fence with a central gate
in it across the fourth side, leaving a generous
gap in line with the front door for the primary
path. If the ground slopes up toward the

house, build steps to provide you with another preposition: UP. Within the courtyard, plant one or two trees appropriate for your climate and the style of your home to provide shade and a semitransparent ceiling for your entrance garden. Position a bench or chairs and perhaps even a little table under the tree. Display sculpture or a garden ornament alongside the path that is in keeping with the artwork and decorating style of the interior. Keep in mind that a lot of windows look out

onto a courtyard. Consider the view from each of them, and from the front door, when designing your garden.

In a garden I consulted on outside Philadelphia, John and Patricia Wells and I developed a design for a courtyard entrance garden. They were collectors of fine modern sculpture, so we designed a bluestone pad among evergreen and deciduous shrubs in the entrance garden for a beautiful abstract bronze, the backdrop for which was the tall

long, flat face to your home, use a concrete-block wall (see figure 1.9) or a picket fence (see figure 1.10) to create a courtyard garden.

A SECRET ENTRANCE GARDEN

Perhaps you want total privacy from the street as well as from neighbors on either side and at the back of your property. However, you aren't sure just how to proceed, or even whether you should totally screen yourself off from your neighbors. Well, plenty of precedents exist for making this supreme gesture in the name of privacy and seclusion, particularly when your home is on a small urban or suburban lot. Utterly surround your home with a garden – no lawn, just garden.

The late James Rose, an influential landscape architect trained at Harvard in the 1930s, wanted total privacy at his home on a corner lot in suburban Ridgewood, New Jersey, a home and garden that is now open to the public for viewing and research. First Rose installed a 6-foot-high Japanese-inspired wooden fence 3 feet in from the sidewalk to the west and north of his home. (The view from the south- and east-facing windows of his home looked into attractive municipal woodland.) He then densely planted the 15-foot space between the street and the front of his home with shrubs and trees on either side of the wooden fence so that his home was completely screened from the street. A solid 7-foot-high gate in a curvilinear path from the sidewalk to the front door further screened a view of the front door from the sidewalk. (See figure 1.11 for a simplified view of this entrance garden on a suburban corner lot.) Because Rose then surrounded his home with trees, shrubs, and perennials (and no lawn), there was no seam, no distinction between his entrance garden and any other part of his garden. His home was literally the center of his

FIGURE 1.10
To enclose the area at your front door, construct a fence that complements the style, color, and materials of your house. Here, a fence runs from the corners of the house and out about twice the height of its front wall. The far gate invites visitors into the side and back gardens.

whitewashed brick wall of their house. When the Wells opened their front door, guests could see one or two other sculptures of a similar style in the entrance foyer. Furthermore, they could look down the length of the front hallway and out glass panels at the back of the hallway to another modern sculpture set in the back garden. At night, these subtly lit sculptures, quietly relating inside to outside, took on an even more important role welcoming guests. No clichés here.

Sometimes you want a courtyard effect for your entrance garden because such an enclosed garden feels so cozy. If you have a garden, and because it was a small suburban lot of less than an acre, he could maintain it.

Willem Wirtz and the late Cy Roossine, garden lighting designers, lived in a densely populated cul-de-sac in Palm Beach years ago when I visited them. I pulled into the parking space on my first visit, and all I saw were trees and shrubs and only the slightest hint of a house within the foliage and a stone path leading to its front door. They had so densely planted the 10-foot gap between their house and the common parking area in the plaza that I barely knew the house was there. When we sat on their front screened porch, only 10 feet from parked cars, we looked into the branching of citrus trees and densely planted understory shrubs; I could hardly make out the outline of parked cars.

Keith Geller, a garden designer in the Pacific Northwest, utterly screened his home from view of his street in suburban Seattle. As I stood on the sidewalk before going up to his home, all I could see was a dense planting of trees, shrubs, and groundcovers on a steeply sloping bank retained by a 4-foot-high concrete retaining wall which every house on that side of the street shared. To reach his house, set some 10 feet above the street and back about 30 feet, I walked up a set of concrete steps, at the top of which I turned right and steps led me up to his front door. His modest home was set within a lot perhaps 75 feet

FIGURE 1.11
By combining screening shrubs along the sidewalk with a wooden fence that meets your municipal code requirements, you can gain total privacy from the street, even if your house is on a corner lot.

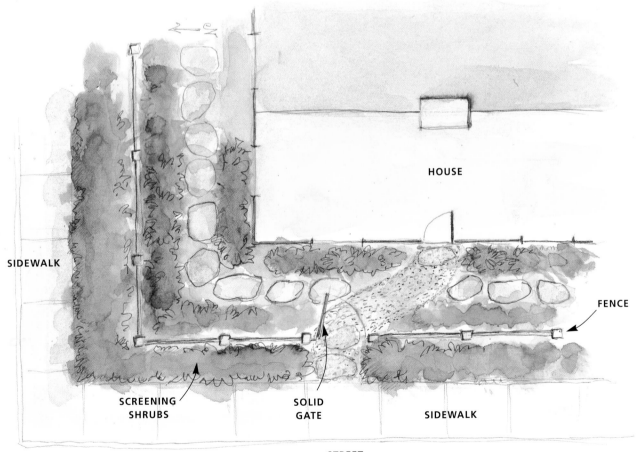

SIDEWALK

HOUSE

FENCE

SCREENING SHRUBS

SOLID GATE

SIDEWALK

STREET

MAKING A SCALED DRAWING

To create a scaled drawing of your home and surrounding lawn, garden, and major trees and shrubs, you will need the following drafting tools:

- Sheets of ¼ inch = 1 foot graph paper, either 18 by 24 inches or 24 by 36 inches
- A triangular scaled ruler that has at least ½, ¼, and ⅛ inch scales
- Erasers and pencils
- Two tape measures at least 100 feet long
- A 24-foot-long metal tape measure
- A roll of 24-inch-wide tracing paper
- 1 roll of masking tape

Begin by measuring and recording the dimensions of all sides of your house, the position of all doors and windows on the first floor, and any existing steps, landings, or porticoes. Then measure out to the sidewalk or street at the front of your home and to the property boundaries if the distances are no more than 100 feet; these measurements will help you see where to locate the house on your drawing.

Start with the scale of ¼ inch = 1 foot. Using your scaled ruler, locate one front corner of your house on the drawing. Do this by measuring from that corner out to the street and then to the boundary closest to that corner, thereby getting two measurements at right angles to one another. Locate that point on the drawing, and then, using your scaled ruler, draw in the outline, or "footprint,"￼ of your house using the light blue grid on the graph paper to help you draw accurate lines.

Having drawn the outline of your house, including all doors and windows, locate any outbuildings on your drawing. The position of the garage, for example, or a garden shed will be easy to locate relative to the walls of the house.

Next, locate all above-ground utilities: propane tanks; satellite dish; placement of spiggots along the foundation of the house; wellheads; telephone poles; and the power meter box affixed to a wall of your home. If you have information regarding all underground utilities – your septic tank and leachfield, cables buried for telephone, electricity or television, as well as buried propane tanks –￼ record them on your drawing.

Once you have included this information, record the location of sidewalk and street, major trees and shrubs, and any existing gardens, patios, and terraces. To locate these and many other elements accurately on your drawing, you'll need to understand triangulation.

Triangulation (SEE FIGURE 1.12)

Having completed the drawing of your house, you'll want to locate key components of your existing landscape on the drawing as well: trees, shrubs, planted beds, the driveway, and so on. The most accurate method is triangulation. It's as simple as can be. Get two tape measures, each at least 100 feet long. Pass a bamboo stake through the hole in the metal clip at the zero

wide and 150 feet deep; the house was virtually surrounded by birches and amelanchier trees underplanted with shade-tolerant woody shrubs and perennials. At the back of his garden, in a pool of light, was a brick sitting area with striking blue-painted chairs and a table. Geller was living in a densely populated suburban community, and yet while I was visiting in his garden and home, I was entirely unaware of other houses no more than 50 feet away.

Notice that each of the examples I cite above are the homes of garden designers, and I could make a list as long as my arm of similar cases if you'd put up with it. But suffice it to say that these are confident people who love plants, love design, and love privacy. You may or may not share their proclivity for separation from the world or have their fortitude to withstand adverse public opinion, but you may well gain confidence by knowing about these examples and thereby decide to increase the level of screening you have already planted so that you can more fully enjoy the privacy you seek.

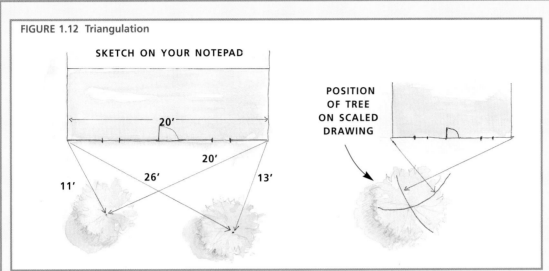

FIGURE 1.12 Triangulation

SKETCH ON YOUR NOTEPAD

20'

20'

26'

11'

13'

POSITION
OF TREE
ON SCALED
DRAWING

end of the tape, and push the stake into the ground at one corner of your house. Then pin the zero end of the second tape at another corner of your house. With tape one, walk to the base of a tree you want to locate on your drawing, pull the tape tight, and record that measurement. Then, using the other tape, measure from the other corner of the house to the base of the same tree and record that measurement. What results is a triangle: the side of your house and the two lines from its two corners to the tree.

Now go to your scaled drawing with a compass. Set the metal point at zero on the scaled ruler, and then pull the pencil end of the compass out until you get to the exact number of feet, at ¼ inch = 1 foot. Set the metal point at the appropriate corner of your house on the drawing and draw an arc to record that distance on your scaled drawing; do the same for the second measurement, and draw that arc. The intersection of those two arcs is the point where that tree is on your scaled drawing.

Tape the completed scaled drawing to a tabletop, and tape a piece of tracing paper over it. You can then begin to sketch out a rough draft of a garden design on that sheet of trace. If you want to try a second design, take up the first piece of trace and lay down a second, and so on.

BETWEEN THE HOUSE AND THE STREET

While it is certainly true that many garden designers completely screen off their home from view, not everyone is a professional designer; nor does everyone want such absolute privacy. Well, there is a middle ground. By designing a low fence, hedge, or mixed planting out by the street, you gain a modicum of privacy in your front garden without appearing to be exclusionary. Here's an example of what I mean.

Amanda and Fred Quinn, who live on a side street in a Boston suburb, asked me to help them design their front gardens. Their long, low house had detailing reminiscent of a cottage. Along the base of the house ran the prerequisite foundation planting within a squiggly, curvy bed, a line that bore no relationship to the house itself. Level lawn stretched from that wavy edge out to a broad curve in the street between 50 and 75 feet away. The first decision we made was to design a 4-foot-high white picket fence to

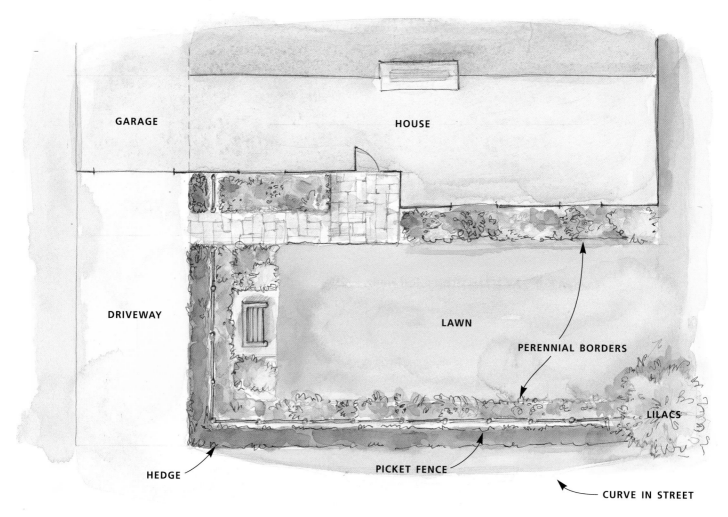

GARAGE

HOUSE

DRIVEWAY

LAWN

PERENNIAL BORDERS

LILACS

HEDGE

PICKET FENCE

CURVE IN STREET

FIGURE 1.13

When installing hedges, fencing, or beds between house and street, follow the lines of the house, not the street, to ensure a visual relationship between house and garden.

separate the front lawn from cars driving by on the street, aligning the fence with the façade of the house, not the street.

There is a big difference between the two. If you align a fence with the curve of the street, you create an amorphously shaped lawn between fence and house that bears no visual relationship to the house or to any beds along it. To establish that relationship, line up the fence with the house and you end up with a long, rectangular lawn between fence and foundation. Then design beds along the house and fence, and the lawn between those beds becomes not a squiggly, meaningless shape but a firm rectangle that draws all parts into a whole. Follow that principle, and all the beds

along the inside of the fence and along the façade of the house will necessarily be in line with one another. The line of your house, not the curve of the street, dictates the lines of your gardens. Coherence results.

Now here's an example of how to break up a foundation planting, because that's just what we did next at the Quinns' (see figure 1.13). Once we located the fence a uniform 45 feet from the front of the house, we decided to use some of the foundation plantings in the beds out by the fence. We transplanted lilacs that had been in full shade by the house and grouped five of them around the far end of the picket fence to give logic to why the fence ended there. We dug up shaded and struggling rosebushes and set them against some of the fenceposts in compost-enriched soil and full sun. We took several junipers battered by snow coming off the roof and put them on the burn pile. We left those perennials and shrubs that were flourishing in the shady foundation planting where they were: *Pieris japonica* 'Brower's Beauty,' hostas, ferns, and epimediums. Then we added shade-tolerant perennials and shrubs to make a lively, colorful garden, not static foundation planting.

We also straightened out the line of the garden by the house so that it ran parallel with the building but 5 feet out from it; in that way, the line where planting bed met lawn related to the line of the front of the house. We then designed a uniform 4-foot-wide bed on the inside of the 4-foot-high picket fence, thereby leaving a rectangular panel of lawn 36 feet wide between the two gardens, as shown in figure 1.13. This was the one flat lawn on the property that the children could use for their games, and it was an area protected from the street by a picket fence that doubled as the backdrop for a mixed perennial and shrub border.

You could use any number of less assertive ways to separate the front of the house from a suburban street with sidewalk, thereby creating a more intimate context for your entrance garden. Plant a row of crab apples or other small trees parallel with the front of your home but out by the sidewalk. Rather than let lawn flow right out to the edge of the sidewalk, plant a 5-foot-wide border of perennials and shrubs that follows the inner edge of the sidewalk – if it runs parallel with the front of the house. Plant an evergreen or deciduous hedge a few feet in from the sidewalk, and then plant a perennial bed along the inside of the hedge so that it can be seen from your entrance garden. Any of these approaches, and countless variations on their themes, will provide you with a feeling of separation between the front of your house and the traffic, and you just might find yourself sitting in or playing with your children in your front garden.

FOUNDATION PLANTING

Foundation planting is a style borne of thinking literally from another century. When the renowned Olmsted Brothers designed a suburban community outside of Chicago in the late 1800s, they installed at least 30 feet of lawn that swept up from the sidewalk to 3-to-5-foot-wide plantings of rhododendrons, yews, holly, and euonymus located against the high front and side foundations of tall Victorian homes. The Olmsteds wanted to create open and democratic front yards, as opposed to the English and European model of the hedged, and therefore more private and supposedly elite, front garden. Well-known American garden writer Frank Waugh took up their banner and popularized the idea in his 1927 publication *Foundation Planting*. We Americans have held tenaciously to his idea ever since.

However, so much has changed in the past hundred years. In the late 1800s, we thought we had just tamed nature and saw ourselves as holding dominion over it; today, we see nature as endangered, in part because of our own actions. More than ever before, we look to natural ecosystems as models for our gardens, and we plant native plants out of deference to the natural world. We have become confident gardeners, and gardening a form of self-expression. More people are now building smaller houses on smaller plots on lower foundations in a variety of styles. A vast range of plants and design ideas are available today, so it no longer makes sense to surround our homes with such a limited range of plants used in such a limited way. Foundation planting has become a safe cliché; it's time to move on.

ACROSS THE FRONT OF THE HOUSE

Now that we've examined entrance gardens as well as the space between the house and the street, let's stand back and look at how to relate these garden areas to your overall garden design.

While designing your entrance garden with its broad primary path, you also need to be thinking about how you can encourage guests to walk from the entrance garden on a narrower secondary path through other front gardens and on into gardens down one or both sides of your home.

Somewhere along your primary path from the driveway to the front door, design a secondary path that will read as an invitation to go across or through the gardens along the front of your home and then turn to show the way down the length of a side garden.

Here's an example of just such a path system around a house I saw in the Garden District of New Orleans (see figure 1.14). To get from the sidewalk to the front door, guests open a wrought-iron gate set in a wrought-iron fence that runs along the 120-foot front of the property, behind which is a tall shrub border separating sidewalk from

FIGURE 1.14
Paths help link front and side gardens; fences and beds enclose those gardens and reinforce the lines of the paths.

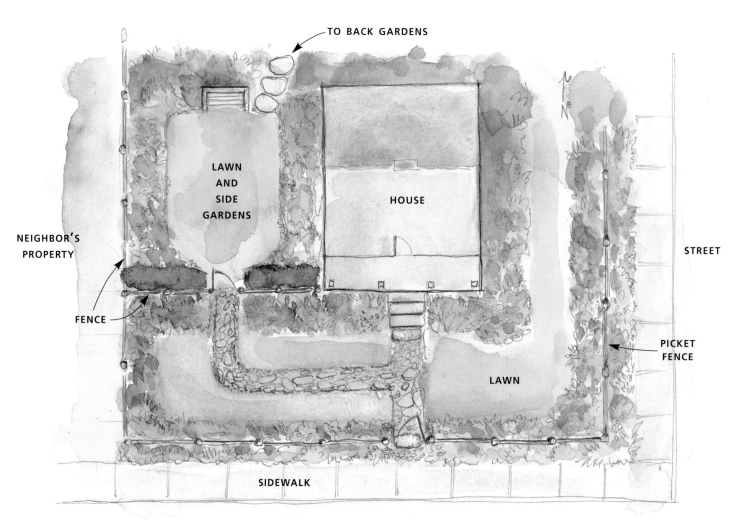

SURROUND YOUR HOUSE WITH A GARDEN

If you live on a small enough property – or you're prepared to put up with "romantic maintenance," wherein you can live with a few weeds and a less-than-manicured garden – consider taking up all your lawn. Utterly surround your house with plants and a sitting area or two so that your home is literally the center of your garden. Paths can then wind and sweep from the doors of your house and through the garden. With wise planting decisions, you can create a garden that need not be high-maintenance yet can bring you extraordinary pleasure.

Diana Guyer did just that around her home up on a ridge from which she looks down on South Kona and the Honaunau Bay on Big Island, Hawaii. When we visited Diana one recent winter, we looked out from a variety of rooms in her open-air home onto a magnificent view through the branches of grapefruit, lemon, lime, and tangelo trees, through the trunks of palms and white sapotes, mountain apple trees, papaya, banana, and breadfruit trees, many of which are underplanted with shade-tolerant coffee shrubs. Sitting areas were paved with stone or crushed gravel, and tropical plants big and small came right up to the edges. Paths wound and swept through all these gardens to link house to sitting areas overlooking a view of the Pacific Ocean that defined the curvature of the Earth.

Beatrice Bowles has surrounded her home overlooking San Francisco and the bay beyond with a series of sloping and terraced gardens of ceonothus and manzanita, fragrant rhododendrons, jasmine, camellias, tree ferns, lavenders, and climbing banksia roses, to name just a few of her plants. Level sitting areas, one directly off the back of her sitting room and a second sitting area higher up, provided me with panoramas I could hardly believe. Both straight and curvilinear paths connect house to garden and sitting areas in the most natural and beguiling way.

You may not have views like these, but if you have a small property, take up all the lawn and surround your entire home with a low-maintenance garden. Your life will change.

private front garden. Guests walk the 30-foot-long, 5-foot-wide primary path straight to steps up to the front porch and front door. But just before getting to the bottom step, they see to their left tightly abutted 3-foot squares of cut stone that run through lawn and then turn right to lead to a second wrought-iron gate in a second shrub border. When visitors open the gate, other 3-by-3-foot pieces of cut stone set in lawn show them the way through gardens along the side of the house. The bluestone path continues to the back corner of the house, where it leads to a bench and a path into the back gardens.

While you will certainly have to modify this idea to make it fit your own garden and house, the central point is the same. It is paths that will help you join your front to side to back gardens – the hipbone's connected to the thighbone. . . . Before you know it, you'll have a unified overall plan for all the gardens around your entire house, and it is the path system that will be able to co-opt any outbuildings and structures into the overall plan as well.

Now, having said all that about the front garden, let me add one more note: some houses are so beautiful, so elegant in their lines and proportions, materials, and architecture, that you should plant nothing but a lovely tree off each front corner and leave it at that. Visit Old Deerfield, Massachusetts, and you'll see what I mean. Sometimes less is more.

THE LINK BETWEEN ENTRANCE GARDEN AND SIDE GARDEN

The broad entrance path leads guests to the front door; while stepping-stones invite visitors to the brick dining terrace. The open gate in the fence, in combination with furniture and umbrellas set in a third garden, is another invitation. Plant a privacy hedge or a shrub border along the street, and you could create private sitting areas at the front of your house too. (FIGURE 1.15)

PRACTICAL PROBLEMS SOLVED

1

POWER CABLES AND ELECTRICAL METER BOXES

If you ever plan to plant trees or large shrubs, it is essential that you know where your power cables are situated below ground or overhead. If your main electrical cable is buried, it will be 12 inches or deeper than frost can reach in a cold winter. Here in the Northeast, that means that power lines are set 48 to 60 inches below ground level; in Kentucky, those lines are buried 24 to 36 inches deep. Check with the field service representative of your power company to find out what the standard burial depth is in your area. Cables typically run in a straight line from the last

utility pole to your meter socket, but that's not always the case. Never plant trees or large shrubs anywhere near buried cable without calling Dig Safe.

Suspended telephone and communication cables are typically 15 feet above your garden; electrical cables are uppermost on a utility pole and are usually 30 feet or so above ground. If either type passes over a driveway, it is usually suspended 18 feet above grade. Before planting any trees that will eventually reach into those lines, look up. Be certain that the branches of the tree when mature will not come within 10 feet of those power lines. If they do, the power company will have no mercy. I watched in dismay one day as a chainsaw-wielding crew hired by the power company cut off half of a crab apple tree in a neighbor's front garden because the tips of its branches were just about to touch

overhead cables. They may as well have cut the tree down, it was so badly misshapen when they were finished with it.

Power lines lead from a utility pole to a meter socket affixed to the side of your house or garage and then on to a breaker panel usually in your basement. A meter socket is a gray metal box roughly 8 inches wide and 12 inches high and is typically screwed to the side of your house 5 feet 6 inches above ground. Set into the center of this small box is a 6-inch-diameter clear glass or plastic cover through which a meter reader, six times a year, can see to record usage. Many homes, particularly those with rental space in them, might have more than one meter. I have seen as many as five of them glommed on to the side of a house; even one is a discordant note in a refined garden.

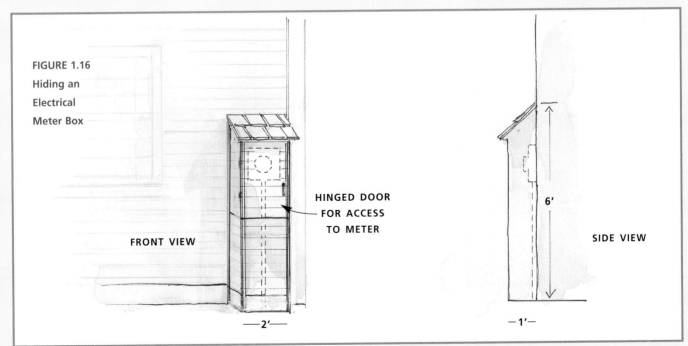

FIGURE 1.16
Hiding an
Electrical
Meter Box

HINGED DOOR
FOR ACCESS
TO METER

FRONT VIEW

—2'—

6'

SIDE VIEW

—1'—

Meter readers and power company employees who service these meter sockets need 3 feet of clearance on all sides. Given those limits, proceed with any screening you would like. Upright evergreens such as *Thuja occidentalis* 'Smaragd,' tall, narrow shrubs such as *Viburnum dentatum* or lilacs, or any number of columnar shrubs will do the job.

But if planting within 3 feet of a meter socket is not feasible or desirable, you can enclose these meters within a small wooden structure which has a door that will provide access to the meter and cable. Build the structure to match the style and materials of your home, as we did. We have a gray-painted clapboard home with white trim and a gray roof. We hired a carpenter to build a 6-foot-high, 2-foot-wide, 1-foot-deep clapboard cover, the front of which is

hinged for access to the meter and cable. He also put a little sloping roof atop the structure and covered it with gray shingles (see figure 1.16).

But there is an even more satisfying, albeit more costly, solution. Many power companies across North America will allow you to build what they call a meter pedestal well away from your home (see figure 1.17). You can set two 4-by-4-inch posts in the ground so that 6 feet or thereabouts is above ground. Bolt a 3-by-4-foot piece of exterior plywood to those posts, and then your electrician affixes the meter socket to the plywood. As long as this meter pedestal is 10 feet from the utility pole and you are prepared to bury the power and phone cable from it to your home, you can avoid having any meter sockets on your home. This meter pedestal can be enclosed within a small

wooden building or painted forest green and screened from sight with shrubs and trees so long as it is readily accessible by a meter reader from your driveway. A client who was renovating an 18th-century home in New Hampshire constructed a meter pedestal and then built an outhouse out of old materials around the meter pedestal; its door had a quarter moon cut into it. Check with your power company to see whether they will allow you to construct a meter pedestal.

Finally, if you are in the design phase of home construction, check with your power company to see whether they are ready to install new meterless technology. In the future, power companies will be removing meter sockets and replacing them with wireless sensors that will enable meter readers to simply drive by your home; receivers mounted

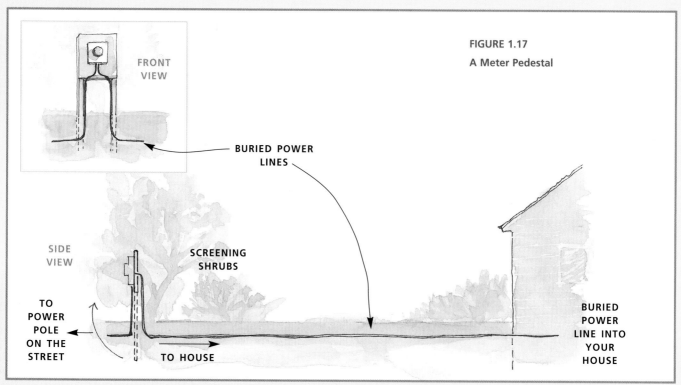

FIGURE 1.17

A Meter Pedestal

FRONT VIEW

BURIED POWER LINES

SIDE VIEW

SCREENING SHRUBS

TO POWER POLE ON THE STREET

TO HOUSE

BURIED POWER LINE INTO YOUR HOUSE

in their vans will take power-usage readings automatically.

The Main Points

■ Look over the meter sockets on your home to see whether they are indeed unattractive and need screening or covering.

■ If you want to screen the meter from view, consider building an architecturally sympathetic box over it, with a door for access.

■ If the built solution doesn't work, consider upright evergreen or dense deciduous shrubs and plant them far enough from the wall of your house so that they won't hold undue moisture against it.

■ Consider removing the meter from your home and installing a meter pedestal at a distance from the house and then burying the lines between it and the house.

■ Consider moving your meter or meters from the house to an out-of-the-way location on the garage or another outbuilding, particularly if you're in the design or construction phase of your home.

■ If you are in the design or construction phase of home construction, check with your power company regarding meterless technology.

2

UTILITY POLES AND THEIR GUY WIRES

Utility poles and the wires they support are one of those necessary but unattractive parts of the modern world we gardeners struggle with.

We're trying to create beauty, yet that 40-foot-high pole with wires and crossbars is in full view from the front door. Just visit Colonial Williamsburg or Amish and Mennonite country in Pennsylvania or Ohio, and you'll see how beautiful our landscape can be without electrical and phone wires draped from utility poles.

Of course, if you are prepared to pay for the service, the power company will remove the pole and bury the lines to your home, but that could cost about the same as a new car. A less expensive but still costly alternative would be to have the pole moved to a less conspicuous spot.

Because utility poles, guy wires, and the protective yellow plastic sleeves covering the base of those guy wires are the property of the utility company, you cannot paint the sleeve; nor can you plant vines to grow up the sleeves and onto guy wires or poles. The only thing you can do to screen the base of the guy wire is to plant shrubs that will mature quickly to heights between 10 and 18 feet high. To screen a 40-foot-high pole, you will need to plant fastigiate trees 20 to 30 feet from the pole, or broadly spreading trees at least 50 feet away. Evergreen trees will clearly do the best job all year-round. The key to selecting the place to plant the tree is to determine the line between the pole and the most important vantage point or points from which you see the pole.

This view might be from the front door, the main window of the sitting room, a bedroom window, or an important terrace or bench in the garden. Stand at that point while a second person takes a tape measure and extends it or a pole above ground level between 10 and 12 feet, that is, the height of a typical 2-to-3-inch-caliper deciduous tree. Try out a variety of spots to find just the right location where that tree will screen as much of the utility pole and wires as possible from as many vantage points as possible and still not be too close to the house or gardens.

The closer you plant a tree to the vantage point, the taller it will appear and the more screening it will accomplish. One very practical way to determine where a tree might be planted is to go into woodland and cut down a 12-to-14-foot sapling, roughly the height of a tree you could afford to plant. While someone holds that sapling upright on the ground at various places, you go from vantage point to vantage point to see what effect the sapling is having on your view of the pole. You might find that if you have three important vantage points, planting one tree close to the main vantage point will solve the problem there. A second tree in the mid-distance could help with screening from a second vantage point, while a third tree way out by the pole and situated in line with the third vantage point will accomplish the task.

Proceed with caution if you are cutting down trees or tall shrubs that are anywhere near a telephone pole. As you prune the lower branches out of trees or lop off the tall branches of a shrub, constantly look into the background to be certain you are not exposing an unsightly view of a pole and all its wires when looking from important vantage points in your garden.

The Main Points

- If a utility pole is sufficiently ugly, call the power company and ask for estimates to remove the pole and bury the lines to your home.
- If removal is not possible, consider using a meter pedestal that will enable you to avoid the full cost of removing a pole and burying all the lines from it to your house.
- If both approaches fail, choose the main vantage points from which to screen a utility pole.
- Plant upright shrubs in the foreground in line with your main vantage points, and you may be able to avoid having to plant large-caliper trees out by the pole.
- Select fastigiate, deciduous, and evergreen trees if you have to screen a utility pole near the pole itself.
- Plant fast-growing fastigiate shrubs near the base of the guy wire and yellow sleeve to at least hide them.

3

GLARING FLOODLIGHTS

Contractors building new homes often install floodlights under the eaves, either at the peak of the garage roof or at the peak of the gable end near the front and back doors. They aim the 150-to-300-watt floodlights down onto the driveway, the front walkway, the area between garage and side door, or directly onto back sitting areas. These lights certainly do a job, but all cause considerable glare and discomfort. Good lighting is achieved by having more fixtures with light of lower intensity close to the area of activity.

Before installing more light fixtures, however, there is one very simple solution that might solve the problem of glaring outdoor light.

If you have large deciduous trees near any of your floodlights, climb a ladder in early evening to loosen the wing nut that holds your individual light fixtures in place. Aim the floodlight up rather than down so that nearby trees are illuminated; then resecure the wing nut. Go back out once darkness has fallen, and I think you'll be surprised at how much light bounces off the leaves of deciduous trees to provide sufficient indirect light at ground level. By aiming one, two, or even all of your existing floodlights up into trees, rather than down into the eyes of family and visitors, you also create a more inviting atmosphere in your garden at night and you won't compromise any motion-sensing switches that you installed for security reasons. If this simple solution doesn't provide enough light, especially during the winter months when leaves have fallen, then you will need to consider installing additional lighting fixtures that may or may not use floodlights.

Lampposts, especially if set within low shrubs and perennials, are useful and attractive at the beginning of the path from the parking area to the front door or around the perimeter of a stone terrace or patio. When choosing lamp fixtures, repeat the style of existing exterior lighting fixtures throughout so that there is a unified style.

Light fixtures attached with U-bolts to metal stakes pounded 2 to 3 feet into the ground can also be aimed upward into shrubs or trees. Such stakes and fixtures can be hidden within a garden

along the front of your house to illuminate the back of the trunk of a tree and its inner branching along the walkway to the front door. Fixtures can also be affixed high in a tree, with light shining down onto the garden, thereby illuminating any entrance walkway. Farther out into the garden, affix downlights where the crosspieces of a pergola or arbor meet the uprights or where downlights could be located at the eave end of the garden shed or small outbuilding.

Nearer the house itself, add wall sconces directly onto the wall of your home. These are often sufficient to illuminate the area around the front door, a small back terrace, deck, patio, or balcony, especially if they are supplemented with candles set into glass sleeves.

Finally, don't rely on light fixtures connected to motion-sensing detectors to scare off deer. Deer are very adaptable creatures. While the surprise of lights suddenly switching on at two in the morning might frighten them off the first two or three times, they will soon adapt and find your hostas and yews just as tasty as they always did – and they'll be able to see them more clearly.

By using a number of smaller sources of light rather than two or three glaring floodlights, you also reduce light pollution. In ever more densely populated communities, neighbors don't necessarily appreciate being surrounded by bright lights at night. If you up the number of fixtures and reduce the bulb wattage for each bulb you use, your garden at night will be more inviting, without compromising security.

The Main Points

- High-wattage bulbs on house and

garage may be aimed down into your eyes; aim them upward into deciduous trees to see whether you still have sufficient light with no glare.

- If not, leave the lights pointed up, and add smaller lights closer to places where they are needed.
- Light the main path to the front door with lampposts, with uplights behind the tree trunks of deciduous trees, with downlights high in deciduous trees, and with exterior wall sconces on either side of the front door.
- Lights on motion-sensing switches will not deter deer.
- Light sitting areas with uplights at the base of trees, with downlights high up in trees, and with candles on the table.
- Don't flood intimate sitting areas with glaring spot or floodlights.

4

CARS, DRIVEWAYS, AND PARKING

Cars take up a lot of room. The standard 12-foot-wide driveway has to be 50 to 60 feet long if you want even one turnaround/parking space in it; a two-car garage has to be at least 24 feet by 24 feet. That's 1,500 square feet of space, just a few hundred square feet less than the average house we build for our families.

Furthermore, cars demand a lot of visual space. Look out virtually any window of your home or from many places in your garden, and you'll probably see a car somewhere. Automobiles are typically 6 to 7 feet wide and 14 to 18 feet long, and many are approaching 6 feet

in height. Most are brightly painted with gloss finishes and large amounts of window and chrome, all of which reflect light. And the remarkable thing is that we don't even see these mammoth things. We are inured to their presence.

We gardeners can do some very simple things about the visual pollution of the car. Here's the simplest. If you have a garage, park your car in it. Get the rubbish cans and recycling bins out of the garage and into a hinged-top hutch you build along the side of the garage. Hang up the hoses now scattered all over the floor. Build an attractive addition onto your garage or a modest outbuilding at a distance from your garage for the lawn mower, wheelbarrows, the chipper or rototiller, outdoor furniture, and garden tools now filling up half the

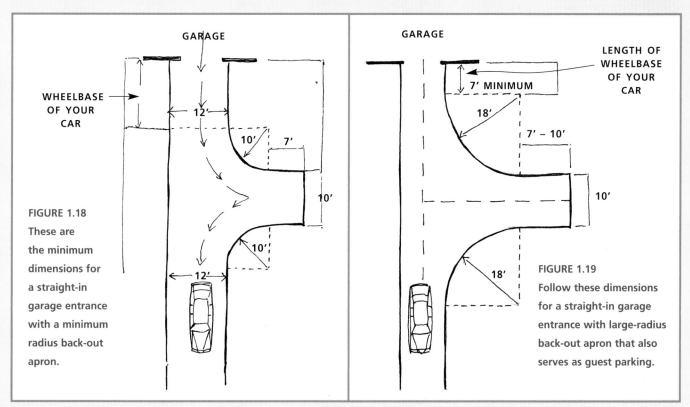

FIGURE 1.18 These are the minimum dimensions for a straight-in garage entrance with a minimum radius back-out apron.

FIGURE 1.19 Follow these dimensions for a straight-in garage entrance with large-radius back-out apron that also serves as guest parking.

garage space. That is, take a fresh look at how you are using that valuable space in your garage, make the obvious changes, and then you can get your car where it belongs – in your garage, protected and out of sight of your home and garden.

Also reassess your driveway. Can you easily and safely back out of your garage, get turned around with comfortable, simple maneuvers, and drive out onto your street or road with good visibility? Is there enough parking space for the growing number of cars in your family? If not, are there alternative parking areas not too far from the house – a meadow, a bit of woodland, or extra lawn – that could be easily turned into a parking space for one or two cars, thereby keeping them off the main driveway? Is there, in fact, far too much space given over to the driveway? Could it be redesigned so as to reduce the square footage for cars and increase the square footage for gardens?

The next thing you can do is take a look at the driveway, the parking area, and the entrance of your garage from various important vantage points, especially the front door, to determine where shrubs could be planted or fencing installed for maximum screening effect. Stand by your front door to see how much of the driveway and how many parked cars you can see. Then consider how you could plant shrubs and tall perennials along part of the driveway edge to create a semi-transparent or solid screen that would block your view of parked cars yet still allow guests unfamiliar with your home a view of the front door as they drive up your driveway.

Also look down the length of the space between your house and garage or other nearby outbuildings. Oftentimes, these two buildings frame a view of a parked car. Consider installing a 6-foot-high fence with a solid door in it that closes off the gap between the front corner of the garage and house, thereby becoming a garden entrance. Or consider building a more open pergola, with uprights and crosspieces between the side door of your garage and house which can support flowering vines that act as a semitransparent screen and a welcoming entrance to the two buildings and the garden between them.

Now go to important sitting areas in your garden: a bench, gazebo or grape arbor, a terrace, deck or patio. Sit in every chair and on every bench in your garden, and look in all directions to see whether you can see a car in the driveway. If you can, think out how shrubs, hedges, or tall perennials such as ornamental grasses could be planted to block the view of automobiles from those important sitting areas. To totally block your view of all cars from all corners of your garden is a tall order, but even if you are able to block views from important vantage points, you are making your garden feel more private and beautiful.

The Main Points
- If you're using your garage to store things and parking your car in the driveway, move the things out and your car in.
- Check to see whether, from the front door and main windows, you can see most of the driveway and cars parked on it.
- Now check to see whether you can see parked cars from other areas of your garden.
- If there is an inordinate amount of driveway, consider removing the unused or unnecessary portions.
- Consider fencing, hedges, or dense plantings of shrubs within garden beds to screen out cars and the driveway from important vantage points.

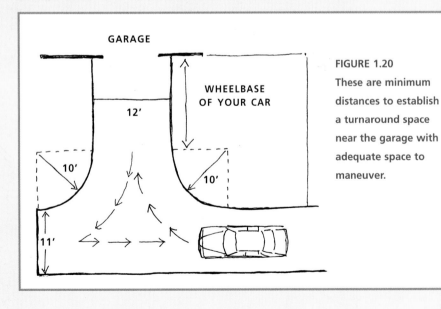

GARAGE

WHEELBASE OF YOUR CAR

12'

10'

10'

11'

FIGURE 1.20
These are minimum distances to establish a turnaround space near the garage with adequate space to maneuver.

FIGURE 1.21 Cobbles laid on the diagonal, in combination with fencing, define this lively garden between parking area and house. This idea would not work where driveways have to be snowplowed.

CHAPTER TWO

SIDE GARDENS

AN ASYMMETRIC

PLAN NOT

ONLY PLEASES

THE EYE BUT

CREATES A NEW

DIMENSION FOR

THE HOUSE.

– THOMAS CHURCH
(1902–1978),
California-based
landscape architect

WHEN LECTURING IN DETROIT years ago about gardening around the house, I asked the audience to picture the gardens along the sides of their homes. I heard someone mutter to her friend: "Oh no! That's where my canoe is, all covered with pine needles." We Americans aren't paying attention to gardens along the sides of our homes. We garden at the front and back; the hallway through the house is the most attractive path between them.

Before you can create engaging side gardens, it helps to understand how they differ from front and back gardens. One primary difference is your awareness of the house itself. As you walk from the parking area toward the front of your house, you see its welcoming face through the branching of deciduous and flowering trees – or at least, you should. With trees between driveway and house, your home feels settled within the landscape; branches reach down toward you,

creating a comfortable volume of human scale to walk through so that the face of the house isn't looming overhead. The portico or porch around the front door provides another sheltering roof over your head. Because guests unfamiliar with your home walk along a pathway from driveway to front door, they have time to appreciate its nature and dimensions. They can also see the destination of that walkway – the front door – so there's a comforting beginning, middle, and end to their journey.

Everything is different along the sides of your house. Walk around the corner, and there is its full length receding off into the distance, with a few shrubs against it and perhaps featureless lawn stretching away with some gardens at its far perimeter. You don't really look at the side of the house; you look along its length to what is beyond – the view through the woods to a neighbor's house, an outbuilding (see figure 2.3), an expanse of lawn, or a

50

FIGURE 2.1 (PREVIOUS PAGE)
A path forms a transition
from front door landing to
side garden while massed
yellow-leaved Hakonechloa
grass brightens up a shady
area. To emphasize arrival,
build a fence and gate off
either the front or back
corner of your house.

FIGURE 2.2 (ABOVE)
This mortared sandstone
path leads from the front
walkway and through a cool
green garden along the side
of the house, where it forms
a generous sitting area in the
ell. Low plantings and high-
pruned trees ensure that
views remain open.

fabulous view of a lake in the distance.
Without a garden and a path through it, the
space remains ill-defined.

When you walk along the side of your
house, you don't so much see it as feel its presence. There might be a few trees or shrubs
along it – and a couple of propane tanks or an
air-conditioning unit – but the space is not
attractive, the house not settled into the landscape.

Without a garden along the side of the
house, there is no path, and without a path, no
comforting destination. Guests don't know
where they're going, so they walk on lawn that
is little more than an implied path from front
to back. And they often walk close to the
house to simply get from point A to B.
Walking close to the house through an indis-
tinct landscape with no clear destination has
an unsettling effect. The side of a one-story
house becomes overbearing; two or three stories are overpowering.

The side garden can play the role of a tran-

sition, a walk-through garden that fuses front
and back gardens into a seamless whole (see
figure 2.4), or it can act as a garden through
which you pass, then open a gate to unveil the
back garden (see figure 2.5). A side garden I
designed for John and Priscilla Hellweg in
Massachusetts, for example, connected front
and back gardens with 5-to-7-foot-long
stepping-stones that passed through an ornamental grass and conifer garden and up to a
brick terrace overlooking the Connecticut
River. But a side garden can also be a destination in itself. I could have set a bench, a sitting
boulder, or even an arbor in the Hellweg garden and made it more of a stopping place had
it not been in full view of the brick terrace
with its chairs, bench, and table.

Side gardens have to have certain charac-

teristics before guests will settle into them. They need to be somewhat enclosed, with a feeling of entrance and exit and perhaps with even a bit of floor and roof and plantings all around. A floor, which only needs to be big enough for two chairs, can be paved with stone, brick, crushed gravel, or wood in any number of styles, while the ceiling can be the overarching limbs of trees, the cross members of a freestanding arbor, or even one that is attached to the side wall of your home.

Designing a side garden is facilitated by the fact that the location of its beginning and that of its end are clearly suggested by the two corners and the side of your house along which the garden will run. The problem lies in establishing its fourth side so that the garden has definition, a sense of enclosure, and appropri-

ate proportions relative to the dimensions of the adjacent wall of your house. If you have a broad lawn between the side of your house and the boundary of your property, you can create a long, rectangular garden that is as wide as the side wall of the house is high. If there is only a narrow slip of lawn between the house and landscape features, such as woodland, meadow, bedrock, or an already-established garden, take up that lawn and foundation planting and allow those existing elements to give you design clues.

Years ago, I designed a garden for Alan and Sally Seymour here in southern Vermont along the south side of their home (see figure 2.6). They live in a long 1½-story Colonial set on flat ground on an east-west line and surrounded by meadows and farmland; a garage is attached at the east end and is set back from the house about 6 feet. Otherwise, it's a long, low traditional home, and that word "traditional" is important. Neither Sally nor Alan nor the colonists would use squiggly,

FIGURE 2.3 (LEFT)
This narrow side garden doubles as a parking space. The double gate allows access, yet when closed separates side from back gardens. Repeating the brick of the house on the ground links house and garden.

FIGURE 2.4 (ABOVE)
This sandstone path repeats the color of the adobe house and wall on either side of it, drawing people down the side of the home to the back gardens. No matter where you live, this principle applies if you have a wall or fence close to the side of your house.

curvy, illogical lines around their homes.

Sally wanted to include an herb garden, a perennial garden under the filtered shade of three black locust trees, and a sitting area somewhere on the south side of the house. We looked to the house for clues and decided that the garden would run east-west, that is, parallel with and adjacent to the full 70-foot length of the south side of the house and garage. Had we run it straight out into the lawn, it would have little relationship with the wall of the house and its doors and windows.

To be certain any garden near a house is in proportion to it, I measure the height of the adjacent wall and flop that dimension down on the ground as a trial balloon for the fourth side. Sometimes the resulting dimension feels too narrow; rarely does it feel too wide. Alan and Sally's south wall was 9 feet high. That was clearly too narrow, so I took 9 as a mod-

ule and considered multiples of that – an 18- or 27-foot-wide bed. (I didn't consider 4 x 9 = 36, because a bed that wide would have been a bit out of scale and the Seymours would have had to hire a full-time gardener.) An 18-foot-wide, 70-foot-long bed seemed a good place to start, so we measured out from the southeast and southwest corners of the house and then ran a 70-foot-long string between the two to see how that dimension looked. In one of those lovely chance occurrences, we found that the line of three large black locust trees were also exactly in line 18 feet out from the west end of the house; so that dimension was clearly our fourth side. The locusts would anchor the garden and give it a feeling of age.

For the sake of privacy from the nearby road, we designed an 18-foot-long, 7-foot-high scalloped wooden fence to screen off the west end of the garden from passing traffic

FIGURE 2.5

On many properties, a narrow strip of land runs between the side of the house and a garage, fence, or wall. By placing a fence and gate across that strip, you separate the side garden from the back garden. Here, fencing extends 8 feet into the back garden, making room for a red cut-leaf maple and a small garden.

SITTING ROOM

KITCHEN

GARAGE

**FENCE
TO SCREEN
ROAD FROM
VIEW**

PERENNIAL GARDEN

SITTING AREA

HERB GARDEN

and to firmly conclude the garden at its west end. The fence, painted the same red as the house, was affixed to its southwest corner and ran out 18 feet south to reinforce the logic of the garden's width. Notice that at the east end of the garden, we did not stick slavishly to the 18-foot width when measuring out from the garage and kitchen, set 6 feet back from the south face of the house. The garden area off the kitchen and garage, then, was 24 feet wide and shared a common outer edge with the rest of the garden. Coherence, you see.

With the fourth side established, we had an area 18 feet wide and 70 feet long for the three areas Sally wanted: herb garden, sitting area, semishade garden. The architecture (and

the three black locusts) told us exactly where each would go.

The 24-by-24-foot space off the gray garage was the sunniest spot along the length of the house. All the signals from the garage – the setback, the different color, the dimensions for the resulting 24-foot-square garden, and the high blank wall to support espaliered apples one day – were right, so that was where the herb garden went. The Seymours' renovated sitting/dining room was 22 feet long, with a door that led out to their new garden area. That 22-foot length established the two ends of the stone-paved sitting area, which would, in effect, be an extension of the interior living space. The remaining 24 feet from

FIGURE 2.6

Sally Seymour's house gave me all the clues I needed to locate three gardens she wanted on the south side of her house: herb garden off the garage, sitting area off the kitchen, perennial garden off the sitting room.

the stone-paved area back to the fence, that is, the old part of the house, would provide the dimensions for the semishade garden under the locusts.

To reinforce the line 18 feet out from the side of the house, and to visually link all three garden areas into a whole, we used a number of devices. First, we designed an open "hedge" of 18-inch-high *Buxus microphylla* 'Green Velvet' to run along the edge of the fourth side. We set the boxwoods every 6 feet along the entire 70-foot outer edge of the garden, creating a suggestion of enclosure, even in the winter. Next, we used only one paving material – cut bluestone – to provide walking surfaces for the sitting area and the two paths that ran down the center of the perennial and herb gardens, laying the stone differently in

FIGURE 2.7

If your boundary line on the east is close to one side of your house, place a fence along the boundary to claim that often-neglected space for a private shady sitting area.

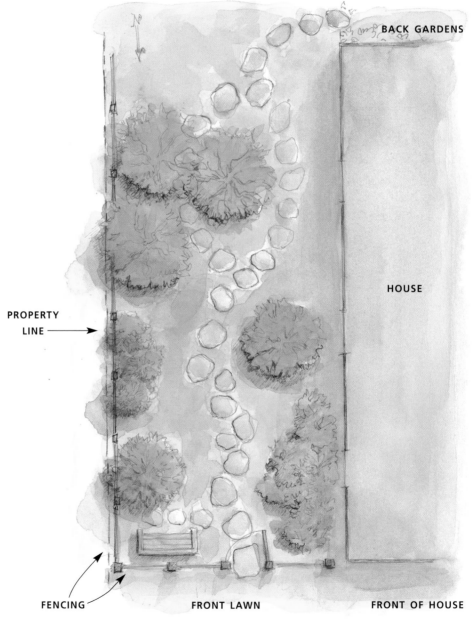

56

each garden to underpin their separate roles. Finally, we set a 6-foot teak bench against the red wooden fence so that people could sit and look east down the full length of the garden and out to the meadow and the Connecticut River Valley beyond.

The spirit and the principles of this design should be useful. Here they are, summarized. First, we consulted the architecture for many of our design decisions: the length and width and position of the garden; the placement and dimensions of the three individual spaces within it; and the placement, direction, and length of the screening, fence, and bench. We gently enclosed the garden along its fourth side with low evergreens, preventing the long, narrow garden from feeling claustrophobic yet visually tying all three separate spaces into a whole. Finally, we used one type of stone for all walking surfaces. With all the shapes and roles of each of these areas clarified, plant choice was easy: herbs in the herb garden; hardy fragrant-leaved geraniums around the sitting area; shade-tolerant plants for the semishade area – heucheras, hostas and ferns, variegated Solomon's seal, and others.

But the unspoken key to this and all outdoor living spaces along any side of a house is sunlight and warmth, as the following passage from Christopher Alexander's book *A Pattern Language* shows:

> People use open space if it is sunny, and do not use it if it isn't, in all but desert climates. This is perhaps the most important single fact about a building. If the building is placed right, the building and its gardens will be happy places full of activity and laughter. If it is done wrong, then all the attention in the world, and the most beautiful details, will not prevent it from being a silent gloomy place.

Had the Seymour garden been along any other side of the house than south, the design would have been totally different. The south side of their house was in full sun from sunrise to noon and in filtered sunlight from the locust trees for the afternoon. There was plenty of light for the Seymours and their family and friends, and the space was used constantly.

THE EAST GARDEN

A garden off the east side of a house is in sunlight from sunrise until midday, when it gradually falls into shade cast by the house as the afternoon lengthens. Given Christopher Alexander's words about sunlight, don't expect guests to linger in an east-facing garden once it goes into shade. They will certainly walk through it and enjoy it, but as for sitting. . . . I can offer a firsthand account of just such a garden I designed 10 years ago.

As part of the gardens around Barry and Elsa Waxman's home set among meadows here in Vermont, I designed a stone-paved sitting area, roughly 20 feet square, enclosed by an arching stone wall and gardens off the east-facing kitchen. The west end of the sitting area came up against the three-story-high gable end of the house, against which I designed a perennial and shrub border. The stone wall acted not only as an enclosure but also as a bench for the sitting area. White birches interplanted with azaleas, dwarf Scots pine, red-leaved barberry, ornamental grasses, and daylilies gathered to the north and south of the stonework, where they received the sun they needed.

The central focus of attention on the stone terrace, however, was the view to the east framed by birches. Guests and family could sit on the stone terrace and look down a sloping lawn to a pond set into the fold of a hundred acres of mowed hayfields and on to a view of the Connecticut River Valley and New

Hampshire beyond. It was a stunning view, but rarely did anyone visit it after one in the afternoon.

We were all flabbergasted. I asked the Waxmans about the area, and they said that shortly after noon, it went into full shade cast by the shadow of the three-story gable end of the house. Certainly family and friends went out there in the early morning with a cup of coffee and the newspaper, but they rarely had lunch there. Even the best view from anywhere around the house couldn't compete with the power of shadow.

On the other hand, family and guests frequented the larger stone patio off the south side of the house. They had lunch and dinner there or read a book or tended the container plantings we set out each year. At night, they lit candles in jars hanging from honey locust trees planted within the terrace that, during the day, provided filtered shade. The east-facing terrace, while used in the early mornings, languished for the balance of the day and evening.

There's a lesson here for all of us. An east-facing garden needs to be designed for living and visiting in the morning, and that typically involves only family and guests who may have stayed overnight. The garden off the east side of your house, which you might even call your Sunrise Garden, requires, at most, a small breakfast area for just a few people and a garden surrounding it that will capture the light of the rising sun. They didn't name a hybrid of the ornamental grass *Miscanthus sinensis* 'Morning Light' for nothing. Grow this extraordinary 5-to-6-foot-high grass and other equally dramatic grasses, perennials, and shrubs, and even cut-leaf maples so that they are backlit by the rising or early-morning sun, and you will see a remarkable picture. Furthermore, your east-facing garden needs to be designed so that light from sunrise on

through the morning can flow right into or onto the heart of that garden. Keep the center of it open so that a pool of light can flow into its center during the hours between 10 and noon.

When it comes to plant choice for your east garden, keep in mind that morning sun is cooler than afternoon sun. Plant moisture-loving perennials and shrubs that appreciate half a day of sun and have minimal phototropic instinct: *Chelone lyonii*, astrantias, eupatorium, aquilegias, ferns, *Fothergilla gardenii*, and *Stephenandra incisa* 'Crispa.' Save your favorite drought-tolerant, sun-loving plants – Russian sage, dianthus, sedums, achilleas, nepetas – for your south- or west-facing gardens; an east-facing garden that goes into shade around midday will not provide the sunlight they need. Keep the perennials low and shrubs and trees spread out to maintain a view; plant shrubs, trees, and perennials high and dense if you want to screen a view.

When it comes to stonework, keep in mind that only by late morning does sunlight begin to heat up stone paving. A stone-paved east-facing breakfast area stays cooler than one in a south- or west-facing garden, especially if it goes into shade shortly after noon.

THE WEST GARDEN

West-facing side gardens and gathering spots near your home are bathed in bright afternoon and evening light. It is during this time, from one o'clock until sunset, that you most often have guests for lunch or dinner or when your family gathers for a meal or games outdoors. So your primary outdoor entertaining area needs to be located off the west, or even sunnier south, side of your house. This fact alone helps with the design of your west gardens, because it demands a broad and spacious stone, brick, or wooden gathering area at the very center of the garden. It, in turn, can be surrounded by shrubs and perennials, as well as trees that will shed dappled shade onto the hardscaping of the sitting area.

To design the sitting area, consult the architecture. Here's an example. I was designing a west-facing stone terrace for Charlotte and Jess Belser here in southern Vermont a few years ago (see figure 2.8). I measured the

west wall of their library and found it was 16 feet high and 20 feet wide. I marked those dimensions on the ground with bamboo stakes and string as an initial idea for a 20-foot-wide, 16-foot-deep stone terrace. The width seemed fine, with the stonework coming directly off each corner of the library wall. However, the 16-foot depth seemed too narrow. We added half of 16 to produce a 24-

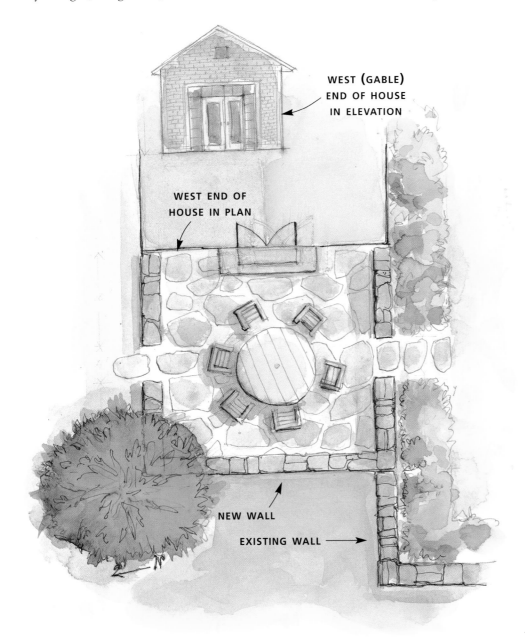

WEST (GABLE) END OF HOUSE IN ELEVATION

WEST END OF HOUSE IN PLAN

NEW WALL

EXISTING WALL

FIGURE 2.8
All the dimensions and proportions for this west-facing outdoor dining area came from the dimensions of the wing of my clients' house. Dining areas are best on the sunny south and west sides, where family and friends gather for lunch or dinner outside.

foot-long terrace, one that would be in sympathetic proportion with the library. I marked it out, and we decided that it would be the most appropriate length.

We then designed two gaps in the wall for access through this side terrace, leaving plenty of room at the west end of the area for a small table and four chairs. In this way the side terrace provided not only a transition space but also an invitation to linger.

Once we had the rectangular terrace designed, I suggested we surround the stonework with a 3-foot-wide shrub and perennial border, leaving room halfway along the south and north sides of the gardens for stepping-stones that would lead into the sitting area. That was when Jess, ever mindful of garden maintenance costs, said he would prefer a freestanding stone wall 24 inches high and wide to surround the three sides of the stone sitting area, with openings in them along the middle of the north and south walls for access. At some point in the future, he said, they might install perennial borders outside the three walls to soften the stony look.

Just as your east-facing garden might be called your Sunrise Garden, so your west garden can be a Sunset Garden, thereby encouraging people not only to pass through such an area but to stay and linger in the extraordinary light at dusk. Because the setting sun has a pinkish red hue to it, plant perennials and annuals with flowers or foliage in reds, yellows, and oranges that will be illuminated in this light. Such perennials as golden-leaved marjoram, aquilegias in yellows and reds, helianthemums, red penstemons, anthemis, rudbeckias, solidagos, *Asclepias tuberosa*, poppies in oranges and reds, and trollius will absolutely glow at or near sunset.

Another way to choose perennials – and annuals – for your Sunset Garden is to choose plants that look or smell particularly good in the evening. For example, some perennials, such as *Cimicifuga ramosa* 'Atropurpurea,' are noticeably fragrant on a still evening, as are annuals such as night-scented stock or *Nicotiana* 'Fragrant Cloud.' White, cream-colored, and pastel yellow flowers also tend to show up especially well once the sun is setting. Unlike blue, dark red, or purple flowers that absorb light, white, cream, and yellow flowers reflect even small amounts of light and are visible much later into the evening. *Lonicera prolifera*, a creamy-white honeysuckle called the moonflower is particularly stunning in our garden on an early June evening.

When choosing perennials or annuals for the Sunset Garden, remember the impact of phototropic instinct. Plant those with it – anthemis and rudbeckias, for example – next to the house; and plant those without it – like penstemons, *Asclepias tuberosa*, and helianthemums – away from the house. Set a chair or a small bench in a paved area among these glowing plants, and you and your guests will be tempted to linger in this side garden, not just pass through it.

THE SUNNY SOUTH GARDEN

The most appropriate area near the house for outdoor living is off the south side, because it is bathed in different kinds of light from sunup to sundown. While south-facing terraces, decks, and sitting areas can certainly get too hot in the southern parts of the United States, trees, awnings, arbors, and other shade-shedding surfaces can mitigate the problem. The Seymour garden I described earlier gives you the principles for a garden that is aligned with the south side of a house.

In a south-facing garden I designed for Tim and Waew Cowles here in Vermont, curved and free-form beds resulted; the architecture, decidedly modern, with lots of glass and white stucco, helped us design gardens in very different ways from those along the Seymours' home.

The Cowles' two-story home is built into a bank and has a sod-covered roof. The house comprises two main boxy structures, with a 30-foot-long one-story-high corridor between the two. The entire south side of all three sections of the house are composed of big sheets of glass. Given that the house is divided into three sections, so, too, would the garden be divided.

The south side of the east wing of the house is 20 feet high and 30 feet long and nearly all

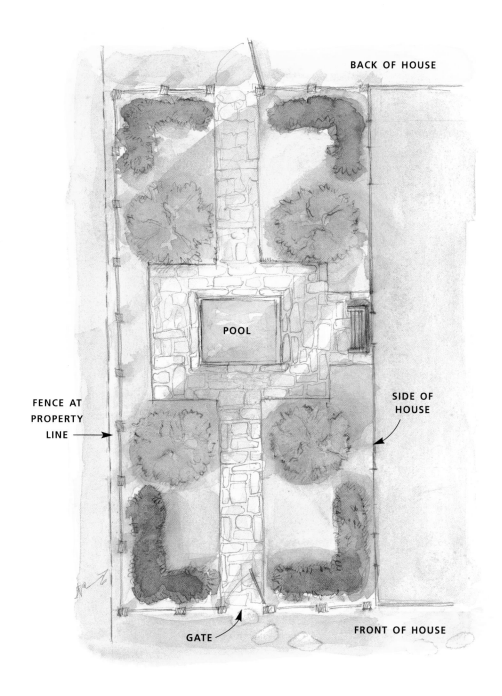

BACK OF HOUSE

POOL

FENCE AT
PROPERTY
LINE

SIDE OF
HOUSE

GATE

FRONT OF HOUSE

FIGURE 2.9
This south-facing formal garden would provide both a place to linger and a passage from front to back gardens. Windows look out onto this garden, heightening the feeling of space.

FIGURE 2.10

Place a trellis on the side of your house or garage, and you can train vines up it. A path, hedge, and raised bed could run parallel with the side of your house, leading to an arbor that draws visitors on. A burgundy-leaved cut-leaf maple off the corner of this house provides strong foliage contrast. (Designer: Freeland Tanner)

glass. Sunlight reflects off the wall of glass during the growing season with such intensity that even lawn will not grow 6 to 8 feet out from the house. To solve the problem, we laid about 150 square feet of flat fieldstones out about 8 feet from the house, leaving 3- to-4-inch gaps between the stones. We then planted several different kinds of thymes, including Hall's wooly thyme, lemon thyme, and *Thymus minus*, in the gaps between the stones. Never have I seen thyme flourish in Vermont the way it did in that heat. Over time, Waew has added her own garden beyond the panel of stone, punctuated with boulders and stone paths which set off a collection of ground-hugging, drought-tolerant plants that spill out to the meadow's edge. The house provided a logical width for the bed; its length just wanders off away from the house. By keeping this entire garden low, the

Cowles were able to sit in their living room and look out over their garden and on to meadow and distant hills and valleys to the south.

In the west wing of the house, used primarily for guests, the south-facing glass panels were not quite so large, and the second floor extends out over the first, providing shade. Over the years, Waew has planted a mixed perennial border that is as wide as the west wing but again flows out to the edge of a stepping-stone path that runs through all of the south gardens, linking one to the next.

The 30-foot-long corridor, set back about 15 feet from the façades of the east and west wings, gave us an entirely different space to work with. First of all, the corridor was not a living space but a hallway joining the two wings. Solar gain was not as essential, so we could design an outdoor living area, the core of which would have to be a group of shade trees. Without them, the heat buildup from the white walls and glass in this narrow, low space would have kept anyone away.

The corridor suggested the 30-foot width for the garden; its length could be anything we wanted, given the spare nature of the architecture. Within a 30-by-30-foot area, we planted six Shademaster honey locust trees, under which we created a crushed-gravel sitting area top-dressed with 1 inch of ⅜-inch peastone. The Cowles then set up a dining table and chairs under the locusts, which, over the years, they have high-pruned to about 10 feet above grade to keep the view of meadow, hills, and gardens to either side intact. To link lawn visually to the peastone-paved area, we planted seven more honey locusts, which spill out onto the lawn and even into the meadow's edge, thereby co-opting lawn and meadow into a relationship with the sitting area.

So what are the principles inherent in this example that you can apply to your very different home and south-facing garden? First of all, sunlight on the south side can sometimes be too hot for comfort. Choose a place along the south side where you can plant shade trees that won't obstruct important views, and design your sitting area under those trees. Take advantage of all that sunlight to grow alpines, drought-tolerant and sun-loving plants, or mixed perennial and low shrub gardens so that you don't block views from your south windows. Finally, if you don't like straight lines at the edges of your gardens, let the south-facing beds flow well out into the lawn; but do find some logical cues to end those beds.

THE SHADY NORTH GARDEN

Gardens along the north side of a house are in shade for longer periods of time, if not all day long, and are therefore only appealing when you sit beyond the shade line caused by your house. Even then, the shade cast by the house seems to dampen spirits. Christopher Alexander writes in *A Pattern Language*:

> Look at the north sides of the buildings which you know. Almost everywhere you will find that these are the spots which are dead and dank. . . . It is inevitable that there must always be land in this position, wherever there are buildings. . . . It is essential to find a way of making these north-facing areas alive. . . . The shadow cast by the north face is essentially triangular. To keep this triangle of shade from becoming a forlorn place, it is necessary to fill it up with things and places which do not need the sun.

If you can, make your north garden one that you stroll through, and if you are shade-

loving, place a single chair or a pair of chairs in it, but don't put a great deal of effort into creating broad stone-paved areas for sitting and outdoor entertaining.

Beverly and Brad Dunbar called me last year to help them solve a problem regarding the fact that no one would sit on the deck or the screened porch attached to the north side of their home. Beverly told me that sitting in those places made her feel cold. Even the dramatic views to the north of farms and fields, meadows and hills would not entice the Dunbars or their guests to linger in either space. We decided to simply leave the deck and porch intact and design a stone-paved sitting area surrounded by richly planted perennial beds off the nearby west side of the deck and house (see figure 2.12).

When designing a garden along the north side of a house, I accept the fact of shade and

FIGURE 2.11

In designing this side garden in Vermont, I enclosed a fragrance garden with a stone wall and then built a stepping- stone path through the garden. That path, wall, and garden link front to back while leaving lawn beyond the wall for play space for Norman and Lyn Lear's daughters. Architect Tim Smith placed skylights in the roof of this north-facing screened porch to bring direct light into the screened room.

focus my attention on shade-loving trees, shrubs, and perennials. Robert and Mary McGrath called me one day just after construction had started on their new home in New Hampshire. Among the design problems we addressed was what to do with the 40-by-60-foot area that had been bulldozed flat for construction between the north end of the house and the native woodland. Rather than take the cue from the house for garden design ideas, we turned to the woodland.

Because Mary's study downstairs and the master bedroom upstairs looked out onto this area, we first opted to gently thin out some of the existing trees, particularly small white pines, to open up a view from the house into the woodland and to increase the feeling of spaciousness. Without such thinning, the interior of the existing woodland was blocked from view by a green wall of foliage. We then designed native plantings in the bulldozed area so that, in essence, we returned the area to what it would have looked like originally: birches, white pines, and red osier, with long sweeps of ostrich and Christmas ferns we transplanted from the woods. A path was not included, because Mary didn't think she would use it. The

FIGURE 2.12

The west side of a house is best for a sitting area; late afternoon and evening is when we are most likely to have time to enjoy it.

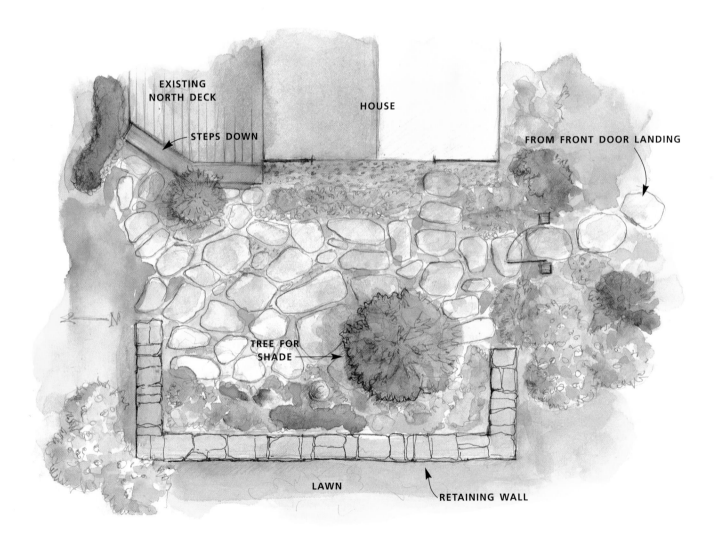

EXISTING
NORTH DECK

HOUSE

STEPS DOWN

FROM FRONT DOOR LANDING

TREE FOR
SHADE

LAWN

RETAINING WALL

THE HOUSE, ITS SHADOW, AND PLANTS

When choosing flowering perennials, shrubs, and trees for gardens near your home and the shadows it casts, you need to understand the concept of phototropic instinct, that is, the proclivity of many plants, both flower and foliage, to lean toward sunlight. If you've ever seen a sunflower, you know that it faces south, toward the maximum sunlight, as do daylilies and virtually all composite plants with daisylike flowers, among many others.

Conversely, several plants generally have minimal phototropic instinct and are well-suited for a long, narrow, shady side garden (see figure 2.13). Russian sage does not lean; nor do the spiky blooms of kniphofia, veronicas, and verbascums, or the blooms of hardy geraniums, dicentras and corydalis,

penstemons or monardas. Lilacs and ninebark will lean toward the light; most viburnums will do so but minimally.

The practical implications of phototropic instinct in plants are clear. Let's say you design a stone-paved sitting area immediately off the west side of your house. You incorporate two perennial beds into the design, one in a 3-foot-wide bed between the house and the sitting area and a second, 3-foot-wide bed along the west end of the sitting area. If you plant daylilies, compos-

ites, or other phototropic plants in the bed by the house, their flowers will face the sun and thus the sitting area. If you plant them in the bed west of the sitting area, you'll only see the backs of the blooms from the sitting area. If you plant phototropic plants in a south-facing garden, as we did at the Seymours', they will get a balanced light from sunrise to sunset and will satisfy you when seen from any direction. A garden along the north side of your home is, of course, the place for shade-tolerant plants,

the vast majority of which have very little phototropic instinct: hostas, astilbes, *Anemone vitifolia*, *Tricyrtis*, *Primula japonica* and *denticulata*, epimediums, *Phlox stolonifera*, and *Mertensia*, to name just a few.

FIGURE 2.13
Even the narrowest of spaces between two houses can be gardened. Mortared paving provides a safe walkway, while tall, narrow, shade-tolerant shrubs and perennials combine to enliven this narrow space. Planted pots emphasize the entrance.

mulch under all these new plants would be leaves and pine needles that we gathered from the nearby forest floor, thereby visually linking the new garden to the natural woodland and making the new plantings look established. If you have woodland or any native habitat not too far from the north side of your home, my work with the McGraths could well be a model for you. That is, rather than let the house generate garden design ideas, let nature point the way.

I was faced with a different problem along the north side of Barry and Elsa Waxman's home in Vermont. The main entrance is near one end of the north-facing porch, the west end of which ends at the ell of the garage. This 20-foot ell established the outer edge of the 20-foot-deep, 70-foot-long entrance garden that ran the full length of the north porch out to the edge of the driveway. I began with an 8-foot-wide, 20-foot-long tightly fitted fieldstone path from the driveway to the 8-

FIGURE 2.14
Because a third of the space enclosed by a stone wall on the north side of our house is in shade throughout the day, we placed a south-facing bench against the wall so that it would be in sunlight.

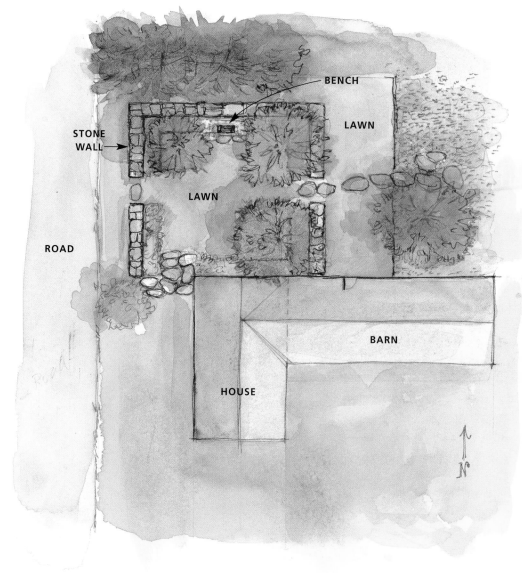

foot-wide wooden steps up to the porch and the front door. I then designed a secondary path 3 feet wide from the garage door to the primary path. Next I included a relaxed tertiary path of stepping-stones that would wander through 50 feet of the 70-foot length of the garden and then split. One spur went south onto a stone terrace, and the other went north across the driveway to a mowed path through a meadow. Where one path met another, I set one or two mossy boulders to mark the junction. I then went across the driveway and meadow to clear brush away from existing boulders on stone walls at the nearby woodland edge to set up an initial visual link between new garden and native landscape.

With the paths and boulder placement designed, I then looked to the woodland for cues as to what trees to plant in the entrance garden. The birch was a natural choice with its upright habit – the north side of the house was three stories high, and I wanted a tree that would get above its roofline as soon as possible to settle the house into the landscape.

Once the birches were situated, I underplanted them with azaleas, ferns, Russian cypress (*Microbiota decussata*), the shade-tolerant blue oat grass (*Helictotrichon sempervirens*), *Vinca minor* 'Bowles,' and hundreds of daffodils, narcissi, and crocuses. During the design work for the entrance garden, I was

certain to keep all woody plants out of harm's way of snow cascading off the roofs of house and garage. Every year since we installed the garden, we have also planted several 24-inch terra-cotta pots with shade-tolerant annuals for seasonal color. Other than two chairs on the covered porch, there was no place in this entrance garden for a chair or a bench. This was a side garden that acted solely as a transition space. Its primary path led between driveway and front door, while a secondary path led down its length toward the east sitting terrace.

Here in our own garden gathered around our 200-year-old farmhouse, we recently built a stone wall to enclose the perimeter of an area roughly 50 feet square along the north side of our house (see figure 2.14). This 2-foot-high stone retaining wall was meant to mimic an old barnyard, with gates at the east and west sides. Within this new area, we will design a garden of low-maintenance shrubs and perennials with a path in sun that runs well beyond the shade line thrown by our two-story house. The path will lead out of the wall-enclosed area and under the shade of an ash tree, where we have set two chairs on stone in full view of our pool garden. This cool sitting garden in the shade of a tree, not a building, will provide us with respite on those hot summer days when the sound of splashing water will be so welcome.

PRACTICAL PROBLEMS SOLVED

1

TOO MANY TREES NEAR THE HOUSE

To decide whether or not your have too many trees around your home, take a fresh look at those trees, first from every window and doorway and then from all vantage points from the front, back, and sides of your house. Trees sometimes provide a feeling of separation and a degree of privacy between you and your neighbors. Other times, trees, such as the grand live oaks of New Orleans or Savannah, provide essential cooling shade. The element of privacy might be particularly apparent from your upstairs windows, from which you look into the branching of trees rather than into your neighbor's windows. On the other hand, you might find, upon reassessment, that the trees around your house are oppressive and block too much sunlight or beautiful views.

When trying to determine what to do about trees around your home, keep in mind that you have a lot of options. The two most obvious choices are to leave them as they are or to cut them down. But in between are many alternatives, all of which gather around pruning.

One method is high-pruning, wherein you cut off the lower branches to lift the tree's canopy. You can high-prune many trees so that as much as the lower one-half of the trunk is limbless. The result is a lofty, regal look to a tree that

almost appears to be floating above your garden. I saw just such a garden in the Berkshire Hills of Massachusetts several years ago. The owner had limbed-up around fifty 100-year-old maple trees so that the lowest limbs on all the trees were 30 to 40 feet above the ground. He then planted vast areas of *Vinca minor* 'Bowles,' ferns, and hostas, and very little else. The house, set at the edge of this remarkable acre of trees and massed perennials, felt as if it were sitting at the edge of a great cathedral. Consider high-pruning some of the trees near your house to lift their spirit and let more light and air get to the house and any gardens planted under the trees.

Another method is thinning. While you have to proceed with care and most certainly consult an arborist, you can thin branches to open up the inner branching. Such thinning will allow more light to reach into the interior of the tree, onto the ground and underplantings, or into your windows and give definition to the nature of the tree's architectural branching structure. One result of thinning is that you can carefully select branches for removal so that your tree becomes sculpturelike in its shaping and form. But let a trained arborist do this and all major tree pruning. I once saw a magnificent 150-year-old beech tree so drastically thinned out by an inexperienced landscaper that the tree was clearly about to die.

A third possibility is shaping. Prune the limbs between the trunk of the tree and the side of your house well above the line where the vertical wall of your

house meets the dripline of the roof. However, leave the branches between the trunk and your neighbor's property so that they arch down, perhaps even to within a foot or two of ground level. The result is to capture that vast volume of space between the ground, your house, and the remaining exterior branches of a tree or trees.

Once you high-prune and/or thin out a tree following wise arboriculture

FIGURE 2.15
Rather than cut the tree to the ground, we hired Gerry Prozzo, a sculptor, to carve The Green Man into the 8-foot-high trunk of a dead butternut tree in our garden in Vermont.

principles, more light reaches the ground, thereby enabling you to grow groundcovers, perennials, and understory shrubs with much greater success. Furthermore, by opening up the interior of a tree, you make sitting and walking under it much more pleasant. Sitting in a garden under a beautifully pruned tree becomes a very real addition to the variety of moods your garden can offer.

If you have to cut a tree down, consider two options I have taken in our garden. When cutting down a 75-year-old butternut tree, I left an 8-foot-high stump of the 24-inch-caliper tree. A sculptor friend then carved the face of The Green Man, a Druidic image symbolizing the meeting place between mankind and plants, in the top 2 feet of the remaining trunk (see figure 2.15). We also had to cut down a black locust tree in the garden, so we left its 14-foot-high trunk standing and trained the white blooming wisteria 'Aunt Dee' to climb it. Don't cut a tree to the ground until you have explored all the options.

The Main Points

- Methodically check to see whether any trees near the house are so tall and broad that they are a danger to the house or, at the very least, are blocking far too much light from the interior of the house.
- Call in a licensed arborist to see whether any of your trees could be pruned, shaped, thinned, or removed to bring more light onto the garden or into your house.
- Decide which trees are so important for screening, for sentimental reasons,

or for pure aesthetic appeal that they should remain absolutely intact and be carefully tended.

- Walk your property to see whether the space under any particular tree or trees would be suitable for a sitting area.
- If you have to cut a tree down, consider leaving 8 to 12 feet or more of the main trunk as a climbing post for a flowering vine.

2

GARDENS ALONG DRIPLINES

Your home may not have gutters along its eaves, so rainwater runs off or snow cascades down onto plantings below along what is known as the dripline; that is, the line onto which water drips from your roof. That falling water splashes mulch or soil up onto house siding, discoloring it or causing it to rot prematurely, or damaging nearby plants; the weight of snow breaks off branches and sometimes whole plants, especially those with brittle wood, such as *Daphne x Burkwoodii*, rhododendrons, or mountain laurel. Walk along the eave sides of your home, and you will see an erosion line on the ground, a line that, below a typical 2,500-square-foot roof, has to absorb 1,500 gallons of water when an inch of rain falls. A variety of solutions – many of which rely on a good understanding of what impact all that water has had on the soil – can be used to handle problems associated with driplines directly below the eave side (as opposed to gable end) of your roof.

Before considering any of the solutions below, check the soil along the driplines of your home to see whether it is compacted or has very little tilth or openness in it. Also have the soil tested for lead from sloughed-off old paint and for pH, especially if you live in an area beset by acid rain. Unlike other areas of your garden that receive more evenly dispersed rainfall, the nutrients in the soil under a dripline have often been leached away and very little organic matter remains.

Rather than reinvigorate the soil between the foundation and 6 inches beyond the dripline, excavate it. In areas of North America where annual rainfall is between 15 and 25 inches, excavate that area down 6 inches (see figure 2.16). Lay a water-permeable geotextile in the resulting trench, and then cover it with 6 inches of $3/8$-inch peastone or some other attractive small rounded stone indigenous to your area. (Avoid crushed stone, as it is often unattractive and coarse and has an engineered look.) When water falls on these small stones, droplets of water disperse, causing no harm or mess to house or plants. Do not use large, flat stones, because such a surface does not break up water into droplets; instead, water splashes off and up onto the siding of the house with damaging volume. Once the small stones are in place, you can amend the soil beyond the backfilled trench and plant as you normally would.

In areas of North America where annual rainfall is above 25 inches, or in the Southwest where periodic torrential downpours happen, huge volumes of water often cascade off a roof. What I did at our own home in southern

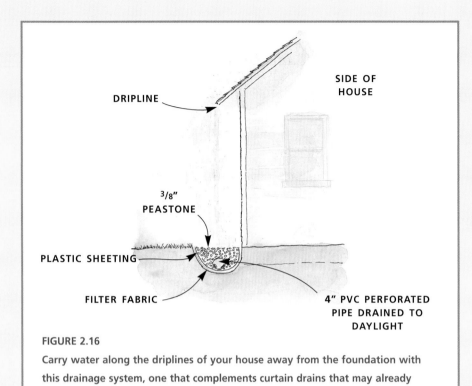

DRIPLINE

SIDE OF
HOUSE

3/8"
PEASTONE

PLASTIC SHEETING

FILTER FABRIC

4" PVC PERFORATED
PIPE DRAINED TO
DAYLIGHT

FIGURE 2.16
Carry water along the driplines of your house away from the foundation with
this drainage system, one that complements curtain drains that may already
be installed around your foundation.

Vermont, where we typically get 44 inches of rain a year and sometimes more than 2 inches in one storm, was excavate 14 to 16 inches deep against the foundation to a point 6 inches out from the dripline. The trenches ended at a low spot at the far end of the house, where they could drain onto the lawn. I then lined the trench with woven filter fabric to protect the next layer of heavy-gauge plastic sheeting from frost pushing sharp stones against it. Next, I spread 2 inches of 3/8-inch peastone in the bottom of the lined trench and set 4-inch-diameter perforated pipe, holes facing down, atop that thin layer of peastone, frequently checking with a spirit level to be sure the pipe was gently sloping so that it would drain. I then filled the remaining

trench with the 3/8-inch stone.

Dormers and especially roof valleys, where two wings of a house meet at right angles, concentrate rainwater coming off a roof. Below such valleys, you'll need larger rounded stones set almost a foot out from the dripline to withstand heavier, more concentrated downpours. I use 3-to-6-inch river rocks set several inches into the peastone below such a valley.

If this drainage system is not screened by shrubs and perennials but lawn runs right up to its edge, there are a number of attractive ways to make a low-maintenance transition between lawn and peastone. Set tightly fitting pieces of cut stone or irregularly shaped flat sandstone, limestone, or mica schist 12 to 16 inches wide in a line between the

lawn and the peastone. If you fit the ends of those stones tightly together, the lawn will not creep between them. Furthermore, the stones will provide a stable, level surface for lawn mower wheels so that you can easily maintain the edge where lawn meets stone.

Of course, in many areas of the country, rain turns to snow in the winter and either blows, cascades, or melts off the roof onto shrubs and trees planted along the eaves of a house. If you live in an area where it snows and you have a slate or metal roof off of which snow will fall, plant only tough, deep-rooted perennials along the eave sides of your house. They die back out of harm's way during the snowy months, and their crowns can survive under mounds of snow for months on end. On the north and east sides, combinations of shade-tolerant hostas, ferns, epimediums, astilbes, and tough groundcovers like *Vinca minor* 'Bowles' or *Geranium macrorrhizum* will do fine. On the south or west sides, plant daylilies, heleniums, asters, Siberian iris, shasta daisies, or other deep-rooted perennials.

If you want to plant shrubs along a dripline where snow damage is a problem, don't resort to unsightly triangular wooden shelters for winter protection. First, plant at least 18 inches out from the dripline. Second, choose shrubs with flexible, not brittle, branches or with a prostrate habit. Third, choose plants that bloom on new wood so that if you have to prune back damaged twigs and branches, the shrub will have time between early spring and midsummer to generate new growth on which they will flower. As a rule, any shrub that blooms after July 4 blooms on new wood.

The Main Points

- Check along the driplines on the eave sides of your house and outbuildings to see whether you have soggy or eroded soil or plants damaged by rainwater coming off your roofs or rotting siding caused by backsplashing.
- Use small particle stones such as peastone or crushed stone that disperse falling water along a dripline. Large, flat stones cause backsplash that will rot house siding.
- With a shovel, explore the nature and condition of the soil along the driplines. Examine or test the soil to see whether nutrients have been leached out of it by excessive water along a dripline. If so, replace it with crushed stone, or have a professionally installed drainage system put in.
- If snow cascades off your roof, damaging plants below, replant with more flexibly branched shrubs or shrubs that bloom on new wood, or rethink the entire design for garden areas under your driplines.
- Collect rainwater from a roof valley for use in your garden during dry periods.

Shrubs with flexible branches:

Andrachne colchica
Cotoneasters
Chamaecyparis pisifera hybrids
Forsythia 'Arnold Dwarf'
Fothergilla gardenii
Kerria japonica
Leucothoe fontanesiana 'Compacta' or 'Nana'
Rhus aromatica 'Gro Low'

Salix purpurea 'Nana'
Sasa veitchii
Spireas
Symphoricarpos hancockii
Taxus densiformis
Xanthorhiza simplicissima

Shrubs with prostrate growth habits:

Cornus canadensis
Cytisus decumbens
Forsythia viridissima 'Bronxensis'
Gaultheria procumbens
Juniperus communis
Leucothoe fontanesiana 'Compacta'
Linnaea borealis
Mahonia aquifolium
Microbiota decussata
Pachistima canbyi
Picea abies 'Nidiformis'
Groundcover roses
Sarcococca hookerana var. *humilis*

Shrubs that bloom on new wood:

Buddleia davidii
Caryopteris clandonensis
Clerodendrum trichotomum
Clethra alnifolia
Diervilla sessilifolia 'Butterfly'
Hypericums
Lespedeza bicolor
Polygonatum aubertii (fleecevine)
Roses
Sorbaria sorbifolia

Snow, Ice, and the Dripline

In many parts of North America, heavy, not powdery, snow often builds up on the roof and then cascades down, damaging shrubs below. It's not the amount of snow that causes damage to foundation plantings and gardens below the eaves but the kind of snow. Hydrologists with the U.S. Weather Service quantify snow as wet or dry by means of a ratio between the number of inches of snow that falls in any given storm and the number of inches of water that snow will produce. The lower the ratio, the heavier the snow and the more damage it does to your shrubs.

The average in New England, for example, is 10:1; that is, 10 inches of snow will produce 1 inch of water. A different situation prevails in the West. Clouds dropping snow laden with moisture at a ratio of 10:1 up to 15:1 can sweep off the Pacific, drop snow onto western Oregon and Washington, and then move on. By the time those clouds reach the eastern slope of the Rockies, the ratio has dropped to 50:1. The moisture-laden snow that falls on homes in New England and the Pacific Northwest sits on the roof and then one day slides off and damages the mountain laurel and rhododendrons planted below. Powdery snow blows off a roof, causing little or no damage.

Extended Roof Overhangs and Resulting Dry Areas

On many modern homes, roof overhangs can extend out from walls as much as 2 to 3 feet. One result is that this broad space near the house remains extremely dry throughout the year and shady throughout the day, making it difficult, if not impossible, for plants to flourish. You can certainly install a drip irrigation system that won't spray up onto the walls of your home the way a pop-up irrigation system will, but even with properly aimed irrigation heads, the soil will still dry out, especially in the winter when the system may be turned off.

The best solution I have found is to make the area under the extensive overhang into an open maintenance path between the foundation of your home and plantings outside the dripline. Excavate 3 to 6 inches of soil from the foundation to about 6 inches beyond the dripline. Lay down a porous geotextile, such as filter fabric or DeWitt weed barrier, then cover the cloth with a 2-to-3-inch layer of 1½-inch crushed stone, and top-dress it with 1 to 2 inches of ⅜-inch peastone.

If you live in the arid Southwest, indigenous gravel could come right up to the foundation. In other parts of the country, where more even rainfalls occur, plant gardens up to that line 6 inches out from the dripline to help soften the exposed foundation, thereby settling your home into the landscape.

If you live in a modern home, the lines of which are simple and geometric, it might be preferable not to plant a garden outside the dripline but to allow lawn to run right up to a black anodized aluminum, steel, or cedar edge set 6 inches out from the dripline. This creates a sleek, simple line that emphasizes clean architecture. Your gardens then could be situated around the outer perimeter of the lawn.

3

BURIED PROPANE OR NATURAL GAS TANKS WITH ABOVEGROUND CAPS

The typical 500-gallon propane storage tank is a metal cylinder around 10 feet long and 3 feet across buried to within 8 to 12 inches of the surface, most often covered with 6 inches of sand and topped with 5 to 6 inches of topsoil (see figure 2.17). So that the tank can be periodically serviced or filled, a 2-foot-high, 14-inch-wide black hinged aboveground cover, called a riser, is situated atop the center of the tank. Open the cover of the riser, and you will find a gas volume gauge, a red regulator, a faucet handle for shutting the gas on or off, and one gas line running out of the tank. Each of these copper or plastic lines, usually buried 18 to 24 inches deep, typically run in a straight line from the riser to a 6-inch-diameter greenish colored regulator affixed to the side of your house before it goes through the wall to whatever appliance it feeds. The hose on a delivery truck is between 100 and 120 feet long, so the tank must be positioned within that distance from a road or driveway.

Because the tank itself is constructed with ¼-inch-thick cold rolled steel, you don't have to worry about damaging your tank with a shovel, though you should certainly be careful when working in the area of the tank and its buried lines. Because the gas lines from the tank to your home are made of soft copper or plastic, you do need to know

where those lines are and how deeply they are buried before preparing holes anywhere from 2 to 24 inches deep for new plants. If you do break a line with a shovel, immediately open the riser, turn the faucet handle clockwise to shut the gas supply off, and then call your gas supplier. Because new codes governing flammable gases do not allow for patching broken gas lines, your supplier will have to replace the entire line from the riser on into your home to the appliance it serves. That can be quite a problem, given all the perennials and shrubs you might have planted above the gas line over the years; so find out exactly where those lines are before planting near them.

The tank itself poses a set of problems for the gardener as well, especially one that has been recently installed. Old codes allowed the tank to be buried as much as 18 to 24 inches deep; new codes in many states require that the top of the tank be flush with the adjacent grade, with 6 inches of sand or topsoil placed atop the tank to create a quickly draining mound. Furthermore, a properly installed tank has 6 inches of sand around its entire exterior, meaning that the soil close to the tank is very quickly draining.

Because these tanks are made of stout steel, you can plant shrubs and perennials to within 12 to 18 inches or so of the crest of the tank in topsoil that gets rapidly deeper as you move away from the top of the tank. But keep in mind that the deliveryman with a heavy plastic hose no longer than 120 feet will have to follow a certain route from his parked tanker truck to the riser of your tank. When planning your gar-

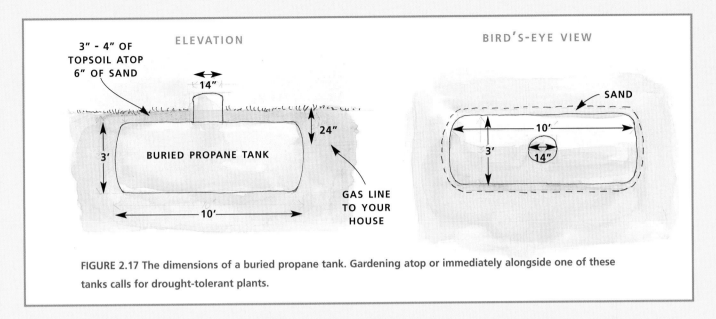

ELEVATION   BIRD'S-EYE VIEW

3" - 4" OF TOPSOIL ATOP 6" OF SAND

14"

24"

BURIED PROPANE TANK

3'

10'

GAS LINE TO YOUR HOUSE

SAND

10'

3'

14"

FIGURE 2.17 The dimensions of a buried propane tank. Gardening atop or immediately alongside one of these tanks calls for drought-tolerant plants.

dens, keep that distance in mind, as well as where the driver parks the tanker truck, so that you don't end up planting fine or brittle-stemmed shrubs and perennials along his required route.

The black metal riser 14 inches across and 24 inches high also poses a visual problem for the gardener. It's pretty ugly. One solution many gardeners try is to ring the black metal dome with evergreens. Such a treatment certainly covers the cap but usually ends up calling attention to the fact that you are trying to screen something. A far better solution is to plant a larger garden, in proportion to the surrounding area, that screens the riser of your gas tank from view.

While you can certainly situate a tank at a far greater distance from the house than the 10-foot minimum, thereby setting the riser out of view

from house and garden, only do so if the gas lines will not run under a driveway or through areas that you will want to garden in the future.

There are also very simple ways to hide the riser from view. I have managed to find a number of hollow logs over the years that I have been able to slip over these 2-foot-diameter risers. Such a solution is appropriate here in the wooded Northeast. In other parts of the country, you could gather a group of boulders around the riser so that although from a distance, it looks like a naturally occurring feature in the landscape, access is still assured for the deliveryman.

The Main Points

■ A propane tank can be buried virtually any distance from a house. To easily hide its black cap, bury the tank

behind distant existing shrubs or an outbuilding and run an unusually long copper line to it from your house.

■ A propane tank deliveryman must drag a stout hose from his truck up to 120 feet to your tank; make sure he has a route that won't force him to damage garden plants.

■ Keep at least 3 feet around the black cap free for the deliveryman's work, but feel free to screen it with plants.

■ A buried cylindrical tank is often 10 feet long, with its top only 6 inches or so underground. Find out exactly where the tank is, and then plant around but not on top of it.

■ Copper gas lines from the tank to your house are only buried a few inches. Know where they are so that you don't sever them with a sharp shovel or power equipment.

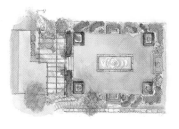

CHAPTER THREE

BACK GARDENS,
PATIOS, AND
TERRACES

THE PATIO

IS THE SLOPE

DOWN WHICH

THE SKY

FLOWS INTO

THE HOUSE.

– JORGE LUIS BORGES
(1899–1986),
Argentinian author

GARDENS AT THE BACK OF YOUR house often appear the easiest to design. You install a sitting area off the back door and surround it with perennials and small shrubs. Just as obvious seems the placement of trees, shrubs, and perennials in separate or linked beds with curvy edges around the perimeter of the big central lawn. Maybe you even place a few island beds in the midst of the lawn. My question is, What do you do with that perimeter garden other than maintain it? You walk off the terrace, walk on the lawn around the perimeter, and walk back on the terrace. There's no destination, no place to sit among the plants, no center to the experience other than one big (or small) central flat lawn. There is no overarching idea to hold such a garden together. While you certainly want to provide play space on a lawn for the kids, once they no longer need it, the lawn becomes a green void that bears little or no relationship to the house, particularly if the

lawn is shaped like an amoeba. To give shape to the lawn, and thus adjacent beds, you can remove some lawn, leaving only geometric panels of green with strong architectural beds adjacent to them (see figure 3.2); or if you have a very small bit of lawn, you can take it all up and replace it with a well-proportioned stone-paved sitting area surrounded by plants (see figure 3.3).

That's what my wife Mary and I did at our own recently purchased vacation cottage with a flat back garden 17 by 35 feet. We left some of the perennials and shrubs in the already-existing perimeter gardens intact but took up the central amoeba of lawn. We replaced it with a 12-foot-diameter stone-paved circle and then surrounded that with an omega-shaped 16-inch-high stone wall, leaving a gap for access. We then linked the existing semi-circular stone landing by the back door to the gap in the omega-shaped wall with a field-stone path. Once all the stonework was com-

FIGURE 3.1 (PRECEDING PAGE) If the area at the back of your house is very small, you can enhance a feeling of spaciousness by installing a pair of French doors that draw the indoors and out-doors together. Potted plants provide summer-long color, while paving provides a surface on which to display them and outdoor furniture.

FIGURE 3.2 An arbor at the back of your lawn with a bench under it placed in line with your back door helps you design the space in between. Take some cues regarding the position of beds, brickwork, and lawn shape from Terry Shane Teaching Garden at the Scott Arboretum, shown here. (Designer: Rodney Robinson of CLRR Associates)

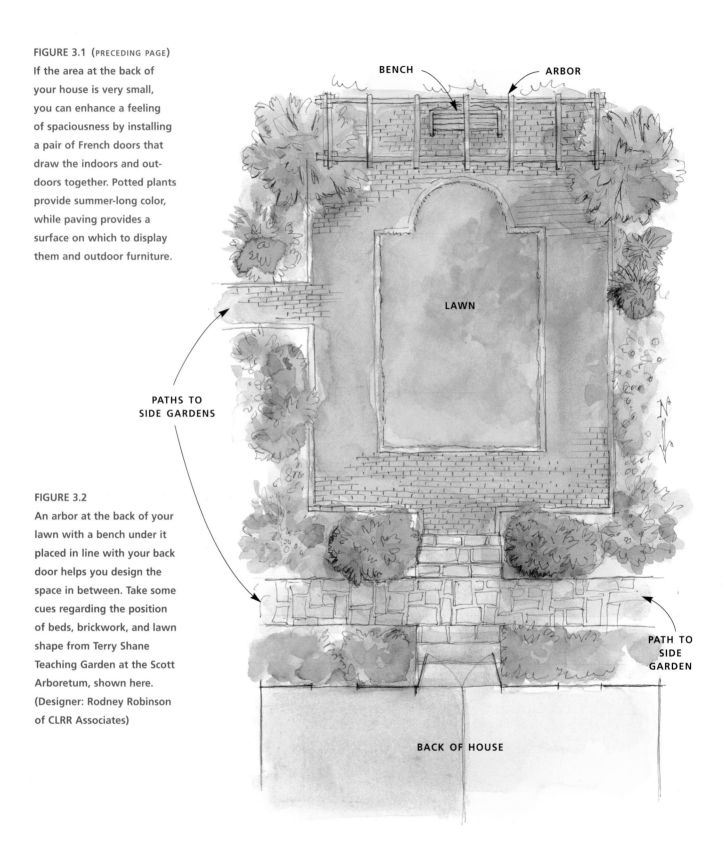

BENCH

ARBOR

LAWN

PATHS TO SIDE GARDENS

PATH TO SIDE GARDEN

BACK OF HOUSE

pleted, we planted new perennials in the open soil between the new stonework and the established shrubs and perennials that we had kept. Now we go out to the dining table set on the circle of stone and read or have meals with friends, all the time surrounded by plants we love. (See figure 3.3 for a variation on the theme.) Even though the lines of the path and garden bear little relationship to the lines of the house, the garden now has a sufficiently strong visual center so that the curving path and surrounding beds feel right and inevitable.

Here's another example, one that comes from a linear back garden I designed for Stan and Cheri Fry in New Hampshire (see figure

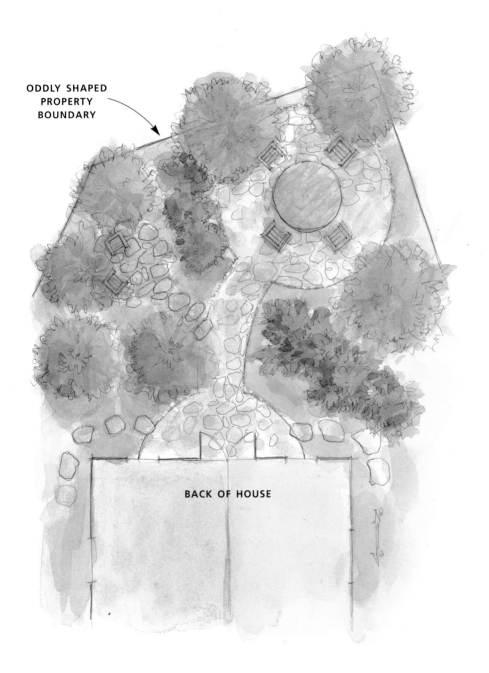

ODDLY SHAPED
PROPERTY
BOUNDARY

BACK OF HOUSE

FIGURE 3.3
The problem of a small, oddly shaped property can be resolved by making strong geometric shapes with stone or brick. Shrubs and trees mask your awkward lot shape because the focus of attention is on the shapes of the paved areas and surrounding plants.

3.4). Before the space roughly 30 feet wide and 50 feet long was reconfigured, the Frys and their guests would sit on a bluestone terrace at the back of their refined white clapboard Colonial and look out onto amorphous lawn surrounded by perimeter plantings. House and garden barely knew each other existed. In the redesign, I first located a rectangular reflecting pool 8 by 32 feet, the long center of which was in line with the center of the bluestone sitting area. I then removed some of the lawn in such a way that the pool ended up being surrounded by 12-foot-wide panels of lawn. To reinforce the rectilinear shapes governing the design of pool and adjacent lawn, we planted open boxwood squares at the four corners of the garden; Stan purchased cast-stone urns to set within each. We then designed boxwood-edged, bluestone-paved spaces for teak benches on the east and

west side of the garden, in line with the single jet of water rising from the center of the pool. At the far south end of the garden, we planted rhododendrons to accompany already-existing ones and used them as a backdrop for a classical cast-stone sculpture, in line with the central jet and the center of the bluestone sitting area. House and garden were in formal harmony.

Now you may look at this example and feel that the cost of a reflecting pool is just too much for you. Take the principle of my example of a central rectangle (in line with steps off the back terrace) surrounded by a lawn, in turn surrounded by plantings. Instead of the pool, plant a formal knot garden, a hedged herb garden, or a mounded rock garden. Change the lawn to crushed gravel, and the surrounding plants to those native to your area. That is, change my formal design to your own less formal purposes.

FIGURE 3.4

Every garden needs a focus of attention. In this formal garden I designed, the reflecting pool is the focus, in line with a sculpture at one end and the steps down from the terrace at the other.

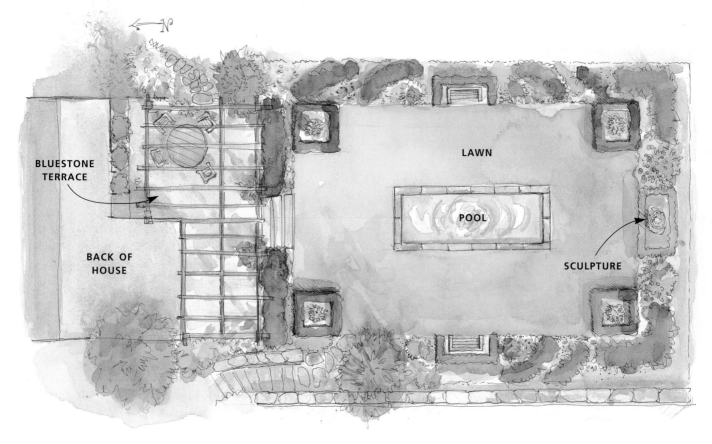

BLUESTONE
TERRACE

BACK OF
HOUSE

LAWN

POOL

SCULPTURE

One of the biggest dilemmas you may be having with the design of your back garden is breaking into the expanse of lawn. The reason the lawn poses such problems, no matter how big or small, is that there are no clues, no context, to help you think about gardening in the middle of a space. That's why you may feel comfortable with perimeter gardening; you see the obvious context of existing trees or shrubs as anchors for beds at the lawn's edge, or you set island beds somewhat arbitrarily into the lawn, leaving the middle open.

The best place to begin designing or redesigning your back gardens is the area adjacent to the back wall of your home. Once you see the back sitting area by the house as its anchor and as the core of your thinking, everything beyond it falls into place. And once you see the back door as the link between outdoor and indoor living space, you have your first clue as to where to set your anchor (see figure 3.5). Let's examine the space just outside the back door in light of two different situations: first, you already have a deck, terrace, or patio there now with some adjacent beds, but you're not really thrilled with any of it; second, there is nothing there at the moment, and you need ideas about how to proceed. Let's look at the former first.

FIGURE 3.5

Landscape designer John Brookes designed this back garden by breaking a long rectangular space into linked rectangular terraces, stone sitting areas, and planted areas. The retaining walls extend the brick of the house into the landscape. The walls are capped with bluestone to echo nearby paving.

FIGURE 3.6 (ABOVE)
Retaining walls create level gardens in ground that slopes down to the back of many homes. Leaving room between the base of the wall and the paved area for perennials and shrubs softens the feel of such small spaces.

FIGURE 3.7 (RIGHT)
Double French doors open to reveal a path and borders in line with the center of the doors. Any back door in your house could help you design a similar garden. A bench set in line with the path is an invitation to explore.

BACK GARDENS DESIGNED FROM EXISTING DECKS OR PATIOS

Let's say you have a long, rectangular deck or stone terrace centered on the back of your home. A set of narrow steps leads from the pair of doors in the center of the back wall of your home down onto the deck. Railing runs around the three sides of the deck with a break in its center for steps down to the lawn. You have planted shrubs on either side of those and around the perimeter of the sitting area and a small tree off each corner of the deck, and that's about it. You sit on that deck and look out at a broad expanse of lawn. What to do?

Here is the core idea of this book. Don't look just to plants for the solution to your

problem. Look to architecture as well, to built surfaces and structures, to help you make appropriate places for plants. First of all, make the steps down from the deck or terrace much wider so that you can display terra-cotta pots with combinations of annuals, still leaving lots of room for walking. If you have a handrail, consider removing all of it along the outer edge of the deck; next, build a step that runs the entire length of the deck and then a second landing, perhaps even 6 to 8 feet wide, which provides additional sitting area before it steps down onto lawn or stone paving. Don't be niggly. Make roomy surfaces that are in proportion to the back wall of your house and to the number of people you entertain. If you don't have the room because of a retaining wall or severe slope at the back of your home, set table and chairs that are in proportion to the space (see figure 3.6).

See your existing deck (or stone terrace or patio) as a shape that can be changed, added

onto, or manipulated in some way to give it greater depth and breadth, more level changes and curving edges or straight edges. Such changes are not necessarily expensive; it's the creativity, the open mind, the new ways to solve old problems that are at issue here. Budget holds your enthusiasms within bounds, but you've got to conjure up the enthusiasm and the creative solutions first.

Now comes the fun part. Once you've got your deck or patio, your terrace or landings right, you can look at these new surfaces, as the starting point for many subsequent plant choices and garden design decisions. Here again, you need to break out of the perimeter garden mold. Look to your back door as a clue for an axis, a line that you can carry right out to the back of your property (see figures 3.7, 3.8, and 3.9). This axis might end up generating straight-edged or curvilinear beds, either of which is fine; but get that axis in mind, because it invariably leads to an overarching idea.

For example, set your new rectilinear deck into a semicircular garden (see figure 3.10). Tap a nail into the center of the bottom step, and tie a long rope to it. Walk with the line until you are off the corner of the back wall of the house; let's say the wall is 36 feet long, so you will have 18 feet of line. Walk with the line taut to scribe an 18-foot-diameter semicircle, marking the outer edge of the semicircular bed with bamboo stakes. Then mark a 15-foot-diameter semicircle with bamboo stakes to mark the inner edge of the 3-foot-wide bed, leaving a smaller semicircle of lawn between the rectilinear deck and the semicircular bed. Now mark three openings that will be paved with stone so that guests can walk down either side of your house through the side gardens and turn into the semicircle. Finally, draw a straight line from the center of

FIGURE 3.8
The width of this house suggested the width of the garden and the placement of the trelliswork; the central back door suggested the location of the path and fountain. The flat face of the house suggested the arbor to break the verticality of the wall and to shade a sitting area under it.

the back door and through the nail in the center of the bottom step to the apex of the semicircular bed. Leave a generous 6-foot-wide gap there for access. What you end up with on a scaled drawing looks something like the protractor you used in the seventh grade; the straight base is your deck, and the semicircle scribes the beds without the three openings. What you have done is directly link bed shapes to an architectural element, thereby drawing house and garden into a relationship based on proportion.

Now you're ready to break into the central expanse of lawn. Stake out the semicircular bed, and stand with your back to the center of your back door. Look down the axis: from where you stand to the nail and through the gap at the apex of the semicircle and across lawn to the back of your property. By seeing the line as an axis, you then have a line along which to place the destination for that axial line: a bench within a garden, a grape arbor, or a group of five crab apple trees with bench and chairs under it (see figure 3.11). The grape arbor, or whichever structure you choose, will in turn anchor plantings along its back and both ends.

Then the question becomes, How do you visually link the semicircular garden in the foreground to the gardens around an arbor 50 or even 100 feet away? That's when the implied lawn path between the two comes into play. That line suggests an allée of trees between deck and arbor (see figure 3.11 again) or two open hedges on either side of the implied path or a stone path with perennial or low shrub borders on either side of it. You take the 18-foot dimension (half the length of the back of your house) and place the crab apples 18 feet on center along the implied lawn path and 18 feet across from one another. Those trees will in turn give you an idea for underplantings, and the whole

back garden soon comes into focus.

And so it goes. That whole natural sequence of ideas in the above examples came from the deck and the back doors of the house. If you follow the spirit of this idea rather than the facts – that is, your house may not be 36 feet wide, and your deck may be a stone patio – you can apply the principles behind my example to make a similar sequence of decisions yourself.

If you like curving, free-form beds, you can use the same principles gathered around axial arrangement. When Bill Patterson from Delaware came to a workshop I offered at the Longwood Gardens outside Philadelphia, he showed me a sketch of his back gardens south of his house (see figure 3.12). Down either side of the center of a 150-foot-long lawn, Bill had planted disparate island beds, some 10 feet long, some 30 feet long, but all of them no wider than 6 feet or so. Each had a different style: a rose garden; an ornamental grass garden; an herb garden; a garden of shrubs with a bench among them. They were not linked but were vaguely in two long lines. Some were separated from others with 5 feet of lawn, others with 15 feet of lawn. Because of the different styles and different amounts of lawn between beds, the back garden was dotty, broken up, and unsatisfying, and Bill knew it. He wanted me to help him pull all these disparate elements together around a unifying idea.

First, we sketched out how to remove the lawn between the ends of adjoining beds so that the seven beds on the right and the nine beds on the left were pulled into two long beds. Seen from a helicopter, these two long, thin beds would look like two huge snakes slithering down Bill's lawn, their full lengths surrounded by lawn (see figure 3.13). The inner curving lines could do what they wanted; the outer bed edges matched the line of

FIGURE 3.9 (OPPOSITE) A boardwalk in line with the back door extends hundreds of feet into a wildflower meadow. Build a boardwalk or path of an appropriate length straight from your back door into the natural landscape, linking house to the natural world.

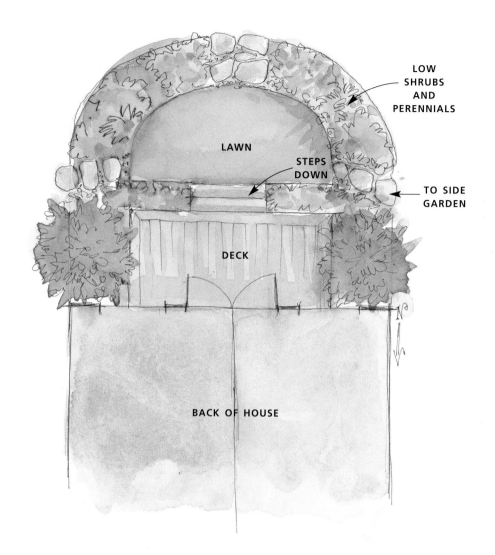

LOW
SHRUBS
AND
PERENNIALS

LAWN

STEPS
DOWN

TO SIDE
GARDEN

DECK

BACK OF HOUSE

FIGURE 3.10

Start with a modest first step
to break into your back lawn
and create a garden. Make
a semicircular garden that is
as wide as the back of your
house, with three paths leading out to link with two side
gardens and the garden at
the far end of your lawn.

the perimeter beds, thereby creating a uniform
5-foot-wide lawn path between perimeter
beds and the long, curvy beds. Where Bill
wanted to be able to walk across a bed, we
sketched in stepping-stones. Lawn paths pre-
viously separated beds; now stepping-stones
with plants on either side joined them.

Second, we set up a transplanting plan so
that, for example, most of the major ornamental grasses in the one grass garden Bill
had were now distributed along the length of
both beds. They acted, therefore, as a structur-
al element, a repeated form down the length
of both beds. We did the same with his rose-

bushes and several *Viburnum carlesii*, as well as
red-leaved barberries. The result was that a
variety of plants could now settle into a new
framework made up of dramatic, large-scale
perennials and shrubs with red leaves or striking flowers all set into two big, bold beds.

Third, we designed an arbor with bench
and chairs under it at the bottom of the garden and on center between the two long, thin
beds and the middle of Bill's back terrace.
When guests came out onto that terrace at the
back of his house, the arbor and furniture
would invite them to walk down the central
lawn, now an implied path, and between the

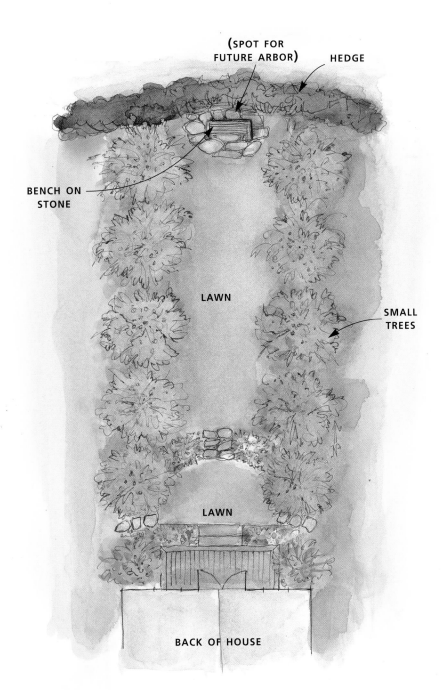

(SPOT FOR FUTURE ARBOR)

HEDGE

BENCH ON STONE

LAWN

SMALL TREES

LAWN

BACK OF HOUSE

FIGURE 3.11
Over time, you can expand the garden in figure 3.10 to look like this. Plant an allée of five pairs of small trees, such as crab apples, and then create a sitting area at the far end of the lawn with a hedge behind it for privacy.

full length of Bill's grand pair of curvilinear beds to sit and look back.

Fourth, the bench and chairs in this and all back gardens played a number of roles in holding this garden together. They acted as magnets to draw people across the full length of the back lawn, introducing them along the way to the full length of Bill's gardens and property. In combination with the arbor, they offered a sheltered place to sit and linger in the garden. Seeing that bench and chairs under the arbor when standing on the back deck of the house also enabled people to fully understand distance. Knowing how large a

BEFORE

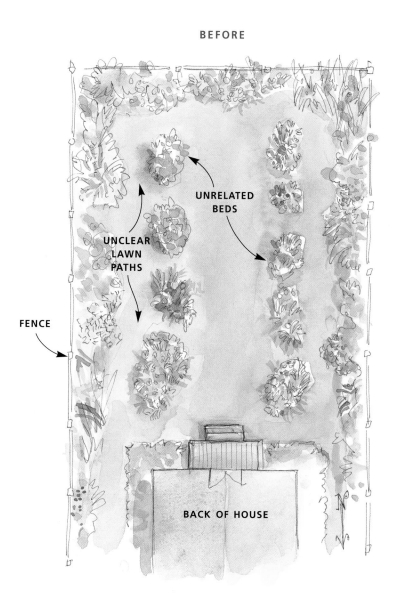

UNRELATED
BEDS

UNCLEAR
LAWN
PATHS

FENCE

BACK OF HOUSE

FIGURE 3.12
BEFORE – Several unrelated beds wander down the length of the lawn. At the end of the garden, there is no destination to draw people deep into the garden.

garden chair or a bench is, guests would be able to read how far away the arbor and chairs were at the other end of the garden. This understanding would, in turn, enable them to comfortably understand scale and distance throughout the back gardens from that vantage.

In the example of Bill Patterson's garden, formerly disparate gardens were drawn together into a coherent whole by a Big Idea, not a set of little ideas. All lines in a garden

need to relate, whether they are curved or straight. Given that the most important lines in your garden are those of your house or other buildings, start with those lines, and the resulting marriage between house and garden will create an overarching harmonious whole. If you have free-form island beds in your back lawn now, apply the lesson learned from Bill Patterson's example and explore ways to draw some or all of them together around your own Big Idea.

NEW BACK GARDENS

Before considering any design ideas, create a ¼ inch = 1 foot scaled drawing of the back of your home, including its wall height and position of doors and windows. Using triangulation, record existing features, such as major trees, outbuildings, boundary lines, even the location of a buried propane tank or septic line at the back of your house. Then lay a piece of tracing paper over the scaled drawing and tape down the four corners. You're ready to go, but take your time.

Stand for a few moments at every back window and door looking out at the existing foreground, middle ground, and background. Beautiful views in one direction might need framing; unsightly views in another will need screening. Flat land gives you broad options; slopes might suggest the location for a retaining wall to create a level plane between house and wall and a sloping garden beyond the wall. Existing trees, shrubs, or perennials that are flourishing might suggest the beginning of a plant list. Native bedrock, fieldstones, or old stone walls might give you a clue regarding what stone to use for a terrace, wall, or stepping-stone path.

Now go out to your boundary lines, or at least to the edges of the area you imagine gardening, and look back at the house. Walk the entire perimeter. Size up everything – light and shade, slope and flat, frame or screen, gravel or topsoil, points of the compass – and record it all right on that top sheet of tracing paper. Now take your assessment sheet off your scaled drawing, and put down a fresh sheet of trace.

What you look for first are potential paths and the sitting areas and even a gazebo or arbor that will act as destinations for them. For example, the immediate destination for the walk out the back door may be onto a terrace, patio, or deck. Start there. Measure the height of the back wall, and flop that dimension down onto the ground as a way to start your thinking. If it's a gable end, measure to the triangular tip of the roof; if it's an eave side, measure to where the sloping roof meets the vertical wall. Literally stake that dimension out on the ground as a rectangle or square with bamboo stakes to see what you see. Then start manipulating that shape in light of questions like these: Will we sit out here, and if so, how many people should the space accommodate? Is the marked-out space too small, too narrow, too long, not wide enough? Will steps be required to negotiate level changes? Do we want gardens on all three sides and perhaps even in a gap between the foundation of the house and the beginning of the paved sitting area?

To help you determine whether to locate a sitting area immediately off the back of your home or away from it, determine what direction of the compass the back of your home faces. Each direction has its own quality of light and will offer many clues as to where you will want to sit; refer back to Chapter 2 for all the details.

Once you have located and designed the sitting area adjacent to the back of your home, you're launched. Stand in the frame of the back door and look out at the distance. Do

you see a place out there for a gazebo or for a simple arbor against or near the house (see figure 3.14) or for any other built garden feature that will act as a destination for a straight path from your back door, across the sitting area and lawn to that structure? (See figure 3.15.) Do you already see the front of a garden shed or the side of another outbuilding that could become the backdrop for a garden and bench which would act as a destination for the path from the back door?

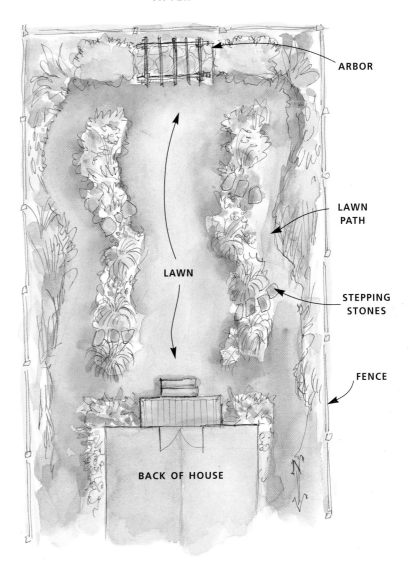

AFTER

ARBOR

LAWN PATH

STEPPING STONES

FENCE

LAWN

BACK OF HOUSE

FIGURE 3.13
AFTER – The arbor and bench underneath draw people down the central or side paths. Short stepping-stone paths allow people to walk through the long beds. The result is an itinerary and a unity that pulls all parts into a related whole.

Take some chairs and a table, set them up on the lawn where your sitting area will go, and take a look around. How can you link the paths coming down either side of your house with this new back sitting area? (See figure 3.16.) Where should plants go around the perimeter of the back sitting area? If you like to cook, perhaps the sitting and barbecue area out by the garden shed could be combined with a culinary herb garden with a lovely pattern to it.

Once you get the sitting area by the house established and link it via a path to a destination out from it, you have two centers for gardens and a link between them (see figure 3.3 again). Each will give rise to ideas for gardens

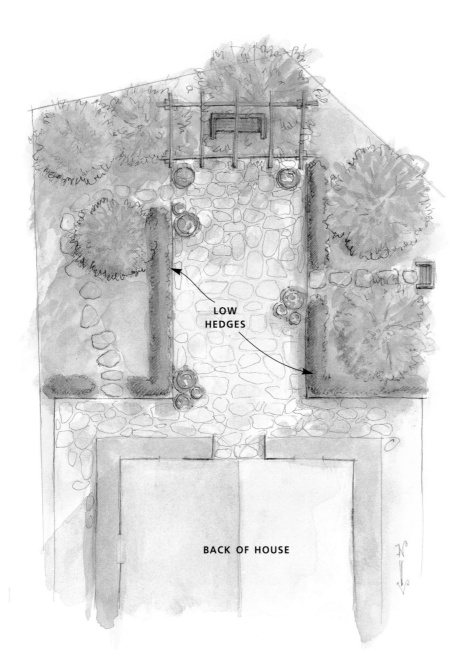

LOW HEDGES

BACK OF HOUSE

FIGURE 3.14 (OPPOSITE) Place an arbor suitable for the style and materials of your house near or at a distance from the back of your house. Create a sitting area under the arbor and take advantage of its columns to frame views. House and arbor act like bookends, holding gardens in place.

FIGURE 3.15 (LEFT) This rectilinear garden resolves an oddly shaped lot while drawing people into all parts of a small back garden. This design would also work well in a rectangular lot. The bench under the arbor and among trees and shrubs would provide privacy even in a suburban setting.

on either side of them or between them. By studying the next three chapters on ells and courtyards, spaces between buildings, and gardens around outbuildings, you'll be able to create new gardens in relation to existing or planned buildings. Then you link the doors in them with paths, and those paths become the spines of gardens. Coherence results if the lines of those paths are all related – that is, if they are all parallel or perpendicular to your house and other buildings or if they curve and

sweep to create pleasingly shaped and well-proportioned beds and lawn.

Let me give you a couple of examples of how I have applied the above process to develop a garden design. The south-facing lawn at the back of Cindy and Gerry Prozzo's home here in Vermont sloped gently away from the house just enough to demand a low retaining wall to make it flat (see figure 4.10). Knowing that the space outside their one-story-high living room was the perfect place to sit out-

FIGURE 3.16
Here, a roomy paved area could support other furniture and planted pots. A low fence around the perimeter increases the sense of enclosure. High shrubs and trees screen the area from neighbors' view.

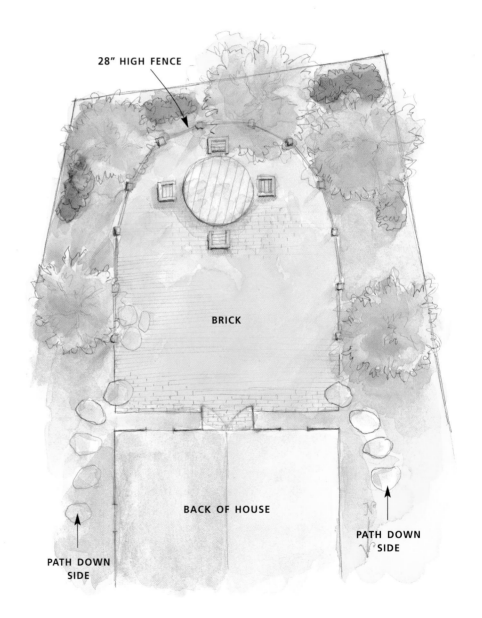

28" HIGH FENCE

BRICK

BACK OF HOUSE

PATH DOWN SIDE

PATH DOWN SIDE

CURVED BEDS AND PATHS IN THE BACK GARDEN

Edges of beds and paths adjacent to them that curve near the back of a house are often unsuccessful because their wiggly lines don't make sense. The curves in this garden do. The broad arcing curves simultaneously define the shapes of lawn paths and beds adjacent to them. The lawn path of uniform width curves from the back sitting area of this house and out, around, and down the slope in one long sweep. The uniformly wide lawn path in the foreground curves around the trunk of the maple, turns to direct you to the table and chairs under that tree, and then leads up the slope where it splits by the large-leaved hosta. All these curves in bed and path are logical. Yours should be too.

doors, I paved a 12-by-18-foot bluestone sitting area, with two wooden steps leading down from the living room door to that paved surface. Because the land sloped gently away from the house, we installed an 18-inch-high retaining wall 20 feet out from the back of the house to level the area. We planted the 2-foot-gap between the foundation wall of their home and the bluestone with small-leaved rhododendrons and evergreen groundcovers. Just below the retaining wall, we planted an Improved Bechtel crab apple, with its tiny roselike pink flowers, and underplanted it with hardy geraniums.

Once we established the design for the back sitting area and set it into a garden of plants on three sides – the fourth was the back wall of the house – we had the core of a design. Now the Prozzos walk off the bluestone area onto lawn, and they have several choices, all of which they can see from that area. In other words, their garden has an itinerary. They can turn right and walk south to the far level sitting area set into the edge of woodland. They can go straight ahead and across lawn to the beginning of a woodland path that leads through the east woods. Or they can turn left and walk across the lawn to a broad stepping-stone path into a semienclosed garden between the east lawn and the driveway. Along these paths are other subordinate gardens: a vegetable garden in full sun; a garden of native drought-tolerant ferns and mosses on a 50-foot-long expanse of exposed bedrock.

Gail Gee, a passionate, indefatigable gardener who lives in a rural area outside Baltimore, Maryland, offers another example on a larger scale. Even though she had already planted wonderful perennial and shrub borders around the perimeter of her back west-facing deck and around most of the perimeter of her large back lawn, the work I did with her holds an important lesson for anyone with a large central lawn out back.

Hers was almost an acre of amorphous lawn in the very center of her back gardens that sloped south to a woodland edge. Even though she had richly planted perimeter beds everywhere, her overall garden lacked a center, a bold, dramatic statement that would act as a focus, an organizing shape that would draw all perimeter beds into a relationship with it. The first problem we had to solve was the fact that the ground sloped down gently from north to south so that any garden we planted on it would not look settled. Geometric shapes in a lawn need to be made on level lawn; slopes are for curves. A 2-foot-high retaining wall running east-west solved the problem of the slope and gave us a broad, flat plane to work with.

After exploring a variety of shapes for the center of the lawn, we settled on a 60-foot ellipse scribed in the lawn in the form of a 5-foot-wide perennial bed, with two buddleia planted 8 feet apart in each of the four beds to provide structure. (This turned out to be a fortuitous shape, because Gail's husband, a non-gardener but part owner of a race horse, saw echoes of a racetrack in this design and he was hooked.) We decided to leave 6-foot-wide gaps at the north and south ends of the ellipse; the south gap would line up with a set of steps down through the retaining wall to an existing gazebo off line but in nearby lawn. The gap at the north end would lead to a new path and grape arbor set into the north perimeter bed. We also designed gaps along the east and west lengths of the ellipse, all in line with the steps down from the deck. The east gap enabled guests to walk down steps from the back deck of the house, into and straight through the center of the oval, and out the other side. They would then walk through an allée of five pairs of trees to a bench set against a handsome little utility shed designed to look like a rustic summerhouse. Whereas the elliptical garden provided a center for the entire back garden and helped us locate three built structures, the center of the ellipse suggested a place for a 12-foot-diameter pool with a single central jet to act as the very center of the entire back garden. To draw the old beds into a new relationship with the new, we reshaped the edges of some of the existing beds near the oval to echo its shape. The result of all this work provided a center, a focus for the entire back garden.

Now I can hear you groaning: An acre of garden? A 60-foot elliptical bed that leads to three outbuildings? Allées and a pool and new edges to all my beds? I don't have Gail Gee's stamina. Well, don't necessarily look at the facts of her design but at its principles. Explore the possibility of creating a shape in the center of your back lawn that is big enough to act as a bold center for all adjacent beds (see figures 3.2, 3.4, and 3.16 again). Let that shape, whatever its size, radiate out to connect to a bench under a group of three small Donald Wyman crab apples rather than a costly summerhouse. Design a crushed-gravel panel edged in brick in the center of your shape to take the place of Gail's pool, and set planted terra-cotta pots on the gravel. That is, take the principles of Gail's garden, or any garden I describe in this book, and apply them to the dimensions, climate, budget, and maintenance requirements of your own garden so that they become realistic, practical ideas for you.

PRACTICAL PROBLEMS SOLVED

1

THE AWKWARD
SPACE UNDER
A RAISED DECK

One of the most difficult spaces to screen from view is that long, shaded area under a deck or porch. Often it is 2 to 8 feet high, with upright posts set every 8 feet or so to support the deck above. It is usually an area where water drips in rows from the deck surface above onto gravel, mulch, or weeds below. The back of the area is often a concrete wall or an unfinished basement wall with a spiggot and hose hanging nearby. This space ranks

among the most unsightly. The obvious solution is to plant a shorn evergreen or dense deciduous hedge to screen the space, but there are many other solutions to consider.

If you have not yet constructed the deck, keep one rule in mind: if at all possible, build the deck of the same material as that of your house. The central problem with decks is that they appear tacked onto homes, a look that no amount of landscaping can resolve. If you have a white-painted clapboard home, for example, build the railings around the perimeter of the deck to echo some architectural element of your home and then paint them white too. Screen the open area between the floor of the deck and the ground with

trelliswork that creates 2-to-6-inch squares rather than diamonds. That is, have the lines of the trelliswork run horizontally and vertically to echo the vertical and horizontal lines of the house, and paint that white as well, or a dark green for pleasing contrast. Shrubs and perennials planted in front of this architectural solution will soften the look and tie deck and thereby house to the garden. Plant a tree or two among those shrubs and perennials to provide shade; as the tree grows, prune the lower branches until you open a view under the branches of the tree to the gardens and views beyond.

Keep one other principle in mind. A deck feels logical and therefore looks best when it holds you perched high

FIGURE 3.17
Climbing and trailing annuals in pots arrayed on a shallow shelf mask the underside of this deck.

above a dramatic drop into woodland or out to the lake, ocean, or valley below. A deck also looks right when it reads as an extension of the first floor and comes out in two or three broad landings that each step down 6 to 7 inches to deliver you with one final gentle step onto lawn or a stone walkway.

The decks that are visually troublesome are in that middle ground 3 to 6 feet above grade, where the logic of the deck is weak: it holds you above a level lawn only 3 feet below and provides an often-pinched sitting area for a few chairs and a table just a few feet above adjacent gardens. It is far preferable to reduce the gap between the surface of the deck and ground level by adding three steps from the floor level of the house down to a roomy deck only 12 to 18 inches or so above grade. Either that, or avoid building the deck altogether by constructing an attractive set of stone or wooden steps to get you from the house down to a stone- or brick-paved terrace or patio.

To keep weeds from taking hold in a space under a deck or porch, remove the topsoil, level or at least reduce the angle of the slope underneath as much as possible, lay down a water-permeable geotextile, and then cover the area with a few inches of 3/8-inch crushed stone or peastone. Do the same under any raised wooden surface, such as an entrance portico, a porch, or a deck, even if it is only a few inches off the ground. If you don't and you leave the subsoil or topsoil in place under a deck or porch, weeds will take hold and make an unsightly area even worse.

The most difficult problem regarding decks 3 to 6 feet or higher is how to screen the area under the deck from view. The classic approach is to tack trelliswork to the deck supports. One of the problems with this approach is that you can still see through the trelliswork to the lawn mower, ladders, blue tarps, and hoses stored under the area. Here are some alternatives to screening this unsightly area.

First screen the area under the deck by screwing or nailing fine-quality exterior plywood to the back of the uprights, from ground level up to the bottom of the deck. Paint it a color that is similar to the dominant paint color on your home. Then affix a trelliswork to that plywood surface, and paint the trelliswork the same color as the plywood. The result is a total screen through which a door could be set for access to the storage space underneath. By affixing the trelliswork to 2-to-3-inch-thick wooden strips, you can create a gap between the backboard and the trelliswork that would support morning glories or other annual vines which could be removed easily in the event that maintenance was necessary. Another option could be to plant a hedge in front of the trelliswork, the hedge acting as a background for a perennial border. Instead of the hedge, a series of espaliered fruit trees could be trained against the trelliswork backdrop.

Evergreen or deciduous hedges or dense plantings of flowering shrubs and evergreens will also screen the underside of the deck from view. Privet, yew, or arbor vitae hedges will work well and will, in turn, form a backdrop for herbaceous perennial borders in front of them. You could also plant a shade tree off one corner of the deck and then plant groups and single specimens of deciduous and evergreen shrubs to set the deck into a richly varied garden that would simultaneously screen the underside of the deck.

If your deck is 4 to 5 feet off the ground and you need to shovel snow off of it during the winter, tall perennials that die down to their crowns in the winter, rather than woody shrubs with brittle branching, will provide a more suitable choice of plants. *Cimicifuga ramosa* 'Atropurpurea,' along with massed tall ornamental grasses such as *Miscanthus sinensis* 'Purpurascens' and *M.s.* 'Morning Light' interplanted with tall perennials such as *Aruncus dioicus*, will totally screen the underside of the deck. Then plant middle-height perennials, such as echinaceas, Russian sage, or heleniums in front of the tall plants and yet shorter perennials, such as peonies, catmints, Veronicas, and hardy geraniums, in the foreground.

I saw another clever solution at Bill Dodge's garden on Kauai. He built a 12-inch-wide horizontal shelf 4 feet above ground level between each pair of uprights supporting his deck (see figure 3.17). Then he affixed an open wire mesh that stretched from the back of the shelf up to the horizontal beam supporting the front of the deck. He then set planted pots on the shelf, some containing climbing vines that twine up the wire mesh support and others that trail down to cover the gap below the shelf.

The other option is to affix open wire mesh, ornamental ironwork, or handsome wooden trelliswork to support woody vines – *Ampelopsis bre-vipedunculata*, clematis, hops, grapevines, honeysuckles, *Akebia quinata*, *Bougainvillaea*, *Hedera colchica* 'Dentata Variegata.'

Climbing annual vines:

Abutilon megapotamicum

Cobaea scandens 'Alba' – cup and saucer plant

Convolvulus tricolor and other morning glory vines

Dolichos lablab – hyacinth bean

Phaseolus coccineus – scarlet runner bean

Rhodochiton atrosanguineum – purple bell vine

Solanum jasminoides – potato vine

Thunbergia grandiflora – blue trumpet vine

Tropaeolum peregrinum – canary vine

Mina lobata – romantic love vine

Humulus lupulus 'Variegatus' – variegated hop vine

Trailing annual vines and plants:

Helichrysum petiolare and its varieties – licorice plant

Ipomoea batatas and its varieties – sweet potato vine

Lobelias in variety

Lotus berthelotii – lotus vine

Pelargoniums in variety, especially the Swiss Balcon series

Petunia hybrid *Calibrachoa* – Million Bells

Petunia integrifolia and other trailing petunias

Plectranthus spp. – Swedish ivy

Scaevola – Australian fan flower

Tropaeolum in variety – nasturtiums

Verbenas in the Tapien and Temari series

The Main Points

▪ The most appropriate deck holds you high above woodland, a valley edge, a beach, or some naturally occurring landscape.

▪ If you must have a wooden deck, get it as low to the ground as possible by creating two or three steps down from the floor level of your house before building the deck surface, thereby increasing its connection to the earth.

▪ Nail vine-supporting trelliswork or wires between existing vertical deck supports; plant flowering vines that will cling to the trelliswork and screen the underside of your deck.

▪ Plant an evergreen or dense deciduous hedge to screen the deck's underside, leaving a gap in a useful but inconspicuous place for access.

▪ Build a stout shelf 3 to 4 feet above grade and between the vertical deck supports. Attach vine-supporting wire between the shelf and the bottom of the deck. Place potted climbers or trailers on the shelf that will grow up and down to screen the underside of the deck.

▪ Screen the underside with a solid wooden siding like that on your house, and then plant a shrub/perennial bed in front of it, with one or two trees for shade.

2

FENCING AROUND SWIMMING POOLS

Many state, town, or municipal codes require swimming pools to be fenced to prevent pets and unsupervised children from gaining access to deep water. Most regulations require fences to be between 42 and 48 inches high, with gates that have latches children cannot easily open. They often call for certain fencing materials or wooden fences with minimum-gap dimensions between upright pickets. Contact the local zoning ordinance department in your town hall, a town or municipal clerk's office, or an architect or pool-installing company to learn exactly what the regulations are in your area. But whether state or local regulations call for protective fencing or not, you might want to consider installing it in any event.

Surround the area around a swimming pool with a 48-inch-high picket fence, leaving plenty of room for pool coping, a panel of lawn, and a 2-to-3-foot-wide perennial border along the inside of the fence. Your home should provide the clues you need as to the material and color of the fencing so that the two appear harmonious. If your home is painted white, paint the pickets white. If it is made of natural or lightly stained wood, construct the fencing with unpainted cedar, which, over time, will fade to an attractive silver-gray.

The placement of the fence relative to the shape, dimensions, and location of the pool is another important consideration. Where you put the fence should produce a useful, roomy space between the pool's edge and the fence, but that space should also be in proportion with the pool. For example, if the 20-by-40-foot pool is surrounded by a 4-foot-wide concrete or stone coping, you can see that each of these numbers has 4 in common. The 4-foot module can become a very helpful design tool for you. For example, you could add an 8- or 12-foot-wide panel of lawn around the perimeter of the pool coping and then a 4-foot-wide perennial/shrub border between the outer perimeter of the lawn and a 4-foot-high fence that will act as the backdrop for the border. By repeating this 4-foot module – or any module that relates to the dimensions of your own pool and surrounding area – in pool, coping, lawn, bed, and fence, every element of the garden will be in proportion with one another. The 4-foot-wide gates that lead into this space should be of a similar style and material as that of the fence.

If codes allow you to install plants rather than a wooden fence to keep the pool area off-limits, there is a virtually invisible alternative. Drive 6-foot-long metal stakes (those with the metal clips every 6 inches or so) 2 feet deep into the ground and 6 feet on center. Then attach wire fencing to them and plant a hedge of privet, arbor vitae, yew, or any other hedging material tight up against the inside of the wire fencing, and tease the foliage and twigs of the shrubs through the gaps in the fencing. In this way, you hide the wire fencing yet achieve a very safe fence that would not be possible with the plants alone.

Another alternative is to install the fencing well away from the pool. Set a 4-foot-high wire fence, a 12-foot-high deer fence, or a split three-rail fence (to which wire mesh fencing is affixed) around the perimeter of your property, and then plant every so often with attractive vines. In this way, the safety fence is perhaps even 100 feet or more away from the pool, yet still serves the purpose of keeping animals and children from getting onto your property. If you use deer fencing, you may need to install a cattle grid in your driveway to be sure that that one necessary opening in the driveway is essentially closed to deer and very young children.

Rather than see the regulations as a burden, look upon them as an opportunity to clearly define the swimming pool and its surrounding lawn and generous gardens as a secret, private space. A swimming pool is a place where you, your children, and friends enjoy one another's company. Such a space benefits from total privacy and, especially, complete separation from the driveway and the arrival of the UPS delivery truck.

The Main Points
- Before building a pool, research municipal codes regarding fencing around swimming pools.
- Be certain to understand the codes regarding position of fencing, the height, materials, width of allowable gaps, requirements governing gaps in gates, and whether or not plants can suffice as fencing.
- Check to see whether codes will allow fencing up to 100 feet or more away from the pool.
- Ask your architect, builder, or pool installer to become an advocate for

you with town officials so that your fencing can be as attractive and unobtrusive as possible.
- No matter what, be certain your pool fencing is sound enough to keep uninvited children out of harm's way.

3

HIDING THE SEPTIC TANK VENT

While many suburban and all urban homes are connected to municipal sewer lines, many suburban and virtually all rural homes have their own septic systems. The location, dimensions, and depth of the septic tank, pump chamber tank and its associated leachfield, which can cover hundreds of square feet, have a considerable impact on planting choice both atop and near the various elements of the system, so it is essential that you know exactly where your system is so that you make informed garden design and planting decisions. A friend once planted a birch tree within 5 feet of a septic line, and within two years, the roots had clogged the lines. He had to uproot an entire garden – trees, shrubs, and perennials – replace all the septic lines, and then replant. I don't want you to have to go through that.

The first thing to understand is the system itself and how it is constructed. The septic tank is typically located between 10 and 20 feet from your house and is connected to the bathroom and kitchen drains from your home by a 6-inch-diameter pipe buried 2 to 3 feet below ground level. Most three-bedroom homes have a 1,000-

gallon tank that is about 5 feet wide, 9 feet long, and 5$\frac{1}{2}$ feet high. Septic tanks are usually covered with 2 feet of topsoil. In the center of the top of this tank is a 2-foot-diameter clean-out cover that must be dug up periodically so that the solids which gather at the bottom can be pumped out with a stout hose to a tanker truck.

You may have a second tank, called a pump chamber. You'll know if you have one of these because you'll see a white plastic walking-cane–shape vent pipe poking up out of the ground 2 to 4 feet from the second tank. If you have one, it is connected to the first tank by a 3-to-10-foot-long plastic pipe. The pump chamber is where gray water from your home gathers to be pumped through pipes up to the mounded leachfield. The pump chamber usually has a tiled cover for controls and electrical lines. But that's not all.

A strong plastic 6-inch-diameter pipe then runs 2 to 3 feet underground from the pump chamber anywhere from 10 feet to any distance the septic engineer called for to the mounded leachfield, in essence a filter for gray water. The location and dimensions of a leachfield are dictated by the drainage characteristics of your soil and usually cover a 600-square-foot area. Most are 50 feet long and 12 feet wide and are comprised of perforated pipes arrayed over 30 inches or so of sand and crushed rock over which a filter fabric is spread and then covered with 6 to 12 inches of topsoil seeded with grass seed and mulched with hay. The gray water is pumped through the perforated pipes, where it filters down through the sand and crushed stone and back into the earth.

There are a number of things you can do to minimize the visual impact of these systems on your garden design.

4

HIDING THE MOUNDED LEACHFIELD

If you are still in the design or construction phase of your home or if you have to redo your leachfield sometime soon, work with an engineer to locate it out of sight from the house. This will often cost extra, because you may have to bury an atypical length of septic pipe with a backhoe. In one residential design, I worked with the excavator and engineer to site the leachfield completely out of sight, some 500 feet from the home, and over the brow of a hill in gravelly, sandy soil. The location required digging a trench through woodland, but rather than go in a straight line, we created three long, broad curves as the excavator trenched for the pipe. Once the pipe was installed and the trench backfilled, we mulched the disturbed surface with processed bark mulch, and now that leaves have fallen on the mulch, it looks and acts like a woodland path.

A different homeowner with whom I worked had a flat, open site, so we worked with the engineer to locate the 3-to-4-foot-high, 90-foot-long mounded leachfield parallel with the house and some 150 feet away from it. Unless the system is failing, there is no unpleasant odor associated with a leachfield, so we created a mixed shrub and perennial garden with a central sitting area that

faced back to the house. In this way, shrubs, kept at least 15 feet from the edge of the leachfield, and perennials planted right up to and on top of the leachfield, masked the unnatural mound and provided a good context for a dramatic border. I planted fountain grass (*Pennisetum alopecuroides* 'Hameln') as specimen plants in the border and massed the same grass in big drifts on the mound to link foreground to background.

In another garden, we actually built up the height of the leachfield to 7 feet above the grade of the adjacent driveway to act as a screening berm, so people in the house could not see the nearby road. We then planted big sweeps of *Hydrangea paniculata* 'Unique' along the lower sides of the leachfield, out of harm's way of the pipes, and seeded the ground under them and up to the top of the berm with chewings fescue grass seed. At the end of the berm farthest from the house, we graded the berm to blend with the grade of existing meadow, so the whole construction appeared like a natural extension of the rolling meadows nearby. To link meadow to berm even more, we seeded all the disturbed soil of the existing meadow with the same chewings fescue seed to further blur the edge between the constructed berm/leachfield and the existing meadow.

Because the soil atop a leachfield is only 6 to12 inches deep and atop sand and crushed stone, you will want to choose only tough, shallow-rooted, drought-tolerant plants to cover your own mounded leachfield. *Sedum spectabile*, nepetas, *Alchemilla mollis*, *Coreopsis verticillata*, echinaceas and mallows, *Solidago rugosa* 'Fireworks,' *Rudbeckia fulgida* 'Goldsturm,' and daylilies, for example, are all plants I would use here in the Northeast. Your plant list may well be very different, but the plant characteristics should be the same: shallow-rooted, drought-tolerant, rugged and not precious. Peony 'Guardian of the Monastery' would not be a candidate; lupins would be. And finally, do not plant vegetables or fruiting shrubs or trees for human or animal consumption on or within at least 50 feet of a leachfield. Far too many household chemicals make their way to a leachfield and can be taken up by root systems.

5
PLANTING OVER THE SEPTIC TANK

There are two limitations to planting atop a septic tank. First, the soil may only be 12 to 24 inches deep, so you can plant virtually any perennials, but don't plant large-scale shrubs like viburnums, hamamelis, lilacs, or hollies. Choose small shrubs, like *Fothergilla gardenii*, skimmia, small-leaved rhododendrons, caryopteris, potentillas, daphnes, and hypericums. And don't plant trees within 25 to 35 feet of a septic tank or pump chamber, and even then, choose small trees, such as crab apples, amelanchiers, crape myrtles, sourwood, or dogwoods. The aggressive and powerful feeder roots of larger trees, especially those of willows, maples, birches, or beeches will insinuate themselves into the joints where plastic pipe meets concrete tank and

plug up your system. Keep them at least 75 to 100 feet away.

The second limitation to planting above a septic tank is that you will have to dig down 2 feet every two years or so to expose and then open the clean-out cover so that the tank can be pumped empty. Given that the clean-out cover is 24 inches in diameter and that you'll need room for the excavated soil and for yourself to work, you should not plant any closer than 2 to 3 feet from the circumference of the clean-out cover. Otherwise, you can plant small shrubs and perennials as you choose.

6
SCREENING THE VENT PIPE

The vent pipe, shaped like a walking cane and arising from the pump chamber, can be anywhere from 2 to 4 feet high. The simplest screening solution I have found for homes in rural sites is to slip a hollow log – ask an arborist or logger for one – over the vent pipe, thereby making it look as though you left a high stump when you cut a tree down. Another solution is to screen it from sight with plants. Because 2 feet of topsoil sits atop the pump chamber, you have plenty of depth for shallow-rooted perennials and shrubs. First paint the pipe green and/or brown, and then plant ornamental grasses, asters, eupatorium, and other tall perennials in a garden large enough that it doesn't look contrived. If the system in the pump chamber needs maintenance, you may have to move some of the plants, but that's a

small price to pay for not having to look at a vent pipe poking up out of your lawn.

Another solution is to move the pipe. Working with your excavator operator or engineer, consider connecting the 4-inch-diameter vertical pipe just where it exits the pump chamber with an elbow piece to similarly sized horizontal pipe buried just a foot or so underground. That horizontal pipe can then go a considerable distance underground before the vertical vent pipe comes up above grade to provide the venting that is necessary. Explore with your excavator operator or engineer various alternative locations for the vent pipe: at the woodland edge, among existing or planted shrubs, or behind the garage or garden shed. Keep in mind that the role of this pipe is to vent the buildup of methane gas in the pump chamber, so keep it well away from open windows or places where people will gather or frequently walk. The height of this vent pipe will vary according to your location in North America. In Vermont, for example, vent pipes must be 4 feet above grade because snow can build up to that height and cover the vent.

Perennials to plant on leachfields:

Achilleas
Artemisias
Asclepias incarnata or *A. tuberosa*
Echinaceas
Hemerocallis
Perovskia atriplicifolia
Rudbeckia fulgida 'Goldsturm'
Solidagos
Sedum spectabile

Native perennial grasses such as fescues or carexes

Ornamental grasses such as *Pennisetum alopecuroides* 'Hameln'

Trees NOT to plant within 75 to 100 feet of a leachfield or septic tank:

Beech

Birch

Cottonwoods

Elms

Poplars

Maples

Willows

Trees that can be planted within 25 to 35 feet of a leachfield:

Cherries

Crab apples

Dogwoods

Oaks

Pines

Sourwood

The Main Points

- See whether you have an "As Built" map that shows the location of the various elements of your septic system. If not, find out who installed the system and get copies of his records.
- Find out where the clean-out cover is buried, and be certain that as you develop your garden design, you keep the area at least 3 feet around it accessible.
- Ensure that you have left enough room for the tanker truck driver to drag his hose to the clean-out cover without damaging your gardens.
- Don't plant anything but shallow-rooted perennials and grasses atop a

septic tank or leachfield.

- Explore the options for locating a vent pipe at a distance from the pump chamber.
- If you are in the construction phase for your home, try to locate a mounded leachfield over the brow of a hill so that the unnatural mound is not visible from house or garden.

7

PORTABLE AND BUILT-IN GRILLS AND BARBECUES

If you enjoy cooking outdoors, you have two options: portable metal units fired by charcoal or bottled gas, and permanent brick or stone built-in barbecues fired by wood or charcoal. Let's look at the portable units first. Charcoal kettle barbecues and the much larger cart-based LP (liquified propane) or natural gas grills are often ungainly, unattractive amenities that need to be stored near where they will be used: on the back patio or deck, near the swimming pool, or at the back of the garage where a sitting and gathering area is.

Charcoal kettle barbecues are typically 36 to 42 inches high. They are fitted with an 18-to-20-inch dome-shaped painted cover which sits atop a similarly sized and colored metal basin for coals and ashes and the metal cooking grate. On two wheels and one leg and weighing only between 10 and 15 pounds, these small units can be readily stored out of sight in an outbuilding or a utility area behind the garage.

The steel-framed cart-based LP or natural gas barbecues are a different

matter. Even though these units are set on four legs fitted with wheels or casters, they are not easily stored after each use because they weigh anywhere from 125 to 175 pounds. They are often as long as 4 to 5 feet when their covers are open, as long as 5 to 6 feet when work surfaces on either end of the unit are attached, and up to 3 feet deep. They are often fitted with three stainless-steel burners, enclosed storage areas and exposed work surfaces, wire condiment baskets and bottom shelves, cooking tool holders and swing-up tables and also come painted black, blue, burgundy, or green. A 20-pound LP or natural gas tank sits on the ground next to the unit, attached to the burners by a 6-to-12-foot-long black hose. These useful and popular things have a lot of physical and visual weight, but they add nothing to the beauty of a garden. I think they need to be screened from view.

In a garden I designed in Maryland, where there is no problem caused by snow sliding off the roof, I created a little screened-off barbecue area along one eave side of the house. The bottom step coming down from the nearby kitchen door gave us a 10-foot dimension out from the foundation. I designed a yew hedge 5 feet high and 10 feet out in line with the bottom step. This evergreen hedge enclosed a 9-foot-wide, 12-foot-long barbecue area with a 3-foot gap in the hedge for access. We used finely crushed gravel tamped deeply as the surface for the barbecue unit. In this way, grease and oils spattering from the barbecue would land on tamped gravel, which could, after each summer, be easily skimmed

FIGURE 3.18
Build a brick barbecue against a brick wall, and it will settle in visually, especially if you can match brick material and color.

off with a shovel and replaced with fresh gravel.

By enclosing the barbecue area with a 5-foot-high yew hedge on two sides, we were able to screen it from virtually the entire garden and nearby swimming pool, yet it was close to the kitchen as well as to the pool, where people gathered throughout the summer. Furthermore, the yew hedge became the backdrop for a perennial garden running along its length. Because the hedge was kept at the 5-foot height – that is, the optimum height of the barbecue unit – whoever was cooking at the unit could see over the hedge to talk with people gathered by the pool, yet those by the pool couldn't see the barbecue.

If your kettle or cart-based barbecue is on a raised deck or balcony, you could screen the unit with richly planted annuals in large terra-cotta containers, or you could purchase a folding painted screen suitable for use outdoors.

Now let's look at stone or hard brick built-in permanent barbecues. These are clearly more appropriate for the gardener, because they can be so easily integrated into the landscape. If you have a brick wall in your garden, build a brick barbecue against it, made from bricks that can withstand the heat of a fire (see figure 3.18). If you have a stone wall or even bedrock and boulders in your garden near where you cook and eat, simple or complex stone structures can be built for about the same cost as you would incur buying a metal gas-fired barbecue.

For example, Jan Brett and Joe Hearne, who have a summer home in the Berkshire Hills of Massachusetts,

asked me to site an outdoor cooking area among outcroppings of bedrock near their house as part of an overall redesign for their naturalistic gardens. We talked about masonry or drywall construction among bedrock and boulders, but the look was not natural enough. As we were looking around the east slope of their wooded property, at a lake's edge we came upon two 3-foot-high flat-topped outcroppings of bedrock with a gap between them of about 5 feet. Rather than build a barbecue in this pristine woods, we asked a metal fabricator to design and construct a stout metal barbecue grill that could span the 5-foot opening (see figure 3.19). We then excavated the woodland debris and topsoil from the area between the two rock outcroppings, carried in six or eight 5-gallon buckets of finely crushed gravel, and covered the area under the metal grate with the gravel and tamped it down.

We then set large, flat stones under the grate that, by stacking in any number of ways, would allow for building wood fires at different heights under the metal grate. Because fire can cause stone to break up or split, we then set 15 or so thin firebricks atop the upper stone, and Joe now builds his fire atop the bricks. To give him even greater flexibility when cooking, we found a 2-foot-square, 1-inch-thick piece of polished soapstone that he could set atop the metal grating to use as a griddle.

You could take the principle behind this simple construction and make your own barbecue. If you have one 24-to-30-inch-high flat-topped boulder near where you want to cook outdoors, set a second one nearby, and have a metal grill made to fit.

The Main Points

- If you find your charcoal or gas barbecue apparatus unattractive, create a hedged or fenced area off the edge of your garden, with crushed gravel underfoot.
- Site such an area close to the kitchen and/or close to the area where you and guests will eat outdoors.
- Consider replacing your cart-based barbecue on a metal frame with a built-in brick or stone one that can be more gracefully integrated into your garden.

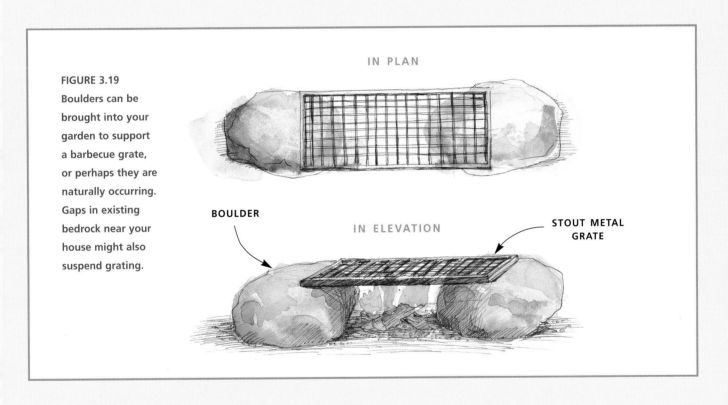

IN PLAN

IN ELEVATION

BOULDER

STOUT METAL GRATE

FIGURE 3.19 Boulders can be brought into your garden to support a barbecue grate, or perhaps they are naturally occurring. Gaps in existing bedrock near your house might also suspend grating.

CHAPTER FOUR

GARDENS IN AN ELL
OR COURTYARD

THE NEW KIND

OF GARDEN . . .

IS DESIGNED

PRIMARILY

FOR LIVING.

— THOMAS CHURCH
(1902–1978),
California-based
landscape architect

A COURTYARD IS AN ARCHITECTURAL indentation formed when two wings come off your house to enclose a three-sided space. An ell is formed when the main body of your home meets a wing of the house or a garage at a right angle to create a two-sided space. Take advantage of the courtyard or the ell by enclosing the fourth side of the courtyard and the third and fourth sides of the ell, and you'll create a happy marriage between house and garden. Pay attention to the location of doors and windows on the two or three sides of your home, and the garden within the space will practically design itself and then ripple out to help you design other nearby spaces.

When Norman and Lyn Lear asked me to design the gardens around their home set among lawn and meadows here in Vermont, part of what I addressed was a space on the west side of their house, just outside the back kitchen door. Featureless lawn grew in the 25-foot gap between the one-story west side of the house out to the top of a retaining wall from which you could look down to a natural pond and spacious rolling lawn beyond. Given that the area was sunny from noon onwards and in close proximity to the kitchen, it was a perfect place for lunch or dinner. The architecture told me exactly what to do with the space. At the south end of the area was a 12-foot-wide setback in the building created by a linking corridor between two wings that each came out 10 feet to create three sides of a space; the fourth flowed out into the lawn.

I designed a 10-foot-wide arbor set into the 12-foot-wide nook in the house and extended it out 16 feet (see figure 4.1). It was as high as the adjacent wall of the one-story wings and linking corridor. Arbor fit house like a glove. I left a 2-foot-wide planting space under the dripline of the three gutterless eave sides of the house for shade and moisture-tolerant ligularias, purple-leaved snakeroot

(*Cimicifuga ramosa* 'Atropurpurea'), and *Hosta* 'Krossa Regal.' *Lonicera tellmanniana* would grow up three of the arbor posts. Stone paving went under and around the arbor, leaving a 2-foot-wide gap of soil between the outer edge of the stone surface and the top of the wall for a low perennial border. The generous field-stone paving provided room during the summer months for richly planted terra-cotta pots. The day the dining table and chairs went in under the arbor, people began to gather in the area for the first time since the Lears bought the house.

Because the ell or courtyard can occur on the front, back, or sides of your home, you need to acknowledge which direction the ell or courtyard faces. What you plant in that enclosed space will in part be determined by the amount of sun or shade the area gets at different times of the day and year. If it's facing south, it will become a hotter microclimate than one-sided south-facing areas because of reflected light from two or three walls of your home and shelter from winds. That enclosed space, especially if it is a court-yard enclosed on three sides, might get hot and dry from lack of air movement, which calls for drought-tolerant plants. If it faces

FIGURE 4.1
Even the shallowest indentations in a house provide clues for garden design. Because the driplines of three roofs shed water onto the ground on three sides of this space, I planted moisture- and shade-loving ligularias and rodgersias in the gap between the stone paving and the wall of the house.

north, it might well stay cool and shady during the growing season and require shade-tolerant plants.

When creating an outdoor living space or simply a walk-through garden in a courtyard or ell, keep in mind that you will be inviting people to come up close to two or three walls of your home. If those walls are two or perhaps even three stories high, you run the risk of making people feel overpowered by all that building. Columnar, upright, or fastigiate trees planted within a tall narrow space will sometimes solve the problem by breaking up the architecture and providing a bit of canopy overhead. A broader sitting area in an ell can benefit from spreading trees (see figure 4.2). Ellen Patterson and I lifted two groups of paving stones from her stone sitting area, dug deep topsoil-enriched holes, and planted two birch trees right into an existing stone terrace

in the ell of her three-story house. Now guests sitting on the patio no longer feel overwhelmed by so much architecture above them.

You also need to consider the role the garden in the ell or courtyard garden will play in the context of the broader design of your entire property. Is the ell or courtyard in a prominent position at the back or front of the house? If so, how can you visually link it to gardens in the distance or to entrance or side gardens? Ellen Patterson and I decided to repeat the same stone paving around her front door and repeat the birches as well, but we built in a difference. We designed restrained, more formal underplantings around the front door, with boxwood-edged beds of July-blooming azaleas underplanted with *Vinca minor* 'Bowles.' In the back ell, we planted the perimeter of the stone sitting area with the nearby woodland in mind: hardy geraniums,

FIGURE 4.2

Two walls of this house provide a protected place for a sitting area. Combined with the tree's branches overhead, such a still corner in an ell holds the fragrance of Brugmansia in the pot and other flowering plants in the beds.

mountain laurel, the fragrant mayflower viburnum (*Viburnum carlesii*), bloodroot, and fall-blooming anemones (*Anemone vitifolia* 'Robustissima' and others).

The position of the courtyard or ell along the walls of your home is equally important to understand. If it's at the side of the house and the view from it is of little interest, create an elegant, restrained garden with sculpture, a water feature, and simple plantings (see figure 4.3), keeping in mind that you'll see the garden from first- and second-story windows year-round. If the courtyard is at the back of the house and overlooks a beautiful west or south view, pave a good portion of it for chairs and tables, and surround the sitting area with gardens (see figure 4.4, and notice what the view looks onto in figure 6.6). Finally, if your

FIGURE 4.3

This urban courtyard garden, the focus of which is the Buddha, is made calmer by the sound of dripping water. Often windows are situated above courtyard gardens, so patterns of garden and paving become important.

105

front door is in a courtyard, you have the best of all worlds. What a marvelous entrance courtyard you could make, with a pair of trees, fragrant flowering shrubs and perennials, and even a place to sit.

Gardening in the Ell

One idea for making the space within an ell comfortable and welcoming is to enclose the other two sides so that you are within a rectangular, square, or curvilinear garden, not a corner. In that way, the two-sided ell becomes a four-sided garden. The space takes on definition, with one or more entrances, a center, and edges. Stone walls, hedges, a low fence, even a simple low perennial bed between the lawn and the garden in the ell will create a feeling of enclosure while assuring you and

guests that you can see and walk out to other parts of the garden (see figure 4.5).

The key to garden design around and within the ell is to look for clues as to where to locate garden entrances, edges, and pathways into as well as through the area. When Clifton and Lyn Cooke asked me to look at their garden in New Hampshire, one of the first areas we looked at was the southwest-facing ell of their home, just off a kitchen wing and sitting room (see figure 4.6). Two adjoining 20-foot-long, 6-foot-wide porches only 18 inches above grade were already built onto each side of the ell, with lawn coming up to the base of the porches. Lyn told me that they loved sitting out in the privacy of the ell in the morning, but the afternoon sun during July and August was sometimes uncomfortably

FIGURE 4.4 (OPPOSITE)
The shallow ell in this home near Ithaca, New York, provides a context for a low retaining wall that pushes the lawn away from the house and provides an informal and level sitting area where two pollarded *Tilia cordata* trees have been planted. The simplicity of the house is echoed in the informal garden. (Designer: Hitch Lyman)

FIGURE 4.5 (LEFT)
This ell at the back of a 200-year-old house provided a context that helped me design a private outdoor dining and sitting area. See figure 4.19 for a detail drawing of the structure Connie Kheel, the owner, built to replace the unsightly metal bulkhead door.

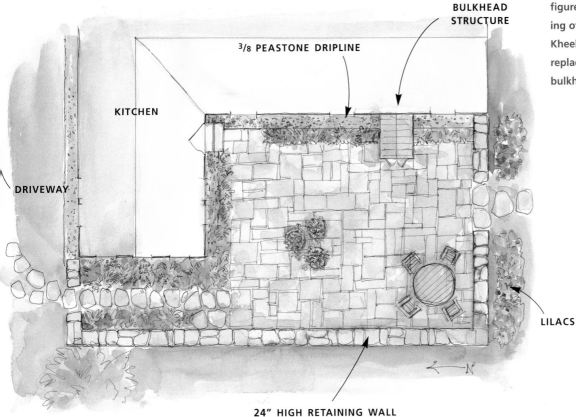

KITCHEN

DRIVEWAY

3/8 PEASTONE DRIPLINE

BULKHEAD STRUCTURE

LILACS

24" HIGH RETAINING WALL

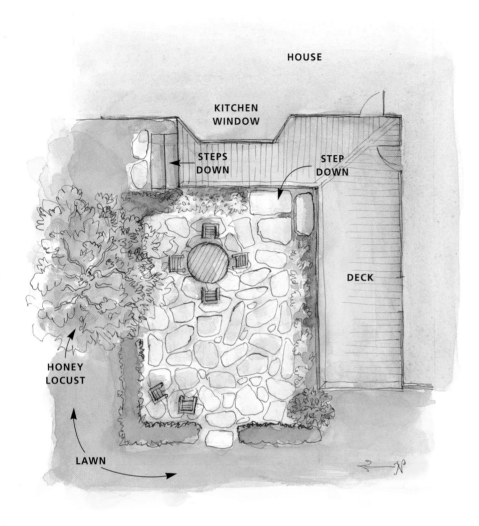

FIGURE 4.6
When a deck in an ell is too narrow for entertaining, extend it with a stone terrace and surrounding plantings so that you step down from the deck into a garden.

'Green Velvet') 2 feet out from the other two sides of the sitting area – the 2-foot width would accommodate perennials too – leaving one gap in the hedge for access out onto the lawn. To provide shade, I located a Shademaster honey locust just a few feet west of the boxwood hedge so that by two in the afternoon, the area would begin to go into shade. As the tree grew, the shade would reach the sitting area sooner.

When designing a sitting area in the ell of Quita Vitzthum's home only 50 feet from a heavily traveled road here in Vermont, the ell gave me a cue (see figure 4.7). Quita wanted a roomy brick-paved sitting area in the south-west-facing ell by her front door. The problem was that the west-facing side of the ell was only 8 feet long, far too short to provide the line for the outer edge of the sitting area. The other side of the ell was 24 feet long, giving us plenty of room for the patio's length. To extend the line of the short side of the ell, I designed a 10-foot-long arbor vitae hedge (*Thuja occidentalis* 'Smaragd'), which ran from that southwest corner of the ell due south and then turned due west to provide the 24-foot-long south edge of the sitting area. (A perennial bed enclosed the fourth side.) The result was a 16-by-20-foot brick-paved sitting area surrounded by perennial beds and hedged for privacy from driveway and road.

Wallace Huntington, a landscape architect who lives in one of the earliest homes built in the Willamette Valley in Oregon, used the space in the southwest-facing ell where barn meets house in a different way (see figure 4.8). A covered porch starts in the ell at the back and goes around the four sides of the house; chairs and tables are set on the porch, particularly on those sides from which the views are attractive. With the porch providing plenty of seating space, the garden in the ell did not need to be a sitting area, such as the ones I

hot. Furthermore, when the Cookes had guests for the weekend, the porch was just too narrow to seat more than two.

The ell told me how to solve the problems. I designed a stone-paved sitting area 18 feet square set into the ell, leaving 2 feet of planting space between paving and L-shaped porch for perennials to hide the underside of the porch and to bring color to the area. I set two 5-foot-wide granite steps in the corner of the porch and just off the kitchen door to lead down to the stone-paved sitting area, matching the steps at the front of the house. I then designed a boxwood hedge (*Buxus microphylla*

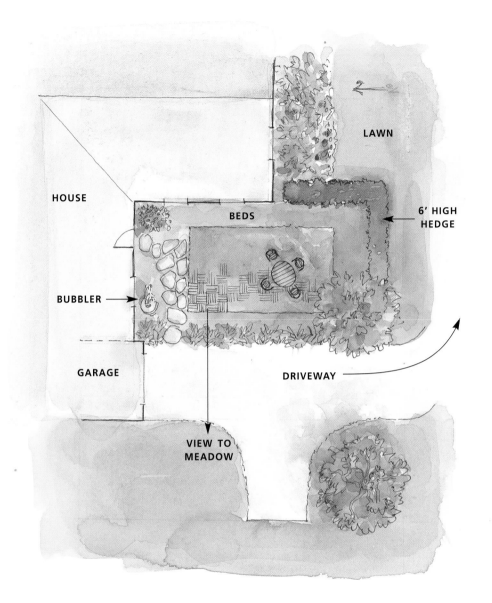

LAWN

HOUSE

BEDS

6' HIGH
HEDGE

BUBBLER →

GARAGE

DRIVEWAY

VIEW TO
MEADOW

FIGURE 4.7
When an ell is too shallow
to embrace a garden,
extend one or both sides
with a hedge to make the
space larger. The sound of
a bubbler in such a small
space adds calm to the
garden only 50 feet from
a nearby road.

designed for the Cookes and Quita Vitzthum, but just a garden to walk through. Given these variables, Huntington created a roughly 20-by-20-foot simple and fragrant walk-through garden in the ell, the edges of which ran up to lawn. A mature fig tree against the barn and a magnificent wisteria growing up a porch column were the centers of attraction. At ground level, Huntington paved a Y-shape path for access from the kitchen door and through the garden to his back and side lawn areas. He made the path with stepping-stones set far enough apart to allow for interplantings of erigerons, dianthus, and even boxwood in the ground as well as in pots set onto the odd stone here and there.

Each of the two spurs of the Y-shape path leads on to other parts of the garden. One goes south to a lawn area with borders around it. The second has far more implications for

FIGURE 4.8
Finding logical edges to gardens is a crucial step in garden design. Here, the outer edge of the porch establishes one edge, and the 2-foot setback in the barn, the second. The result is a harmony between house and garden.

the power of paths to literally and visually link one garden area to the next. As you stand at the end of the west-facing path in Huntington's ell garden, you look down the length of a long, narrow panel of lawn, a panel that ends parallel with the end of the barn. At the end of the lawn panel, which acts as an implied path, is a pair of standing stones on either side of a central set of steps that lead on into other parts of the garden. Those two standing stones also frame a view of a beauti-

fully crafted summerhouse about 100 feet south of the steps.

What I'm driving at in this description is that once you design the path and/or sitting area in the ell of your house, look out to distant areas of your garden from a bench or the end of a path to see whether you can use either to generate sites for other paths, gardens, and structures at a distance from it. In that way, all parts of your garden fit into a larger, all-encompassing plan.

Sometimes the ell can form two sides of an entrance garden, thereby easing the design for your gardens around the front door (see figure 4.9). This was the case in the ell in a Connecticut suburban home of white-painted clapboard that I visited a few years ago. In the 25-foot area between driveway edge and front door, the owner designed a 6-foot-wide brick path that went toward the front door on the diagonal and then broadened out to a 10-foot-square landing by the front door. She planted both sides of the brickwork with a profusion of flowering shrubs and perennials and anchored the plantings with an uplit *Styrax japonica* tree, which arched over much of the landing/walkway to the front door for a feeling of enclosure from above. The landing by the front door was wide enough to allow guests to gather there and also provided room for richly planted terra-cotta pots.

In a garden I saw here in Vermont, the designer built a square deck set into an ell and raised about 2 feet above the adjacent gardens so that the deck stopped 2 to 4 feet from the corner of each end of the ell for flowering and fragrant shrubs. A door led from the center of each ell onto the deck – one from the kitchen and one from the sitting room. Steps directly out from the two doors led from the deck down into gardens planted around its perimeter. The steps directly opposite the sitting room door, the more important of the two

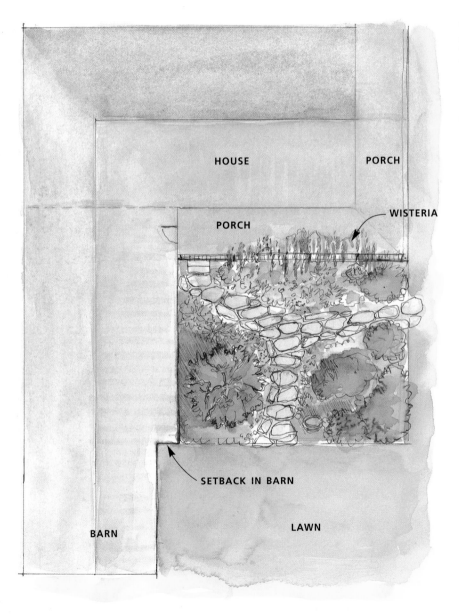

HOUSE   PORCH

WISTERIA

PORCH

SETBACK IN BARN

BARN   LAWN

FIGURE 4.9 (PRECEDING PAGE) The ell of this house provides the dimensions and feeling of enclosure for an intimate terraced entrance garden. Catmint planted along the outside of the stone path ensures that guests pass through, not next to, a garden as they walk toward the front door.

rooms, were 8 feet wide; those across from the kitchen door were 4 feet wide. Two trees planted within the beds surrounding the deck, as well as out in the lawn, provided shade and a bit of break from all that architecture when looking back at the house from the lawn.

This same deck could, of course, have been stone paving at ground level, with steps coming down from the house to the stone patio surrounded on all sides with a garden. In fact,

a garden I designed for Cindy and Gerry Prozzo is organized in just that way (see figure 4.10). Their patio is made of tightly fitting cut stones to create a rectangular sitting and dining area surrounded by gardens. Crab apple trees provide shade for this south-facing garden, while stepping-stones enable the Prozzos to move from the sitting area out into other parts of their garden.

As I have said before, and may well say

FIGURE 4.10 Keep the placement of windows and doors of your house in mind when designing a garden in an ell. All winter, you will look out onto that garden from the interior, so build in year-round interest with evergreens, trees that hold colorful fruit through the winter, ornamental grasses, and plants with handsome branching.

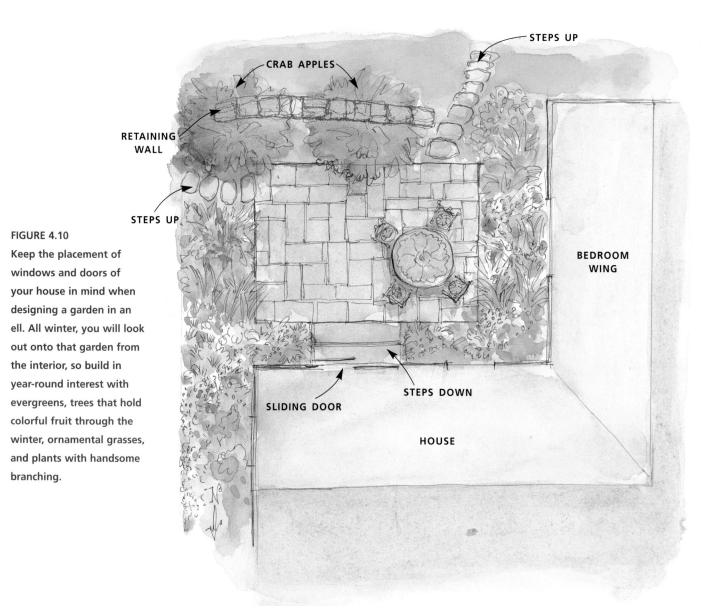

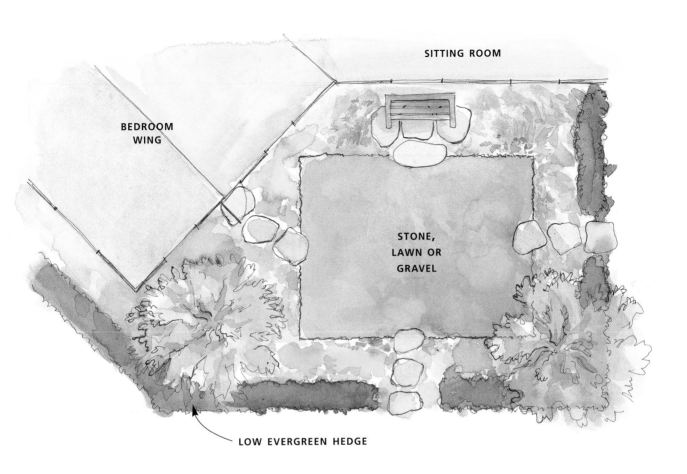

SITTING ROOM

BEDROOM WING

STONE, LAWN OR GRAVEL

LOW EVERGREEN HEDGE

FASTIGIATE DECIDUOUS TREES FOR COURTYARDS AND ELLS

Acer x freemanii 'Scarlet Sentinel'
Acer platanoides 'Columnare'
Acer platanoides 'Olmsted'
Acer rubrum 'Columnare'
Acer saccharum 'Goldspire'
Acer saccharum 'Newton Sentry'

Acer saccharum 'Temple's Upright'
Araucaria bidwillii
Carpinus betulus 'Fastigiata'
Crataegus monogyna 'Stricta'
Crataegus phaenopyrum 'Fastigiata'
Magnolia virginiana 'Henry Hicks' or 'Santa Rosa'
Populus nigra 'Italica'
Prunus avium 'Fastigiata'
Prunus sargentii

'Columnaris'
Prunus serrulata 'Amanogawa'
Pyrus calleryana 'Capital'
Quercus petraea 'Columna'
Rhamnus frangula 'Columnaris'
Tilia cordata 'Chancellor'
Tilia platyphyllos 'Fastigiata'
Ulmus carpinifolia 'Dampieri'
Ulmus glabra 'Exoniensis'
Ulmus hollandica 'Klemmer'

FIGURE 4.11 (ABOVE) Sometimes a bedroom wing meets the main house at an oblique angle. Resolve this odd angle by capturing the space with a hedge that parallels the wall of the main house. You can then create a rectangular, square, or free-form sitting area within that ordered space.

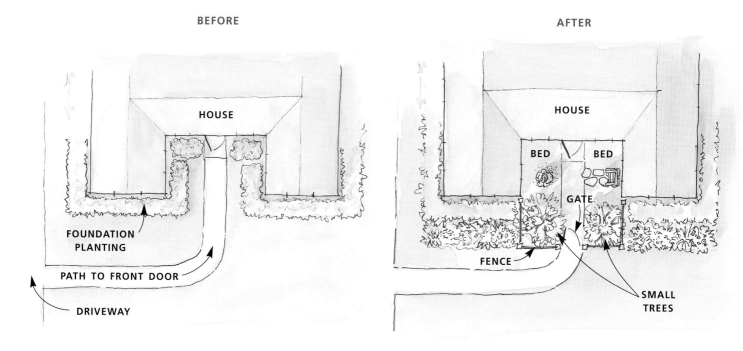

BEFORE

AFTER

FIGURE 4.12
BEFORE – Holding fast to foundation planting, even in a courtyard, results in a lifeless experience for guests and family.

FIGURE 4.13
AFTER – Enclose even a small courtyard with a fence or hedging, and you create a welcoming garden around your front door that you can sit in.

again, to make this book really work, you need to bring a creative mind to the images that I paint for you in words and that Janet Fredericks paints for you in drawings. Work with our images – change them, shift them this way and that – and ask what alternatives there are to images we provide. Bring your creative mind to our images, and this book will provide no end of springboards for your own garden designs.

GARDENS IN THE COURTYARD

If the ell of your house establishes two sides of a garden, the courtyard establishes three, so you only need to determine the fourth and the path through it to any major or minor doors on the three sides of your house. It's a snap.

When I first walked to the front door of Spice Kugle's home in Vermont to begin an overall plan for her, I found myself standing in a shallow courtyard (see figure 4.14). The west-facing wall of the front foyer was 20 feet long, with a central front door. Kitchen and

sitting room wings extended out 10 feet at either end of the foyer wall, stopping within 2 feet of the driveway edge. We started our garden design work for her entire garden right there by the front door.

We designed a 24-inch-high freestanding stone wall to run from the inner corners of the kitchen and sitting room wings to a 4-foot-wide gap for a path leading straight to the front door. Because the shady west side of her home was set into thinned woodland, and given that snow would cascade down from all three sides of the roof, I designed an entrance garden which comprised herbaceous perennials that would die down out of harm's way every autumn: ferns, hostas, epimediums, bloodroot, and the fall-blooming *Anemone vitifolia* 'Robustissima.' China Boy and China Girl hollies, away from potential cascading snow, marked either side of the entrance path.

Jorge and Wendy Crespo have a much larger north-facing courtyard into which they wanted to build lots of curving beds and paths. Set within three sides of their home in

New Hampshire, their courtyard was approximately 30 feet wide and 50 feet long. Given that the Crespos love curving lines and sweeps of color, they worked with their stonemason to create broad, curving stone paths that lead from the kitchen door and their bedroom door and wind on through this space to a point where it leads off to a big lawn area. In other words, they wanted to garden the entire courtyard area, so curving paths through a densely planted garden felt right. Had they chosen to plant curvy foundation plantings along the three walls of the house, with an amorphous central lawn in the middle, the resulting garden, bearing no relationship whatsoever to the house, would have been unsatisfying.

Both of these examples show the fourth side of a courtyard garden being determined by drawing a line between the inner corners of the two wings, but don't feel you have to remain loyal to that line. I once saw a formal entrance garden at the front of a whitewashed brick home in suburban Connecticut that used the courtyard garden to dramatic effect. A straight 6-foot-wide bluestone path led from the driveway edge to the formal front door 40 feet away. The front door was central on a 24-foot-wide wall at either end of which two wings of the two-story house extended out toward the driveway 16 feet. Rather than enclose the 16-by-24-foot courtyard with a fence or hedge, the designer created a 24-foot-wide garden that ran the full 40 feet from inner wall to driveway edge, a garden bisected down its length with the 6-foot-wide bluestone path. Down either side of the pathway, he planted three uplit paperbark maples (*Acer griseum*) exactly across from one another and underplanted them with *Pachysandra termi-*

FIGURE 4.14
Three walls of a house often shade a courtyard garden for most of the day, so I planted a shade garden that echoes the mood of the nearby Vermont woodland.

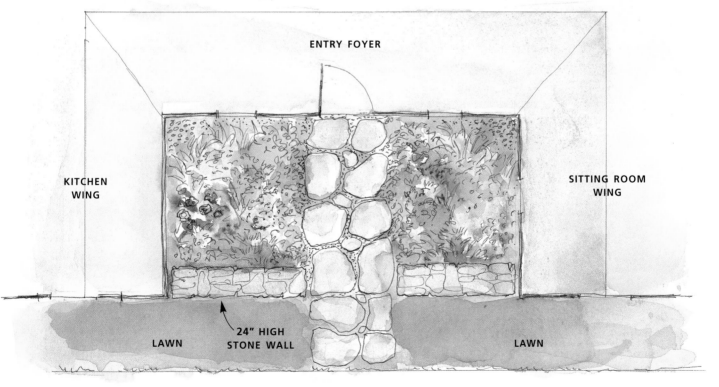

FIGURE 4.15

The rectangular beds in the courtyard and the central path follow the lines of the two wings of the barn in which Laura Fisher designs fabrics that reflect the style of her exuberant garden.

Manor House is an exterior door situated at the end of the longest corridor in the house. This door is in a tiny inset in the house, a veritable mini-courtyard. Open that door, and you look down a birch allée hundreds of feet long that ends in a stone pavilion overlooking woodland. The path is gravel; *Vinca minor* grows under the birches. Even the tiniest courtyard (see figure 4.16) can, in combination with inner corridors and exterior doors, generate ideas well beyond its limits.

ELLS, COURTYARDS, AND WINDOWS

An unusual number of windows often look out onto gardens bounded by two or three walls of your home. If second-story bedroom windows overlook a courtyard or an ell, don't block views with the branching of newly planted trees, and be sure to prune existing trees to open views down to your garden. Create pleasing geometric or curving patterns that can be especially appreciated from above, or, if your house is at the seaside (see figure 4.17), plant heat-tolerant free-form gardens. Those same important windows can often generate the placement of paths, sculptures, garden furniture, and special plants. To help you put your windows to practical use when designing your gardens, rank them according to their importance. Windows looking out from a sofa centrally located in a sitting room have more sway over elements of a garden design than do windows looking out from a utility room or a guest bathroom. Keep fragrance in mind too. An enclosed and protected courtyard or ell can hold fragrance longer than gardens along the more open side of a house; place strongly scented perennials and flowering shrubs near windows that can be opened or next to a bench or chairs you set into the courtyard garden.

nalis 'Green Sheen.' A matching pair of handsome cast-stone urns framed either side of the front door. The drama of this entrance garden came from its restraint and from the way the designer used the courtyard to generate the dimensions of this tasteful garden in front of an elegant whitewashed brick colonial.

Had this courtyard been at the back of the house, the line of paperbark maples could have extended well out into the back lawn before scattering into lawn and nearby meadow. Visit Stan Hywet Gardens outside Akron, Ohio, and you'll see this idea at work on a remarkable scale. Off the back corner of the

ELLS AND NATURALLY OCCURRING FEATURES

Sometimes you want to site your house in a certain place on your lot, and natural features such as bedrock or an old live oak force you to create an ell in the house to literally make room for them. Because that prominent and natural feature often has more visual power than the house, it, rather than architecture, becomes your springboard for garden design ideas.

Robert and Joan Marandino were building their new home on a 1-acre corner lot in a suburb of New York City and asked me to help with the garden design. A massive old outcropping of bedrock had forced the architect to create an ell in the northeast corner of the house; the base of the outcropping was only 8 feet from the house. Given the large size and beauty of the lichen and moss-covered bedrock, it, rather than the building, generated the idea for

FIGURE 4.16
Tiny courtyards need not dissuade you from going all out. This small space contains annuals, perennials, shrubs, vines, planted pots, a birdbath, two chairs and a bench on a paved area, a wooden balustrade, and hanging baskets.

FIGURE 4.17
This ell and the large windows on the one wall gave rise to a mass planting of miscanthus grasses and *Chrysanthemum parthenium* that spills out toward the beach. There is no path, no access through this space. A naturalistic garden ties the house to the natural landscape.

a naturalistic garden – and no lawn – across the back of the house. Also acknowledging 100-year-old oaks growing along the boundary line, I designed a garden of understory plants – witch hazel hybrids, Japanese cut-leaf maples, and *Hydrangea paniculata* 'Kyushu' underplanted with a variety of groundcovers. The more formal gardens, with flowering borders, ran along the front of the house.

Linda Punderson lives high on an east-facing 40-acre meadow in central Vermont, and she sited her house purposely so that the back

ell in her house fit into exposed bedrock, thereby linking house to landscape. Linda then looked to the bedrock, not the architecture, for inspiration. She planted drought-tolerant plants – alpines and low ornamental grasses such as *Helictotrichon sempervirens* – among crevices in the bedrock and then carried that same planting style right up to both sides of the ell, with broad stepping-stones through the garden for access. As with Joan Marandino's garden, all the flower beds and borders ran along the front of her house.

PRACTICAL PROBLEMS SOLVED

1

THE ELL, THE COURTYARD, AND DRAINAGE

Water sheet-drains off a roof; that is, rain falls on a roof and then drains from it in a sheet as long as your roof is. Water is dispersed and falls on what is called the dripline, a problem area that I explore in Chapter 2. However, when two sections of roof come together at right angles, as they do in an ell or courtyard, those parts of the roof near the intersection drain to a common point, the valley, down which the water runs in a stream. If your home is not or cannot be equipped with gutters, this stream creates a drainage problem. Without some accommodation being made for the force of this water falling 10 to 20 feet, considerable erosion takes place.

Most homes built over the past 25 years or so have what is called a curtain drain built against the exterior of the base of your foundation. Stout perforated PVC pipe is set into freely draining crushed rock that typically extends from the concrete foundation wall out about 24 to 36 inches (see figure 4.18, parts 1 and 2). This system collects and carries away some rainwater falling off your roof, but more important, it carries groundwater away from your home. Check with your builder or the previous owner to see whether a curtain drain was installed. Also try to determine where it drains; in the parlance of

builders, you need to ask, "Where does the pipe come to daylight?" Try to find the end of the pipe somewhere at a low point 20 to 50 feet away from your home.

One of the problems is that small grates set at the end of the curtain drain system often fall out or are damaged by string trimming, lawn mowing, heavy equipment, or the force of water running through it. Those grates are there to keep small animals like chipmunks from scurrying up the pipe, nesting there in dry weather, and clogging the pipe.

If you want to be certain that the system is in fact draining water away from the base of your foundation, dig down 1 to 3 feet in the area just below the valley until you expose white filter fabric, which contractors usually use to cover the crushed rock of the curtain drain. Put a hose on top of that cloth, turn the hose on, and then explore low spots, banks, or slopes 20 feet or more from the house, listening for the sound of flowing water. If you find where the drainpipe comes to daylight, you know the curtain drain is working and you

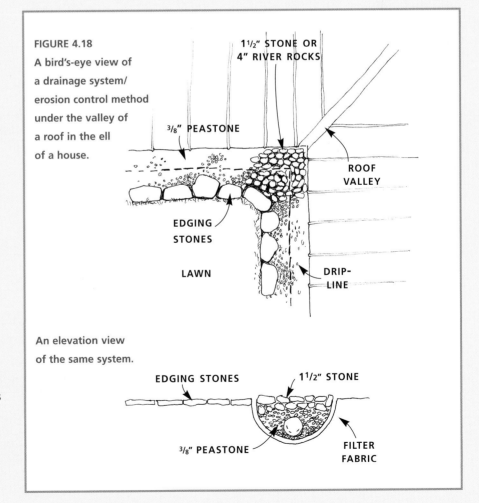

FIGURE 4.18
A bird's-eye view of a drainage system/ erosion control method under the valley of a roof in the ell of a house.

1½" STONE OR 4" RIVER ROCKS

³/₈" PEASTONE

ROOF VALLEY

EDGING STONES

LAWN

DRIP-LINE

An elevation view of the same system.

EDGING STONES

1½" STONE

³/₈" PEASTONE

FILTER FABRIC

can check to see that the grate is set into the end of the pipe.

If you find the soil under the valleys in your courtyard or ell to be badly eroded, you might even excavate all the soil out 3 feet or so beyond both foundation walls under a valley and all the way down to the fabric of the curtain drain. Backfill that hole with 1½-inch crushed stone, and top-dress with more attractive 3-to-4-inch rounded river rocks. In this way, you can ensure that the excessive water draining from a valley does not destroy nearby gardens. Do not place flat stones atop the river rocks, as they spray water back up onto your house siding; smaller river rocks break up water into smaller droplets that aren't so damaging. Use flat rocks or steel edging to separate garden soil or beds from the river rocks.

If you discover you don't have a curtain drain, turn to the section on driplines near the end of Chapter 2 on side gardens for information regarding how to drain water that falls from the roof away from your foundation and adjacent gardens.

If the style of your home allows for this or if you live in an especially dry area of the country, place a collecting barrel under the valley and atop any of the above stony surfaces. The barrel will fill and overflow quickly in a rain, but that's fine; excess water will drain away. After the storm, you'll have a barrelful of water for use in the garden. Another very attractive solution – especially on homes of modern or Far Eastern design – that the Japanese employ is to affix a chain from the lowest point of the valley to within river rocks at ground level.

When it rains, water trails down the chain links, thereby defining the beauty of falling water.

The Main Points

■ Examine the ground under each valley on your house to see whether there is a drainage or erosion problem. Excessive water coming off a valley may require a special solution to the drainage or erosion problem.
■ Check with your builder to learn whether a curtain drain was installed around the base of your foundation wall. If so, ask him where it drains, that is, "comes to daylight."
■ Find out whether the curtain drain is still functioning. If not, explore with your landscaper how to install a suitable drainage system with PVC pipe and crushed rock along the driplines of your home to carry the rainwater away from your foundation.

2

HIDING CELLAR BULKHEADS

Bulkheads are cellar doors that extend out from the basement wall or foundation anywhere from 4 to 7 feet, depending on the angle at which they are set. When open, they lead down a set of steps into the basement. Bulkheads typically comprise two doors, each about 3 feet wide, that open in opposite directions to create a 6-foot-wide opening. Because they are often made of pressed metal, they're ugly.

If you are still designing your home or if you are at a stage in construction where you still have some design

options, find a place for the bulkhead that is out of sight of what will become the most important vantage points from your garden or home: the entrance walkway; the back terrace; important windows; a gazebo or pergola out in the garden.

Another approach is to try to find a way to hide the bulkhead, and this approach need not necessarily rely on plants. For example, you can hide a cellar door under the surface of a porch, as clients of mine, John and Connie Kieley, did during the design phase of their new home in New Hampshire. Part of their porch floor is a hinged door with a recessed handle. They pull up that door to expose a second metal cellar door under the porch which opens for infrequent outdoor access to the cellar. (A door inside the house provides access too.)

Sometimes rethinking the whole notion of the bulkhead is appropriate. I was designing a stone terrace and surrounding gardens at the back of a classic 18th-century farmhouse that Connie Kheel was restoring off a dirt road in New York State when we realized there was a problem. The only place she could gain exterior access to her cellar was off the southwest corner at the back of the house, where a bulkhead would jut out into the only space we had for an outdoor sitting area. We certainly did not want to attach a bulkhead there, where it would be an unhappy presence on a terrace where family and guests would gather.

We decided to have the steps built down to the cellar as planned and then build a 6-by-8-foot extension to the house in the far corner of the terrace

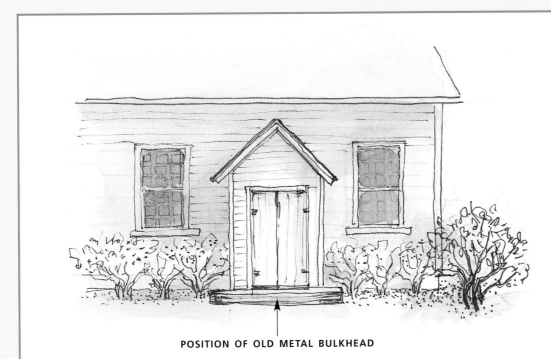

FIGURE 4.19
Replace an unsightly metal bulkhead with a structure that complements the style of your house. See figure 4.5 to see how this structure relates to the whole garden area at the back of this house.

POSITION OF OLD METAL BULKHEAD

(see figure 4.19). This 8-foot-high extension shared the same white-painted clapboards and gray trim, the same roof pitch and roofing material, as well as a door similar to all others on the house. The result was that this little extension, providing roomy access to the cellar, felt architecturally right.

It also solved a problem of architectural scale. Before the 8-foot-high cellar door extension was built, the 16-foot-high back side of her two-story house felt barnlike and imposing. Once the old-fashioned small-scale extension was built, the back wall looked more interesting and felt more nostalgic, and the architecture stepped up gradually from terrace level to its surrounding stone wall to top of extension to top of the west wall and on up to the roof peak. The extension helped screen at least a part of the nearby road from the dining table and chairs set on the terrace.

A problem turned into several solutions.

Even if you have an existing bulkhead, you can still use this idea. Remove the unattractive bulkhead frame and door, but leave the stairs down to the cellar just as they are. Then build an architecturally appropriate extension of the house around the perimeter of the stairs that uses the same siding, roofing, door, and paint color as those of the main house. The two sides of that extension might even prove a good surface for trelliswork that support vines or espaliered apple trees.

But then there are times when the bulkhead needs to stay right where it is. Whether it's made of wood or metal, painting it using the same colors as those of the house will help a great deal to blend it visually. At Colonial Williamsburg, for example, all the wooden bulkheads are painted the

same way: the color of the bulkhead doors match the color of the trim on the house; the color of the bulkhead's frame and sides match that of the walls of the house (see figure 4.20). At Hartwell Perry's Ordinary, for example, the clapboards on the house and the frame and sides of the bulkhead are painted white; the trim on the house and bulkhead doors are painted brown. In other traditional homes, I have also seen the entire bulkhead painted the same color as the walls of the house, as we have done here at our 200-year-old farmhouse. This approach throws even less visual emphasis on the bulkhead. I then planted a *Viburnum lantana* 'Mohican' on one side of the structure and an aster garden on the other, and within the ell of the house, to visually screen the bulkhead.

In one garden I saw in northwestern Connecticut, the designer was faced

121

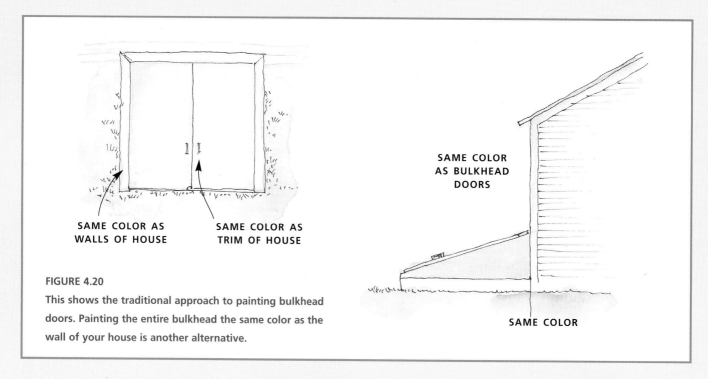

SAME COLOR AS
WALLS OF HOUSE

SAME COLOR AS
TRIM OF HOUSE

SAME COLOR
AS BULKHEAD
DOORS

SAME COLOR

FIGURE 4.20
This shows the traditional approach to painting bulkhead
doors. Painting the entire bulkhead the same color as the
wall of your house is another alternative.

with two one-door bulkheads 4 feet apart set on a bias in the ell of his home (see figure 4.21). Rather than try to mask such mass right there in full view of the kitchen and the entrance to his home, he made a statement of it. He built a 12-inch-wide, 4-foot-long connecting shelf – on which he could display small planted pots – between the top of the two bulkheads and paved the area between and in front of the two bulkheads with tightly fitting Pennsylvania bluestone. He then set a 4-foot-long bench on the stone paving between the two bulkheads and painted the wrought-iron bench and bulkheads a gray-green, the same color as the nearby shutters. The bluestone provided a surface for walking as well as a place for potted plants. He then installed a picket fence and gates on the other two sides of the ell and planted an intimate herb garden, right there

outside his kitchen windows, in full view of the bench.

Paint color, plants, and a stone retaining wall can all be combined to reduce the visual impact of a bulkhead. In a garden I designed for Sue Byers here in Vermont, I ran 12-inch-high retaining walls up to a point on each side of a metal bulkhead that was 12 inches high. I then asked the contractor to bolt 4-foot-high wooden supports to either side of the bulkhead to hold the doors open, thereby keeping their weight off nearby shrubs and perennials. Because the bulkhead was under the eaves of the house and was therefore covered most of the winter with snow, I was forced to plant only perennials to screen the bulkhead. Being on the shady side of the house, I chose large-scale, shade- and moisture-tolerant perennials to plant along the sides of the bulkhead: *Ligularia dentata*

'Othello,' *Hosta* 'Krossa Regal,' and *Rodgersia pinnata* 'Elegans.' These 3-to-4-foot-high perennials screened the mass of the bulkhead from all side views. Had the bulkhead been at the gable end of the house, I could have used shrubs that matured or could be kept at 3 to 4 feet to do the same job: *Pieris japonica* 'Mountain Fire,' *Daphne x Burkwoodii* 'Carol Mackie,' or, in more native gardens, *Ilex verticillata* 'Red Sprite.'

FIGURE 4.21 (OPPOSITE)
One bulkhead is unsightly enough. Here, *two* bulkheads were necessary, so the designer featured rather than fought them. The bench between the two, painted the same color as the bulkheads and shutters to unify all the parts, looks out onto a simple herb garden in the kitchen ell. (Designer: John Saladino)

The Main Points

- If you find your bulkhead is out of sight from most of the important vantage points of your garden, simple solutions such as screening the sides with shrubs or perennials, combined with paint colors that match those of your house, will suffice.

- If your bulkhead is in full sight of important walkways, could the entire frame, doors, and stairs be removed, the cellar wall filled in, and the hole in the ground backfilled and planted?

- If it can't be removed, perhaps cover it with a wooden structure with a standard door that opens to provide access to the bulkhead door. In this way, the solution is in sympathy with your house.

- If you're in the design phase of your home, set the bulkhead in the most inconspicuous, least visited area of your house.

- If none of the above ideas work, make a feature of it, with a shelf along its top for potted plants, painting it a color which echoes that of the nearby wall of your home.

3

AIR-CONDITIONING CONDENSERS

Air-conditioning condensers are typically 2-to-3-foot cube-shaped units with metal louvered sides that allow for the ready passage of air. A large fan is set horizontally and under a protective open grid in the top of each condenser. The fan draws air through the four radiatorlike sides of the condenser to cool the system and then blows that air straight up. These condensers are typically placed at gable ends of a house, either singly or in groups of two or three, depending on the size of the house. Once units are installed on concrete pads about 6 inches larger on both sides than the condenser, water and electrical lines are run from them into the house. There is little or no heat buildup around such a unit that would harm plants.

If you are in a construction phase and can choose the placement of the condensers, select a gable end so that snow, ice, and rain do not fall off your roof onto the units. Also choose a wall of your home, the area around which will be the least visited by guests admiring your garden. If at all possible, avoid placing the condensers within or near the entrance garden or along any of the three walls of a courtyard where you are likely to create a sitting or entrance garden. For example, when working with John and Connie Kieley on the garden design for their new home in New Hampshire, we first roughed out the complete garden design, including the driveway and parking. Only then did we decide that the west gable end of the house would be the least frequented area of the garden and therefore the most appropriate for the condensers. Andy and Christine Hall were developing a faithful reproduction of an 18th-century house in Vermont and certainly did not want modern condensers, even if set behind fencing or plantings, anywhere near the house. They had them installed some 100 feet from the house behind a utility shed and paid for the trenches, extra insulation around the pipes, and a beefed-up unit that could accomplish the job of cooling their home from that distance.

But often units have to be placed where they have to go, or they already exist. Then, the only solution is to screen them from sight. Because service access is gained from the top of the unit and no doors on the sides need to swing open, it is possible to fence or screen condensers for both sound and sight with plants to within 2 to 3 feet of its sides. That 2-to-3-foot gap will provide sufficient room for air movement and for the serviceman to work around the units. While new models are relatively quiet, they do whir audibly, so if possible, position them away from patios and terraces or important windows through which sound can readily pass.

One option for screening is to build a 4-foot-high picket fence around the condensers, but allow no part of it to come closer than 24 inches to the unit. The fence slats should be set so as to leave $3/4$-to-1-inch gaps between the pickets. The type of wood and the way you finish it – painted, unpainted or stained, rough or finely finished – should match the style, color, and finish of your home. For example, in a garden I designed in Maryland around a beautifully crafted home with white-painted trim, we screened the AC units with finely built 4-foot-high white-painted trelliswork that formed 3-inch open squares, not diamonds. Because the trelliswork fencing was sited off a gable end of the house and because snow cascading off the roof to damage fencing is never a problem in Maryland, it was out of harm's way. The posts used to support the trelliswork shared the same finial details as those used on the gateposts and fenceposts of a 3-foot-high white-painted picket fence around a nearby herb garden. The color white and the use of similarly designed posts to support both picket and trellis visually linked fencing and gates into a coherent whole. My client then planted a hedge of *Abelia grandiflora* along the front of the trelliswork, leaving a gap in the hedge for the door to allow access to the units. Over time, the *Abelia* would muffle more and more sound and screen fencing as the shrubs grew taller and denser.

To further mask the units, I have seen fencing built 2 to 3 feet away from AC units around all three sides (the fourth side being the house), and then a removable louvered frame was set in a frame atop the fence so that it rested 18 inches above the horizontal fan. In this way, the entire unit was visually screened, albeit with wooden louvers and fencing that allowed for ample air circulation.

If a built solution to the problem is more than you want to tackle, you can screen the unit with an evergreen hedge so that the inner branches are never allowed to get closer than 2 to 3 feet from the sides of the unit. Just be certain that if you live in a snowy part of North America, you don't resort to plants for screening AC units unless they are well out beyond the dripline where snow cascades off the roof.

You will find dense plants such as flourishing rhododendrons, yews, arbor vitae, or evergreen azaleas will provide better sound abatement than will fencing. If the units are positioned away from the main entrance and other paths used year-round, deciduous plants, which remain leafless during the winter, will be appropriate as well. When choosing plants, keep the amount of sunlight that reaches the area in mind. The south side of a house gets sunlight nearly all day; the east side gets half a day of sunlight that is cooler than half a day of sunlight off the west side of your home. The north side gets little or no sunlight. The less sunlight that reaches sun-loving plants, the thinner their foliage will become over time and the more you will see and hear the units.

The Main Points
(if you are still in the design or construction phase)

- Determine which side of your house will be least visited. This might be the side where both the sound and sight of the unit will cause the least problem.
- If you have a choice, situate AC units on a gable end, out of harm's way of the snow, ice, and rain shed by the roof.

- If the AC units are truly egregious to you, explore with your installer the cost of locating the units well away from the house.
- Finally, if the units must go along one wall of the house, design attractive trellislike fencing with an access gate and then plant in front of the trelliswork, being certain the trellis is at least 24 inches from the sides of the units.
- The tops of the units can also be covered with metal or wooden grating.

The Main Points
(if your AC units are already in place)

- The side of the house your units are on, and thus the amount of sunlight they will get, will to a large degree determine which plants to choose for screening. Whenever possible, choose evergreens.
- Picket, board-and-batten, or trellislike fencing can all be installed at least 24 inches away from all sides of a unit; paint the wood the same color as nearby house siding. Shrubs can then be planted to screen fencing.
- If you've made a lot of changes to your home, and the AC units have become even more of a visual and sound problem, ask your air-conditioning installer about costs involved in moving the units.

CHAPTER FIVE

GARDENS BETWEEN
BUILDINGS

ARCHITECTURE,

INTERIOR

DESIGN, AND

GARDENING

ARE ALL ABOUT

BALANCE AND

SCALE.

– JOHN SALADINO,
contemporary
American interior
designer

T HE SPACE BETWEEN BUILDINGS provides you with just what you need as a garden designer: context. First, design a path to link doors that face each other from the side of a garage to the house, for example, and then design a path down the length of the space between the buildings. Site an arbor against the sunny wall of one of the two buildings that will act as a destination for that central path. Arbor uprights provide supports for vines, and the space on either side of the arbor suggests a place for perennials, shrubs, and perhaps even trees underplanted with shade-tolerant groundcovers. If the buildings are close together, you might even take up all the existing lawn between them, build your paths, and then plant a garden in the entire space with fencing and gates at either end (see figure 5.2).

By creating a garden between two buildings, you draw two major structures – a house and garage, a garage and a smaller outbuilding

– into a sound visual relationship with one another. The buildings anchor the garden, making its placement feel inevitable. A garden between two buildings is often made so strong in its juxtaposition with the two buildings that the lines of architecture and garden generate other lines and ideas in nearby or even distant garden spaces (see figure 5.3).

For example, the south side of our two-story barn is 50 feet across the driveway from the north face of our garden shed (see figure 5.4). As you will read in Chapter 6 on out-buildings, we created an herb garden off the east side of the garden shed and then planted a black haw hedge (*Viburnum prunifolium*) down two sides of the herb garden.

To link shed to barn visually, I planted a yew hedge from the southeast corner of the barn due south to where it met the black haw hedge, leaving two gaps in it for access (see figure 5.4 again). Instantly the hedge pulled the garden shed, herb garden, and barn into a

FIGURE 5.1

I sited the garage after this house was built so that I could fence in a rectangular entrance garden using the near corner of the garage and the far corner of the house as logical starting points for the fence. The west side of the garage is a backdrop for the grape arbor and sitting area.

visual relationship with one another, but other things happened as well. The spring garden, just 20 feet east of the new hedge, was now screened from the driveway, making it much more appealing and private.

Years later, the line of the yew hedge gave me another idea. I left a rectangular panel of lawn 15 feet wide and parallel with the hedge but took up all of the lawn east of that line. I then extended the spring garden into the newly opened soil. By removing all but a 15-

foot-wide rectangle of lawn where amorphously shaped lawn had been, I created a strong 15-foot-wide, 80-foot-long green rectangle that sweeps guests from the herb garden to the pool garden at the back of the barn (again, see figure 5.4).

While you may not have a 150-year-old barn and garden shed, the space between any two buildings will provide you with similar clues. Look closely at the way your two buildings are aligned, and you may be able to draw some strong, simple lines in the form of hedges, fences, and perennial beds between them. The colonists created such lines between house and outbuildings; you might take a cue from them.

Visit Colonial Williamsburg in Virginia or the small gardens of Charleston, South Carolina, and you will see how successfully our forebears sited small outbuildings such as the kitchen, a wellhouse or laundry, a one-horse stable or utility shed, a henhouse or dovecote and then gathered gardens around them and between them and the house.

These outbuildings were invariably set at right angles to one another, and then joined to the main house or one another with picket fencing. A 30-foot-long brick path, for example, leads from the side door of the Taylor House at Colonial Williamsburg to the side door of Mr. Taylor's office 20 feet away (see figure 5.5). A white picket fence runs parallel with the path, linking the facing front corners of house and office; a privet hedge runs along the back of the white picket fence to screen the path and back gardens from the nearby sidewalk.

FIGURE 5.2
The garden between the Benjamin Powell House and an outbuilding in Colonial Williamsburg in Virginia shows how you can take full advantage of a space between two buildings. Use your imagination to conjure up alternatives within this rectangular space.

At the Severinus Durfey House in Williamsburg (see figure 5.6), a brick path runs parallel with the back side of the house and extends about 20 feet beyond its two ends. Two hundred and fifty years ago, the Durfeys placed a delicate garden shed at one end of the path, a henhouse at the other end. White picket fencing runs from two corners of these outbuildings to enclose back and side gardens around the house. The side fencing joins up with pickets and a gate along the front of the house to enclose the front gardens. It's all so simple, so inevitable, so clean – and such a lovely model for any recently built home on a small lot in a suburban community.

The space between two buildings is often geometric, because the exterior walls of two buildings built near one another are often parallel or perpendicular. This space between buildings can be a long, narrow, and level rectangle (as between a house and garage), or it

THE URBAN GARDEN

The space between two buildings in an urban setting is often tall, with many windows looking down on your garden. Such a garden needs to include trees as well as architectural elements, such as an arbor or pergola, that will, in an open way, create a 10-to-12-foot-high "ceiling" for at least a third of your garden. It is often best to place such an architectural element at the back of the garden so that from all the rooms of your apartment, the furniture under the "ceiling" reads as an invitation from within to come out, all the way to the back of your garden, no matter how small it might be.

Long, narrow urban gardens need not be linear. These two examples show the use of curvilinear lines to shape integrated beds, paths, and paved sitting areas.

THE NATURE OF THE SPACE BETWEEN

As you sit at the kitchen table, set two cereal boxes close to one another, leaving about 12 to 16 inches between them. Move the boxes closer together and then farther apart, and see what happens to the void between them. Now place various objects between the two cereal boxes – a knife and fork, another smaller box, a yogurt tub, an upside-down plastic bowl – and see how the nature of the volume between the two cereal boxes changes. The knife and fork horizontal on the table will make the space feel quite tall; a 10-inch bowl upside down will shrink the space between. Such a simple exercise will help you understand this fascinating concept of the space between.

FIGURE 5.3 (OPPOSITE)
I used a fence, based on the design of the porch railing, to create an entrance garden between house and garage for Kirsten and Andy Peterson in New Hampshire. The bluestone path leads to the front porch, while stepping-stones lead the way into the back garden and swimming pool.

FIGURE 5.4 (BELOW)
Even when two buildings are 100 feet or so apart, a hedge or fence can visually link the two while creating a useful gardening space between them.

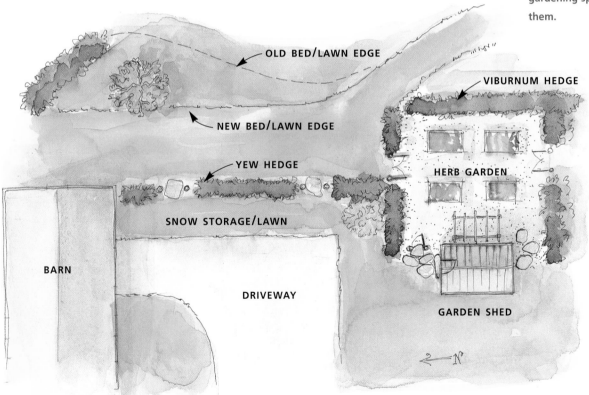

OLD BED/LAWN EDGE

VIBURNUM HEDGE

NEW BED/LAWN EDGE

YEW HEDGE

HERB GARDEN

SNOW STORAGE/LAWN

BARN

DRIVEWAY

GARDEN SHED

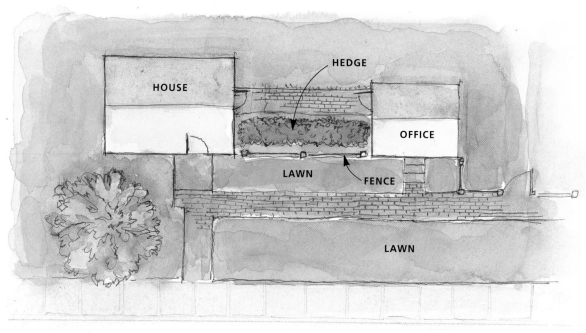

STREET

FIGURE 5.5

When the fronts of two buildings are 20 feet or so apart and in line with one another, you can link the two facing corners with a fence or hedge. By not placing a gate or walkway through that fence and hedge, you increase privacy for your back garden, as they did here at the Taylor House at Colonial Williamsburg in Virginia.

can be a square space between a kitchen wing and the side of the garage of similar dimensions. If you are designing a home and garage or if you are designing an outbuilding and its placement near your house, make sure you think about the shape and proportion and the resulting volume of the space between the two buildings vis-a-vis the building walls themselves. The Japanese designers call this space the *ma*.

Anne Jelich, a garden designer on the Eastern Shore of Maryland, and her family bought a house a few years ago with a stunning view of the Choptank River. The front door of her home was off the gable end, but there was no feeling of entrance, no separation between driveway and front door. Anne decided to move a 12-foot-long antique utility shed that was on the property so that it would anchor the far end of her entrance garden (see figure 5.7). She set the outbuilding

40 feet from the end of her home, roughly twice the height of the gable end of her house, lining up the central door of the shed with the front door of her 24-foot-wide house. She then ran an unpainted cedar fence from the corner of the house nearest the driveway out to a point parallel with the back of the utility shed and then a 6-foot section of fence to connect fence to shed. She did the same with a yew hedge off the other corner of the house.

House, outbuilding, and connecting fences created an enclosed rectangular space 24 feet wide and 40 feet long, with a bluestone path from the front door and through a gate in the cedar fence to driveway. She then designed a central square pool and ran a bluestone path from the doors of shed and house to the pool's edge. Other bluestone paths, all at right angles to one another, created a four-quadrant garden; at the center of each she planted a pink-blooming crape myrtle underplanted

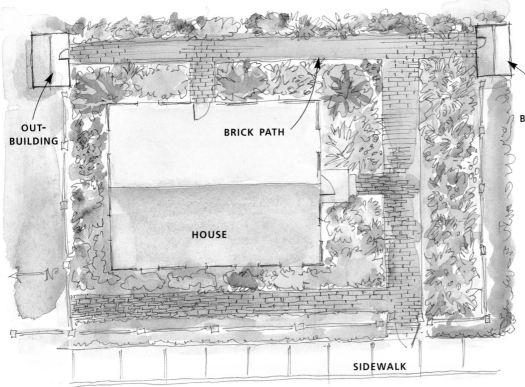

OUT-
BUILDING

OUT-
BUILDING

BRICK PATH

HOUSE

SIDEWALK

STREET

FIGURE 5.6
To increase the usefulness
of a small lot, set a garden
shed and/or an office at
either end of a long path
at the back of your house.
The siting of two small outbuildings at the Severinus
Durfey House at Colonial
Williamsburg provides
some cues to this classic
approach to design.

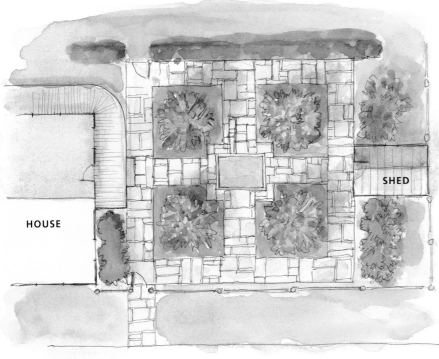

HOUSE

SHED

DRIVEWAY

FIGURE 5.7
Because small buildings
can be readily moved,
reposition a small outbuilding on your property so
that you set up a relationship
between it and your house.
You can then create a garden
between them. Anne Jelich,
a garden designer from the
Eastern Shore of Maryland,
did that very thing.

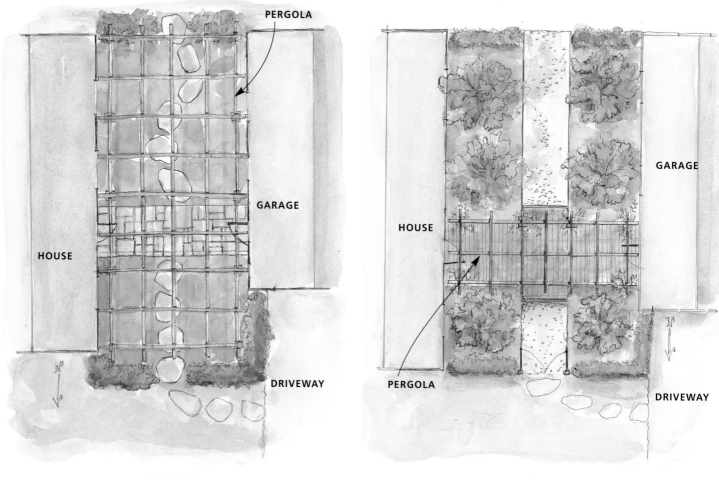

FIGURE 5.8   FIGURE 5.9

FIGURES 5.8, 5.9, 5.10, 5.11
You can garden the space
between the facing sides
of your house and garage
in any number of ways.
Here are four alternatives to
inspire your thinking. Notice
that built structures such as
a pergola or arbor can assist
you in creating an enclosed
space.

with herbs and perennials. She also planted 2-foot-wide perennial borders along the inside and outside of the fence and hedge and festooned the utility shed with climbing roses. A bench placed centrally in the bed along the fence allows guests to sit there and look across the garden and yew hedge to the broad expanse of the Choptank River. Everything fits into place, in large part because of the visual weight and structure of space provided between house and outbuilding.

While the proportions and dimensions of the walls of any two buildings and the ground between them can differ widely, the spaces

between any two buildings have a lot in common. One side is often shady, the other sunny. The buildings frame views in two directions, and typically, it's the sides of buildings that face one another. The closer the two buildings, the more you are aware of the verticality of the space between them and the more vertical become the two views they frame. The further apart the two buildings, the more horizontal the space and view. If they are too far apart, say, five or more times the height of the highest wall of the two buildings, there may be only the most tenuous of relationships between the two, or none at all, particularly if

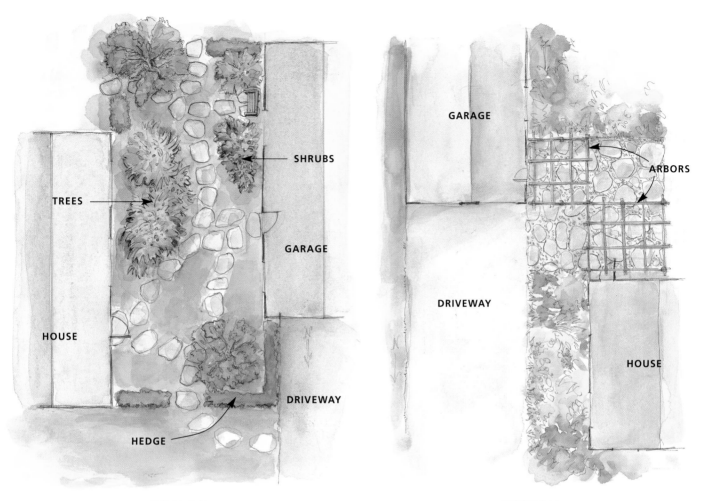

FIGURE 5.10   FIGURE 5.11

they are set at an odd angle to one another.

To understand the nature of the space between two buildings on your property, go out and stand in the middle of the space and slowly turn a full 360 degrees to take in the space and its surroundings. Try to see the space as a volume, with height, depth, and breadth. If it's narrow, perhaps the space could become a transition area between two larger spaces; if it's sufficiently wide, the space could become a garden in its own right, with fencing at either end and a sitting area on the south-facing side of one of the buildings. Walk close to the wall of each building and

look out, or stand with your back at various points along each wall. See what you eye focuses on as you look in all directions from a variety of vantage points. Walk down the middle of the space, paying attention to what you see in front of you and from side to side. Then step 20 to 30 feet back from the front and then from the back of the space to see what is the foreground, middle ground, and background between the two buildings.

For example, if you stand in the driveway looking into the space between your house and garage, you might see the wall of the garage on your right and the wall of your

home on your left. You might also see two propane tanks against the wall of the house and three first-floor windows that look onto or into the space. Do you notice that both sides of the buildings are eave sides that shed considerable rain and/or snow and ice onto both sides of the area?

What do you see way back in the distance? A bit of woodland, a fabulous view of a church steeple, a view of a nearby building that needs screening out, or trees with a beautiful view beyond? (See figure 5.12.) Do you see the potential for adding a garden between the two buildings that is linked with a path to areas in the background? Do you see the opportunity for connecting the corners of the two facing buildings with a fence or hedge at either or both ends of the space? Perhaps you have an existing breezeway between two parts of your house; such an opening can generate a garden on either side of it (see figure 5.13).

Now walk into your backyard, and look between the buildings toward the driveway. Do you see cars passing by on the street? Or do you see across the driveway to parked cars or to woodland or perhaps a neighbor's garden?

Next go into each of the buildings, and

FIGURE 5.12 (ABOVE)
When designing a space between two parallel buildings, take advantage of the fact that they frame views in two directions. If either view is unsightly, screen the poor view in the background and plant a set of handsome trees or a garden in the foreground.

FIGURE 5.13 (RIGHT)
You could use the space between two buildings or even the uprights of a breezeway to frame views into parts of your garden at a distance. Mark Ingmire from South Miami took full advantage of this roofed space between two parts of his house to frame a view of the pond and tropical garden at the back.

A GARDEN BETWEEN BUILDINGS

Here is the sequence I followed to design this entrance garden for Cindy and Gerry Prozzo in Vermont. The photographer was standing where the Prozzos park their car at the end of their driveway. A birch tree, which was part of the design, stood to his right.

- Design the primary path from the driveway to the front door and from the front door to the wood-pile. Decide on the choice of stone in light of what already exists around the house.
- Design a secondary path from the front door land-ing to the back woodland garden, repeating the same stone.
- Choose and site trees to set at the driveway end of the path and near the front door.
- Select upright evergreen shrubs to screen the utility area behind the front door porch.
- Choose mounded ever-green shrubs to provide winter interest along both sides of the path.
- Site flowering herbaceous plants, some of which will offer color through foliage as well as flower.
- Choose a ground-hugging perennial to act as a living grout between the stepping-stones.

look out any doors and windows into the space. Which windows do you look out from frequently, even daily, and which do you rarely look out of? Do the windows and doorways frame attractive or unsightly views? Are you aware of long blank walls that could in fact serve as a uniform background for a tree, shrubs, espaliered fruit trees, or vines on trellises? I certainly was when I was helping Sue Byers here in Vermont. From her screened porch, a place where she and her husband sit most every summer evening looking west to the sunset, she also could look north across 18 feet of lawn to the blank back wall of her garage. We used that south-facing white wall as a backdrop for a 6-foot-deep, 24-foot-long perennial and shrub border, at the center of which we planted a Prairiefire crab apple.

Rank not only the windows but also the doors in both buildings in order of priority.

FIGURE 5.14
Even a tall, narrow space between house and garage can give rise to a formal garden. By fencing off the view at the back, I was able to design an intimate formal space for entertaining.

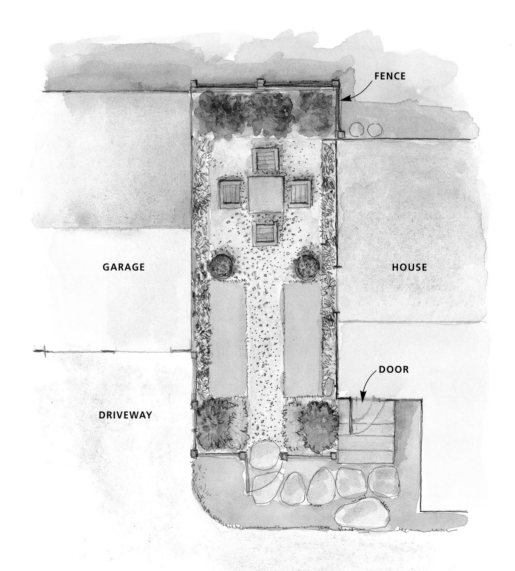

The most important doors will later help you locate paths into, and a water feature, sculpture, or planted pots within, a garden between buildings. Also keep in mind that if your home is small, a garden and sitting area with furniture outside a prominent window will make your home feel bigger. When we look out the windows of our vacation cottage, we see the outdoor dining table and chairs surrounded by gardens; that sight makes our cottage feel bigger.

Finally, consider practical issues. For example, do you need to keep this space open to gain access to the back gardens with your lawn mower and garden maintenance equipment, or is there an alternative route? Will snow cascade off your roof, possibly damaging a fence or arbor, trees or shrubs?

Answers to these questions will help you decide whether you want to garden between the two buildings or not. If you see the potential for a garden in such an area, the nature of the views from either end of the space will give you design clues. If you stand in the driveway and look down the length of the space between house and garage to attractive views of the back garden, then you will want to frame and thereby feature the beauty of the view with trees, upright shrubs, or the columns of a pergola. If, when standing at the back of the space and looking toward the front, you see parked cars or vehicles passing by on the street, then you will want to screen off that view with a hedge or fence, with a solid door or gateway set in it for access, as in the garden I designed for Pam Matweecha (see figure 5.14). This, in effect, will become your garden entrance.

If the view from both back and front is unsightly, then you will want to enclose the space between the two buildings with a hedge or fencing, perhaps, to make a secret garden. Place a solid door in the front to screen views out to car and driveway, but use an open wrought-iron gate, for example, in the back. Don't create claustrophobia. As John

POSITIVE OUTDOOR SPACE

Outdoor spaces which are merely "left over" between buildings will, in general, not be used. There are two fundamentally different kinds of outdoor space: negative space and positive space. Outdoor space is negative when it is shapeless, the residue left behind when buildings – which are generally viewed as positive – are placed on the land. An outdoor space is positive when it has a distinct and definite shape, as definite as the shape of a room, and when its shape is as important as the shapes of the buildings which surround it. . . . It seems likely that the need for enclosure goes back to our most primitive instincts. For example, when a person looks for a place to sit down outdoors, he rarely chooses to sit exposed in the middle of an open space – he usually looks for a tree to put his back against; a hollow in the ground, a natural cleft which will partly enclose him and shelter him. . . . To be comfortable, a person wants a certain amount of enclosure around him and his work – but not too much. . . . People seek areas which are partially enclosed and partly open – not too open, not too enclosed. . . .

Make all outdoor spaces which surround and lie between your buildings positive. Give each one some degree of enclosure; surround each space with wings of buildings, trees, hedges, fences, arcades, and trellised walks, until it becomes an entity with a positive quality and does not spill out indefinitely around corners.

Excerpted from A Pattern Language, *by Christopher Alexander et al.; p. 518; Oxford University Press, New York, 1977.*

FIGURE 5.15

By building a stucco wall between the corners of two stucco buildings, this designer created a space for a courtyard garden. The wall in turn provides a handsome backdrop for trees, dark foliage perennials, and a raked gravel garden. You could use a fence, hedge, or stone wall to do the same between two wings of your house.

Saladino wrote, "Landscapes should have openings everywhere so your eye is never stuck."

One other element of the space between two buildings is that you have two walls facing each other, so you can create a view across the width of the space as well as down its length (see figure 5.15). For example, one sunny expanse of wall might be a good place for an arbor, under which paving might be laid to support a table and chairs. When you sit there, your attention is directed across to the wall of the other building set within your new garden. See that facing wall as a place to display a fine plaque, trelliage, or a humorous painted wooden figure; or it could provide a surface on which to paint trompe l'oeil or to form the backdrop for a sculpture on a pedestal. Trellises affixed to walls can support fine climbing vines; your choice will depend in part on the degree of sun or shade the vine will get and how often you will need to paint the wall behind the vine (see figures 5.16 and 5.17).

Once you have taken a close look at this space between the two buildings, you need to assess the nature and mood and style of the two buildings. Make a scaled drawing of the lengths and heights of the buildings' two facing walls, including all windows and doors and their heights above ground level. Then, on another sheet of graph paper, sketch a scaled bird's-eye view drawing that shows the shape of the ground between the two buildings, as well as the walls of the two buildings, including the location of windows and doors. Record on this drawing where water drips off the roofs and how far out the driplines are from the foundation of each building. Look closely at the ground for erosion and other indications of drainage problems. Record where visible utilities are located: meter boxes, overhead power and phone lines, propane tank caps or whole tanks, the satellite dish, outdoor spiggots and related hoses, or clotheslines. Can any of these discordant elements be easily moved? Also record the location of buried utilities: water, natural gas or power lines, propane tanks, irrigation lines, or invisible dog fencing. All of these will have an impact on the design of your garden.

Finally, take a close look at the details of the two buildings; they will give you a clear understanding of the mood and style of the two buildings and thus help you determine the mood and style of the garden between them. What materials are they made of? What paint color, if any, did you use on the walls and trim? Are the buildings formal or informal, suburban or rural, cozy or stark, modern or historic? Does any stonework or paving already exist between the two buildings or in view from the area between them? What is or might be the relationship between this space and already-existing or planned garden areas on either end of it? Are there existing paths that might give you clues as to where new paths through this new garden might go? The path, after all, is the very first thing you need to design in a garden, and its

FIGURE 5.16 (BELOW LEFT)
Sometimes all it takes to link two buildings is a section of roof that results in a breezeway. That new space between buildings, in concert with a fence in the background, can give rise to gardens that settle house and outbuilding into the landscape.

FIGURE 5.17 (BELOW RIGHT)
Here, a stuccoed wall with a doorway built into it joins two buildings, and the wall supports trelliswork for a rose. There is no end of possibilities for the tall, narrow garden behind or in front of that wall.

FIGURE 5.18
The demands of the site for the Brine's home in New Hampshire required that the garage and house be set at an angle to each other. Their architects designed this pergola to link the front porch to the side garage door. Pergola uprights frame a view of the Connecticut River and provide a garden entrance.

location will in turn help you break the larger design problem down into smaller, more manageable parts.

Once you have closely examined the two buildings and you've prepared a scaled drawing of the walls and the ground between them, examine the drawings with a scaled ruler to see whether there might be a dimension or some proportion that they share. For example, if the wall of your two-story house is 20 feet high and the wall of your garage is 10 feet high, then they share a 5- or 10-foot module. Then you might find that the space between those two walls is 15 feet wide and 30 feet long, thereby confirming the 5-foot module as the dimension all measurements have in common. That might suggest two 5-foot-wide beds on either side of a 5-foot-wide central path. You might plan a 5-foot-wide, 10-foot-long arbor centered on one of the 30-foot-long walls, thereby leaving two 10-foot spaces on either side for trellising. Those modules help create sound, appropriate proportions.

GARDENS BETWEEN NONPARALLEL BUILDINGS

What if the walls of the two buildings are not parallel, thereby creating an oddly shaped space between them? Karen Brine, a client and avid gardener who lives in New Hampshire, was faced with that dilemma when designing a garden in the 16-foot gap between the end of her house and garage at odd angles to one another. First she designed cut bluestone paths that went straight from both the steps off the end of the front porch and from the side door of the garage, the roughly 8-foot-long paths joining at an angle between the two buildings (see figure 5.18). She then installed a similarly angled white-painted pergola over this path to link the two ends of the buildings. Next she ran a field-

stone path from the nearby driveway, under the pergola, between two pairs of columns, and through gardens between house and garage to her back lawn. That is, she surrounded the bluestone path with gardens, thereby reducing the awareness that the buildings were set at an odd angle to one another. What she also did in this deceptively simple design was to use the uprights of the pergola, combined with two upright granite fenceposts at the beginning of the fieldstone path out by the driveway, to act as the entrance to her garden. As you stand out by those two standing stones, you can see a remarkable view of a broad bend in the Connecticut River framed by the two central uprights of the pergola. What Karen was also acknowledging is that the beginning of any path, whenever possible, should direct one's attention to a fabulous

FIGURE 5.19

Long lawn paths edged with an allée of trees or shrubs can help draw a relationship between a house and a distant outbuilding. In this garden I designed for Tyler Jenner outside New York City, I drew a strong line between the outbuilding and a window in the sunroom. Placing the bench against the outbuilding strengthened the connection between the buildings and thus the coherence of the garden.

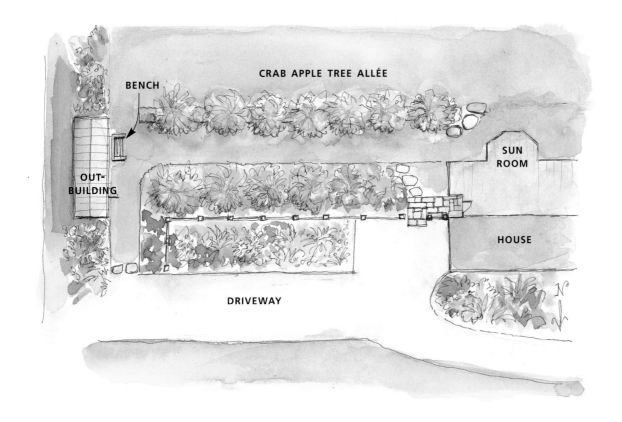

CRAB APPLE TREE ALLÉE
BENCH
OUT-BUILDING
SUN ROOM
HOUSE
DRIVEWAY

TRELLISED WALKWAYS

Trellised walkways have their own special beauty. They are so unique, so different from other ways of shaping a path, that they are almost archetypal. . . . We shall try to define the places where a trellised structure over a path is appropriate.

■ Use it to emphasize the path it covers, and to set off one part of the path as a special section of a longer path in order to make it an especially nice and inviting place to walk.

■ Since the trellised path creates enclosure around the spaces which it bounds, use it to create a virtual wall to define an outdoor space. For example, a trellised walk can form an enormous outdoor room by surrounding, or partially surrounding, a garden.

Therefore: Where paths need special protection or where they need some intimacy, build a trellis over the path and plant it with climbing flowering vines (to create filtered light underneath, where you walk). Use the trellis to help shape the outdoor spaces on either side of it [see figure 5.20].

Excerpted from A Pattern Language, *by Christopher Alexander et al.; p. 810, Oxford University Press, New York, 1977.*

view at the end of the path. That is particularly relevant when setting a path between two buildings, where views are so concentrated between walls.

Gardens between Distant Buildings

There is one final subject to consider, and that is when two buildings are set so far apart that they don't appear to have a relationship to one another. This was the first problem I addressed when Tyler Jenner, who lives in a suburban community just north of New York City, asked me to help pull her garden together. In solving that problem, we solved several others simultaneously (see figure 5.19). As we sat in her screened porch, we looked down 100 feet of amorphously shaped lawn to a garden shed that had once been a children's playhouse. It was a lovely little building but was largely ignored by the existing garden design, even though the door of the screened porch and the door into the shed were directly in line. Running parallel with this line, but set back some 10 feet, was a white picket fence separating garden from driveway. We decided to plant five disease-resistant 'Sugar Tyme' crab apples 18 feet on center along that fence in a 6-foot-wide bed and then to underplant the entire 100-foot length with evergreen *Geranium macrorrhizum* 'Ingwersen's Variety.' The trees would form a semitransparent screen between lawn path and driveway. We then designed a matching set of five crab apples set 18 feet out in the lawn, thereby forming an allée. When seen from the porch, the shed, formerly unrelated to anything in the garden, became the focus of attention from the screened porch and the anchor for the allée and related beds. When we fully understood the new role of the shed, we placed a simple bench in front of the shed window, in line with the center of the lawn path, to draw people toward that end of the garden.

FIGURE 5.20
The line running due south from our front door to a 75-year-old apple tree 200 feet away provided the main axis for our garden. This rustic arbor helps draw people from the front door, across the lawn and through the arbor to the gardens around the apple tree.

PRACTICAL PROBLEMS SOLVED

1

CLOTHESLINES

You may still enjoy drying your laundry on a line. Given that most laundry rooms are situated near the back of the house, the problem for the garden designer is to find a utilitarian place near there for a clothesline that won't take undue attention away from the garden or impede progress through it. I have solved this problem in a number of ways.

The simplest approach is to use a retractable clothesline widely available in hardware stores. Affix the retracted line in its spring-loaded case off the side or corner of your house or garage, and screw the stout second hook into a post set within a hedge or attach the second hook to an outbuilding or garage. In this way, the laundry can dry in an airy open place, and then the line can be retracted.

Another solution is to hedge or fence off a utility area somewhere near the laundry room, perhaps at the back or far side of the garage or garden shed. That utility area could enclose space for laundry and many other utilitarian purposes as well. The dimensions of the back of the garage or other outbuilding will give you appropriate dimensions for such a utility area. For example, plant an evergreen or deciduous hedge from each corner of the back of the garage out two-thirds of the length of the building, say 18 feet or so, leaving a central gap for a solid door, an open

gate, or simply an opening. Then plant a third hedge parallel with the back of the garage to enclose the utility area. (These hedges will in turn form backdrops for gardens outside the hedge.)

Inside the hedge, provide a structure for drying clothes by simply setting two stout posts in the ground and attaching a 4-foot-wide crosspiece, with bracing atop each post. Three or four lines could run between the two crosspieces. Given that the clotheslines might take up an area 4 feet wide and 12 feet long, you'll have room for other utilitarian roles for the space: a lean-to off the back of the garage for firewood; four raised beds for a small cutting or herb garden; a workbench against the back wall for propagating and potting up plants.

Ruth Leys, a client who lives with her family outside Baltimore, loves to see her clothes flapping in the wind in the long, narrow space just outside her kitchen window. However, she's not convinced her guests share her enthusiasm. We decided to separate the back wooden deck from the side utility area with a 7-foot-high fence with a door built into it. The fence became a support for clematis, a backdrop for potted plants set on the wooden deck, and a visual barrier between the furniture on the deck and the clotheslines. Now this sounds like a no-brainer approach, but I bring up this simple solution by way of reminding Americans, in particular, that it is okay to build fences within the interior of your gardens. We have difficulty fencing off spaces within our gardens. It's not in our blood the way it is

among Europeans, and Ruth is originally from Scotland.

Mary and I like to see laundry drying outside too. Because we have set black locust posts on either side of many entrances in our garden, we also set five posts about 8 feet out for the east end of our barn. I then screwed eyebolts into the barn siding and strung clothesline between post and bolt. Because there was a precedent in the garden for these posts, they look appropriate in the garden, albeit in an out-of-the-way section of it.

2

EXTERIOR CLOTHES DRYER HEAT VENTS

Virtually all modern clothes dryers are fitted with a 4-inch vent pipe that runs from the back of the dryer and through the wall of the house to the outside. The average temperature of that forced hot air is between 200 and 225 degrees F. (In fact, the dryer can produce temperatures up to 280 degrees F before a thermal cutoff shuts the machine down automatically.) When the dryer is going through its 30-to-40-minute cycle, that air can dry out the foliage of shrubs or perennials planted within a 4-to-5-foot range and perhaps even further, depending on wind or air circulation in that area of the garden.

Broad-leaved or needled evergreens simply cannot flourish or even live within several feet of a dryer vent. In areas of North America where winter temperatures regularly drop below freezing, the hot air from the dryer thaws and dries out evergreen foliage, yet the roots of the plant, being in frozen ground, cannot replenish that transpired moisture. At the very least, the branches in harm's way of the vent die.

But the problem is bigger than evergreens. Throughout the growing season, the foliage of any nearby plants dries out. During the winter, if the vent is directed toward the ground, the hot air will thaw soil in its immediate area, and then, when the dryer shuts off, that soil will freeze again. That freeze-thaw cycle two or three times a week is enough to kill plants.

One simple thing you can do is add a 10-to-15-foot-long flexible metal or plastic extension to that 4-inch vent pipe so that the hot air comes out at a point where it will not harm plants. You will have to check that pipe monthly to remove lint from its entire length, as well as affix wire mesh to the far end of the extension to prevent small animals from crawling up the pipe.

If you can't add an extension to the pipe, you can place a boulder, a flat fieldstone on edge, or a metal deflector in the soil 12 inches out from the vent pipe to deflect the hot air to reduce its impact on nearby plants.

The Main Points:

- Consider whether you should design a utility area where a clothesline could be set up out of sight from your garden.
- If such a solution is not feasible, think about how to make the clothesline a feature rather than an eyesore or purchase a retractable clothesline that can be pulled out only when you have laundry to dry.
- Find your clothes dryer heat vent. If plants are suffering from the vent's exhaust, shield the end of the vent with a boulder or flat stone on edge or extend the length of the vent pipe and direct the heat to a place away from plants.

CHAPTER SIX

OUTBUILDINGS AND GARDENS

G AZEBOS, GARDEN SHEDS, AND EVEN your garage can play important roles in your garden. At the simplest level, trelliswork affixed to a wall of a small building can support vines or espaliers. One wall of an outbuilding can act as the backdrop for a hedged herb or vegetable garden, or you could completely surround a small building with gardens, as we did with our 12-by-18-foot weathered shed. You can place a gazebo at the far end of a straight lawn path to act as the destination for that path, or you can hide it among trees and shrubs so that it becomes the heart of a secret garden. Well-designed utility sheds can provide a backdrop for an equally well-designed garden. But above all, the position, dimensions, proportions, and materials of an outbuilding provide many of the clues you'll need to develop the gardens near or around it.

When we began developing our 1½-acre garden 18 years ago, we started by designing

the gardens around our 150-year-old wooden garden shed. The reason we started there was that the building gave us a context for our design decisions and an anchor for any garden we designed around it (see figure 6.3). We knew that somewhere in our 1½ acres, we wanted a four-quadrant herb garden, and the area off the east wall of the 12-by-18-foot shed seemed the perfect spot. First we built a rustic grape arbor parallel with and close to the back of the shed. We made the four corner posts out of black locust logs that we had cut from our woodland; we built the upper deck with long-lasting pressure-treated lumber, which has gradually disappeared under the mass of rambling grape vines. Randomly shaped fieldstone paving, with thyme between them, went in under the arbor to support a simple teak bench and two metal chairs I had inherited from my grandparents.

The proportions and dimensions of the four-quadrant herb garden came off those of

FIGURE 6.1 (PAGE 149)
This guesthouse is made cozy by setting it under the branches of a mature tree and at the end of a crushed gravel path through an informal garden. Such buildings tame wild places.

FIGURE 6.2 (OPPOSITE)
Designer Lynden Miller designed this section of her own garden using the toolhouse–potting shed as a visual anchor. As you walk toward the area, the roofline behind the yew hedge hints at what is to come. The hedge, in combination with the white-painted fence, provided her with a logical place for the white structure.

FIGURE 6.3 (LEFT)
Our garden shed helped us find the right place and the right design for our herb garden. Proportions, dimensions, placement of hedge and arbor, size and layout of beds – everything came from paying attention to this building.

the shed. Each boxwood-edged quadrant was just a bit bigger than the 4-by-7-foot door leading into the north end of the shed. The peastone paths between them were the width of that door. The hedge around the perimeter of the garden was as tall as the eave sides of the shed. To allow room for garden and path, we situated the black haw (*Viburnum prunifolium*) hedges down two sides of the garden as far away from the building as the shed door was tall. We then planted an arbor vitae hedge to enclose the east end of the space.

FIGURE 6.4

Leave the sides of a gazebo open if they all look out on attractive views; build a solid wall on sides where the views are unsightly. We left all four sides open to frame views of our garden and meadow.

The informal mood of the old weathered building helped us choose traditional plants for the garden; hardy VanBuren and Aurora grapes growing up the locust posts; climbing hydrangea on the shed; a weeping pea shrub (*Caragana arborescens* 'Pendula') at the center of each quadrant, with annual and perennial herbs around them. We set a classic armillary sphere on a pedestal in the center of the pea-stone paths as a gently contrasting formal note. The result is a shady, intimate sitting area under the arbor for a hot day, with the fragrance and sight of nearby herbs in full sun.

Because the walls of outbuildings are smaller than those of a house, they provide cues for smaller gardens near them. Outbuilding walls, often around 8 feet high, provide a dimension that is just right for a pair of small trees, such as crab apples, planted 8 feet out from one of the walls to form the canopy over a bench and two chairs set against that wall. The trees can be underplanted to surround the sitting area with a richly planted garden anchored by building, trees, and furniture.

If you see an appealing outbuilding in a

garden you visited, or one you see on the Internet, be careful not to necessarily think, "I want one of those in my garden." Outbuildings need to meet three fundamental principles of placement and construction before they have a sense of belonging: elements of construction shared with those of your house or other buildings; appropriate placement for both function and looks; gardens around them, not foundation planting.

First, an outbuilding needs to have some visual echo of your home or other outbuildings – especially if it is in sight of your home – so that its design, style, colors, materials, and detailing feel related on some level to the house, the most important building in your garden. Perhaps an outbuilding shares some architectural elements and detailing of a certain period, or it has similar siding, roofing, or paint color. Our home was built in the late 1700s; our garden shed was built in the mid-1800s of similar materials and roofing; our gazebo (see figure 6.4), built just five years ago, has a similar post-and-beam style as that of the shed and barn attached to our home.

Materials, style, even the bracing methods and materials are shared across all three structures. Our gazebo has, in the parlance of landscape design, a "site-specific character." It is of the place.

You can also use paint color to underpin visual continuity across buildings large and small. Nancy McCabe, a garden designer in northwestern Connecticut, used a dark green paint on the trim of the doors, windows, and fascia boards of her home and then repeated that same color on both a nearby arbor leading from her front to side garden and the trim on a nearby garden shed (see figure 6.11). Robert Dash, in his garden on Long Island, painted the arch over several doors of his summer home and another in a garden shed the same striking yellow. A common color across disparate buildings will help draw them into a relationship. Or, as tradition has it here in New England, paint your house white and the barn and all outbuildings barn-red. Andy and Christine Hall painted all the 19th-century outbuildings in their garden to match the red of their barn, the dominant functional

FIGURE 6.5
A form or shape on your house can be repeated in many garden elements. Here, John and Fiona Owen repeated the Gothic arch from their home into details for benches, a doorway, and even informal twig edging at the front of small borders.

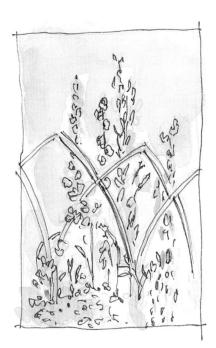

FIGURE 6.6 (BELOW)
From the back door of Hitch Lyman's Greek Revival home near Ithaca, New York, you look across an informally planted terrace, meadow, and pond to a most unexpected Greek Revival temple built to draw and then stop the eye. The contrast between informal garden and formal folly is the source of this garden's strength.

FIGURE 6.7 (OPPOSITE)
This outbuilding in Gordon White's garden in Austin, Texas, contributes a great deal to this spare, geometric garden:
- The dimensions and proportions of the reflecting pool and garden
- A backdrop for the bench
- A tour-de-force use of yellow and green paint to brighten a shady area
- A focal point in line with the glass door at the photographer's back
- A place to store garden tools

building on their property, and all the outbuildings were thereby visually related.

Even when garden sheds and gazebos are built at a distance from the house, their construction still needs to echo some architectural element of the house so that you set up a visual relationship between the dominant house in the foreground and the subordinate building in the middle or background. We visited John and Fiona Owens' garden years ago, the center of which was a renovated

desanctified church. Its stained-glass windows were in the form of the Gothic arch (see figure 6.5). The Owens echoed that shape in all their trelliswork, in the backs of custom-made garden benches and chairs, as well as in gates and doors at transition points throughout their garden. This leitmotif had a unifying effect across all parts of the garden, even when one couldn't be seen from the other.

The second key to establishing that sense of belonging is the siting and context of the

ASSESSING AN OUTBUILDING

To help you choose a pre-fabricated outbuilding or to inform your work with a designer/carpenter who might build a garden shed for you, I turned for advice to Jonathan Jesup, a carpenter who since 1979 has specialized in the design, construction, and restoration of 18th- and 19th-century buildings.

Jon's central advice gathers around the precept that form follows function. If an outbuilding's purpose is functional, then a building should appear and be functional. Ornamentation should be kept to a minimum, because if we follow the logic of this book – buildings as the center for gardens – then we need to view buildings as backdrops to the gardens we design around them. When you look at a catalog of prefab outbuildings, you will see that the designers are trying to make the buildings themselves look appealing; in fact, that will later become your job as a garden designer. Keep the building simple, and it will settle into your garden gently and appropriately and not draw undue attention to itself.

Here are Jon Jesup's observations about what qualities to look for when purchasing or designing a functional outbuilding for your garden:

- Look for **classic elements of design** which will ensure that your building will relate to the architectural precedents in your area. Look for historical design elements that reflect local styles and materials. Avoid the modern or the momentarily popular, and your building will visually withstand the test of time.
- Also keep in mind the **size of the building and its door(s) relative to its function.** Measure your lawn tractor, wheelbarrows, and so on, to get a handle on the minimum square footage your equipment will require and how much space you'll require to move easily about in it.
- **Measure the space where the shed will go in your garden** to be sure the building will look neither cramped nor out of scale with its surroundings.
- **Simplicity of design and materials** is important. Avoid buildings that have been designed to look

unique through the use of a roundheaded door or Palladian windows, for example, or over-ornamentation.

- **The placement of windows and doors within well-proportioned wall space** is a most important design element. There needs to be a balance between the openings for windows and doors in relation to solid wall space. Badly designed buildings are often too small to support the openings for doors and windows.
- When assessing **windows**, keep in mind that windows do two things: let in light and break up expanses of wall. Many small buildings are dark; if you make sure there is plenty of window space, you won't need to electrify the building. High windows set into the gable ends are excellent; they leave lots of wall space for storage and hanging things and the high light shines down on work surfaces. Avoid picture windows. Individual panes of glass should be small, and the longest dimension of the individual panes should be vertical rather than horizontal for the most attractive look.

- **Doors** should be made of wood, not aluminum (once dented, always dented). Paint or stain any cross bracing on the door's exterior the same color as the rest of the door. Cross bracing painted a different color is too blatant a shape in the garden. Before looking at garden sheds, measure the width of a lawn tractor or other wide equipment again to be sure the door will accommodate your maintenance equipment.
- The **pitch of the roof** is a key element in the design of a good outbuilding. Be sure the pitch is sufficiently steep that you see plenty of the roof from a distance. Most are too low, making a small building look squat. Pitches of 9/12 to 12/12 look best. That is, a 9-inch rise (height) for every 12 inches of run (width); 12/12 would be a roof at a 45-degree angle. Long, narrow buildings (8 by 16 feet, for example) can benefit from an even steeper pitch: 12 inches of width for 16 inches of height.
- **Eschew the purely decorative** – shutters, cupolas, window boxes, fussy painting, and fancy hinges. An

outbuilding is and must appear to be functional.

- **Foundations.** Use something as uncomplicated as large stones at the four corners, a simple free-standing stone wall set on 8 inches of 1½-inch crushed stone on all four sides, or concrete-filled sonotubes in the corners masked with fieldstones around them. You can also just dig a hole in the ground and use the earth as the form for the concrete.
- **Eaves** that hang out over the top of the side walls 6 to 12 inches or thereabouts make a building look better and protect the side walls by keeping rain away from the building. Many prefab garden sheds have only 2-inch eave overhangs; don't buy one of them.
- The **roof should have visual and actual thickness** and look solid. Prefab buildings often do not have a fascia board nailed to the rafter tails, something that gives a roof a look of solidity. Be sure that the fascia boards on either side of the structure are in place, adding visual weight and covering the rafter tails, which can

often make a small building look busy.

- **Framing** is pretty standard: 2-by-4-inch or 2-by-6-inch boards throughout. Check to see whether smaller framing boards have been used. If they have, which is unlikely, don't buy the structure.
- The **flooring** should be made of sound 1-inch rough stock or ¾-inch plywood. Avoid particle-board flooring.
- If **the interior walls** are built of vertical boards, look for bracing to prevent swaying, or "racking" in builders' parlance. Exterior plywood sheathing solves the racking problem so that interior bracing is unnecessary, but plywood has a poor appearance from the outside. (Most often, a utility shed is one board thick, so the exterior and interior walls are the same material.)
- Vertical board **exterior siding** on top of the plywood sheathing is a solid, albeit costly, solution. A grooved and milled plywood called T-111 is an attempt to combine the stability of plywood and the vertical board appearance, but it is short-lived and truly unattractive. Avoid it. Solid

wood ages with grace, but it is more expensive than plywood.

- The **roofing material** is typically limited to asphalt shingles; darker colors are visually more appropriate. Combined with generous eaves, such shingles are perfectly adequate and long-lasting. Cedar shakes are more attractive and costly and will weather to a dark or silver gray.
- **Hardware – hinges, door latches, window hardware** – should be strong, simple, and functional. Their color should not make them visually obvious and should echo or share the color of the walls, the door, or window trim so that they don't appear to busy-up the look of the building.
- **Paints and stains.** Use stains rather than paints, and even then, choose stains that have as little color pigment as possible. Jon used a stain with only 2 percent pigment in it so that it would make the siding on his garden shed look older than it really is. Paint is often too fussy from a visual as well as from a maintenance point of view. If you have other painted structures – a

white arbor, fence, or trellising – close to the outbuilding, paint only the trim, the fascia boards, and the window surrounds of your outbuilding white and use a clear stain or sealant on the walls.

Before you buy a prefab outbuilding, check with a carpenter you respect regarding his or her costs to custom-design and build an outbuilding for you. With those figures, you can go to a catalog or a prefab outlet to do some comparison shopping. Finally, call your town hall or local municipality office, and speak to the zoning administrator regarding setback regulations – that is, how far your building must be from boundary lines – before getting too far into the construction or purchase of an outbuilding. Also check with the zoning administrator about permitting requirements and whether or not your building will become a taxable amenity on your property. In Newton, Massachusetts, for example, you are not allowed to build an outbuilding 100 square feet or larger any closer than 8 feet to a boundary.

FIGURE 6.8
The back of a garage is often a neglected space. Here, Stan Fry and I developed a design for a garden in scale with the back of his garage. From the bench, you look across his New Hampshire garden to a view of Mount Monadnock.

building itself in light of its function. The function of a gazebo, for example, is to provide a sheltering structure in which you sit to look out onto a wonderful view. If a gazebo is located too close to a garage so that both can be seen in one eyeful, it will remain subordinate to the larger garage and its role as a lookout will suffer. If you site the gazebo out in the middle of the lawn, with just a few shrubs and perennials around its base, it will also lack context, appear lost in space, and not play a role in focusing your attention on a view. However, place a gazebo among a group of trees at the end of a long, straight path through gardens, and its role in providing an appropriate destination, as well as a place from which to look back up the length of the path, will make it feel right and settled (see figures 6.6 and 6.12). That is, its placement is appropriate to its function.

The same would hold true for a utilitarian garden shed. Place it where it will function well, but make a feature of it only if it has good proportions and detailing and visually echoes your house. Associate it with the working part of the garden – close to the vegetable and cutting garden or to paths that will enable you to get the stored lawn mower out easily. If it is a building of little distinction, screen it from view with hedges or fencing.

Or tinker with its design. I saw a garden outside Akron, Ohio, in which the gardener had affixed a 5-foot-deep porch with a wooden floor along one side of an undistinguished garden shed. She then set a bench against the wall and under the porch and grew vines up the vertical supports for the 5-foot-deep roof. She painted the entire structure dark green so that the porch didn't look added on. That color caused the building to recede into the background of shrubs and small trees which grew nearby, providing the

little structure with a context, with its own place in the larger garden.

When small buildings are appropriately located in the garden, they act as magnets to draw guests along your itinerary by acting as a promise of shelter and enclosure, as well as a place to sit and talk or to look out onto the garden or back at the house (again, see figures 6.6 and 6.12). In acting as a magnet, the building – and its placement – needs to live up to its billing. The uprights and crosspieces of an open-sided gazebo, for example, should act as frames for views out from them. Don't frame something unsightly, especially if you are going to place a bench, table, and chairs against one side of the gazebo. Be sure that at least the dominant side, the one with furniture associated with it, frames a good view.

Having said that, some outbuildings are so utilitarian, so lacking in grace, that they should either be screened from view or moved to where they can be their own functional selves. Professional building movers versed in the ins and outs of such a move will know exactly what to do. A local historian came to our garden one day and saw that our garden shed, 10 by 18 feet, had hinged vertical board siding, which suggested to him that it had been a tobacco drying shed and therefore would be around 100 years old. That gave him the clue that it had certainly been moved 8 miles over the ridge from the Connecticut River Valley, where 19th-century farmers had grown small fields of tobacco. He said, "That's the size building the kids could have moved here with a sled and a team of oxen on a Saturday afternoon." You'll be surprised how easily small buildings can be moved.

Now let's take a close look at the third principle gathered around outbuildings – how you can garden around a variety of different outbuildings.

THE GARAGE

Often, either the back or one side of your garage faces the back gardens. If that is the case with yours, use that blank wall, or any of the other three sides, as the basis for a garden that is in some way linked to the larger design for the gardens at the back of your house. When sizing up the various sides of a garage, consider sun and shade, wind, nearby and distant views, soil, and the use to which this new garden area will be put. All of these elements will help you design the garden once you have chosen the right wall. Here are three examples of gardens I've designed off the back or sides of garages that might spur your imagination.

In a part of Stan and Cheri Fry's garden in New Hampshire, Stan had already trained three espaliered apple trees against the west-facing back of his three-car garage (see figure 6.8). I thought this a particularly clever choice of plant, because he had trained them flat to the garage so that if snow did slide off the garage roof, it would do no damage to his two-dimensional espaliers. As handsome as the espaliers were, Stan asked me to design a garden along the back of the garage, for it was in full view from a nearby raised porch along the back of his elegant 19th-century home.

I stood on the deck, raised some 6 feet above grade, and looked down at the back of the garage only 15 feet away. The pattern of the espaliers was not evident, because the back of the garage ran parallel with the length of the deck on which I was standing. All I saw, consequently, was foliage flat against the wall and gently sloping lawn running up to the foundation of the garage. Then I walked down the stairs from the deck and stood with

FIGURE 6.9 (BELOW)
The back of a barn or larger outbuilding can provide a logical place for a roomy arbor where bench and chairs can be set to look out at a distant view or nearby garden. Choose the materials and design for structure and furniture in light of the building itself.

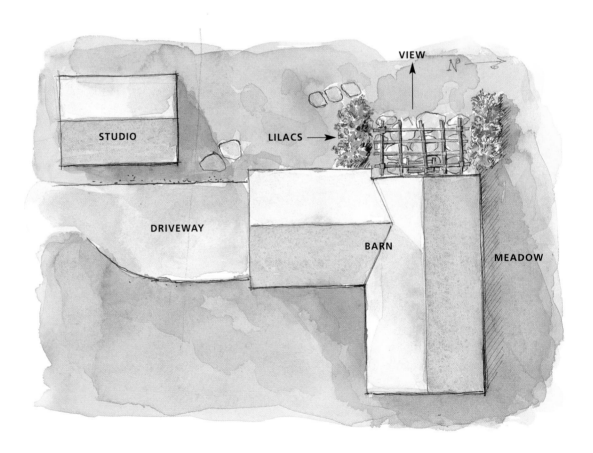

my back to the middle espalier and looked west. It was a gorgeous view that went across many gardens already in place and through a notch in woodland to the peak of Mount Monadnock some 20 miles away. There, against those espaliers, in the center of the back wall of his garage, was a perfect spot for a two-person bench.

I got my measuring tape out. The garage wall was 24 feet long and 8 feet high. Given that Stan likes straight lines and formal gardens near his house, I took the 8-foot dimension (the height of the garage wall) and doubled it to produce a garden 16 feet deep and 24 feet long. That 16-foot dimension gave me the position for an 18-inch-high, 24-foot-long retaining wall that would run parallel with the back of the garage and level the garden between it and the back of the garage. Next I designed two 18-inch-high, 16-foot-long yew hedges that started at the northwest and southwest corners of the garage and went out to meet either end of the retaining wall, leaving a 3-foot-wide gap on the south side for access. I then connected those two hedges with a third, which would run 24 feet along the back of the retaining wall to enclose the entire space with a boxwood hedge. After several attempts at a design within the enclosed 15-by-22-foot space – allowing for the thickness of the hedges – I settled on a classic 19th-century approach reminiscent of the circle in the square. I designed a 2-foot-wide peastone path shaped like the handle and frame of a magnifying glass with a 3-foot-diameter circular garden in its center of Germander (*Teucrium chamaedrys*) and an armillary sphere on a pedestal in its center. I set a dark green metal bench (the same color as the trim color on the garage) in the center of the west-facing wall and a continuous curving herb garden around the perimeter of the path. The pattern of path and garden would be especially appar-

ent from the vantage point of the raised deck nearby, where the light color of the path material – ⅜-inch gray peastone – would contrast with the dark greens of the herbs.

My next example gathers around the notion that we sometimes don't see what's right in front of our faces. Martha Lapham asked me to consult on her garden in Vermont. As I always do, I asked to see all around the exterior of her house and out-buildings before beginning to develop design ideas. As we walked between the back of her studio to the west side of her 18th-century barn, I looked out at the most wonderful view of a meadow that sloped away from the barn and out over woodland to Lake Champlain and the Adirondacks in the distance. (Now I can hear you saying, I don't have that magnificent view; what's this got to do with me? I say, plenty if you have even one outbuilding.) I asked Martha whether she had ever considered sitting at this spot in the evening, and she admitted she hadn't. Well, that's changed, and it might well for you if you reassess views from all sides of your outbuildings.

Together, we designed a rustic arbor off the west side of her barn and within a 2-foot set-back along that west wall (see figure 6.9). We used old cedar posts for uprights and weathered split chestnut rails to echo the weathered barn siding and set the arbor at the west-facing back of Martha's old barn. Next we designed fieldstone flagging, which comprised flat stones from nearby stone walls, to be set under the arbor and fitted moss from the ground along the north side of the barn in the gaps between the fieldstones. Martha purchased an antique wooden bench to sit under the arbor. To tie the arbor to the ground and the nearby gardens, she planted a hardy wisteria 'Aunt Dee' on one corner post and three lilacs off the south end to screen the view of driveway and parked cars.

Martha and her husband tell me that they now sit under that arbor most evenings during warm, pleasant weather. They had lived on the property for 30 years before the arbor went in and had never once sat and admired that view. Look out from every side of your house and outbuildings, and you, too, might find a view that will justify a modest arbor or sitting area which will, in turn, give rise to garden design ideas around it.

Jeff and Susan McCanna had only 75 feet of open space at the back of their attached garage in a small New Hampshire town. It was pretty much the only garden space they had. The design that I developed for them may well give you lots of ideas about how to design your own garden in the small space behind your garage or other outbuilding.

The first controlling fact of the design was that the McCannas needed a turnaround space in the driveway. They wanted to be able to reverse out of their south-facing garage, comfortably back into a space, and then drive down the driveway parallel with the south side of the house and out onto the street. The turnaround required a space 10 feet wide and about 18 feet long. The balance of the backyard could be garden (see figure 1.18).

I designed an 8-by-12-foot arbor against the east-facing side wall of the garage to take advantage of the longest view on their small property. To separate the arbor and its related gardens, we hedged off the parking/turnaround area with lilacs and built a gate within that hedge for access. The entire length of the garden off the garage wing of this modest house was as wide as the garage; the arbor was two-thirds the width of the garage and lined up with the center of the gable end. We paved under this arbor with loosely fitting field-stones interplanted with burgundy-leaved ajuga. I gathered planted pots near the four rectangular cedar posts and then planted kiwi

vine (*Actinidia kolomikta*) on the two front posts – one male and one female so that the female would fruit. We then set a 6-foot-long teak bench under the arbor, and there, in the hedged garden within a densely populated New England village, my clients had absolute privacy. The east end of the garage, in turn, generated all the lines of the garden, including a second hedge 50 feet out from and parallel with the east wall of the garage. Behind that hedge, we designed a utility area for brush, compost, and a leaf pile.

GARDEN SHEDS

Garden sheds, tool or potting sheds, or simple utility structures are often informal, unpainted utilitarian structures. They are frequently positioned away from the main lawn or garden areas and sometimes have a potting bench or wood storage or a lean-to roof jutting out from one side, under which garden maintenance equipment is stored. Such practical buildings can give rise to equally practical garden areas: a cutting garden or vegetable garden or even a small nursery area for divisions of perennials, seedlings, or propagation.

Sometimes a simple garden shed can be co-opted into the garden proper. Nancy McCabe, a Connecticut-based garden designer, used a small garden shed to a wonderfully simple yet rich effect (see figure 6.11). The shed, 8 by 12 feet, is set about 18 feet off the northwest corner of her home; the west walls of the house and shed are parallel with one another. Wanting to increase privacy in her back garden and at the same time create a garden entrance, McCabe planted a hemlock hedge from the northwest corner of her house to the northeast corner of her garden. In the center of the 16-foot-long hedge, she left a 5-foot-wide gap into which she placed a dark green wooden archway that would act as the entrance to her back garden. The hemlock

FIGURE 6.10 (OPPOSITE) Take advantage of the synergy between a small outbuilding and an intimate garden. Garden anchors shed; shed anchors garden—a gentle interplay between a cottage garden and functional shed.

FIGURE 6.11
Nancy McCabe, a garden
designer in northwestern
Connecticut, sited her garden
shed about 18 feet from and
in line with the north end of
her house. The shed provides
a logical end of the hedge
and marks the back corner of
her entrance garden.

hedge, anchored at its far end by the shed, in turn formed the background for beds that came up to both sides of it.

LOOKING AT THE GRAND VIEW

Small buildings and gazebos are also valuable in creating an intimate place from which to see an imposing view. As British garden designer Penelope Hobhouse wrote, "No matter how panoramic its scope, a view of surrounding countryside becomes a genuine garden picture only when it has been framed." Sometimes a vast view – a great expanse of prairie, the Smoky Mountains, a large lake or ocean – without something in the foreground can lack depth, and make you feel insignificant. I stood under a magnificent oak in a seaside garden in Marblehead, Massachusetts, and looked out at sailboats, fishing vessels, and the far shore of the harbor. The overarching branches framed my view and helped me understand distance and depth. When I stepped out from under the tree's branches, the view flattened. The principle is this: if you have a grand view, provide a comforting little building or structure from which to see and frame that view.

Patrick Chassé, a landscape architect working here in the Northeast, designed a delicate white-painted trelliage gazebo covered with clematis vines for a garden in Manchester on the Sea in Massachusetts. It was set on the crest of land near the house and overlooked a 180-degree view of the Atlantic Ocean. Four people could sit in this intimate space to look out at a dramatic view framed by the clematis-covered gazebo. When I sat in the gazebo, I felt enclosed, embraced, and safe as I looked out over this vast expanse of water that stretched out to the horizon from the shore some 75 feet below me. When I got up and walked no more than 50 feet away and stood on the crest of land where there was no structure or fence – just a low garden between me and the vastness – I felt more exposed and vulnerable, and the view had flattened.

Furthermore, that little building played a big role in providing Chassé a context for gardens on either side of it that ran along the edge where lawn met the top of the slope down to the ocean. The gazebo anchored the garden while acting as an invitation from the house to come view the panorama yet remain safe sitting there well above the breaking waves of the Atlantic. It also played the role of an intermediate destination between the house and the nearby top of a wooden staircase down to the beach. The staircase alone might have been insufficient to draw me across 50 feet of lawn to the edge. Architecture and garden worked together to tame the ocean and put me at ease.

The same principles would apply for any grand view from your garden: a gazebo set within a copse of trees looking out at a view into the Sawtooth Range in Idaho; a little rustic wooden structure set within native shrubs near the line where lawn meets prairie in Utah or at the edge of the Sonoran desert; a 19th-century gazebo near a 19th-century home at the edge of the palisades overlooking the Hudson River.

THE GAZEBO TO DRAW YOU INTO THE GARDEN

While our gazebo certainly overlooks a view, it is by no means a grand and imposing one. Ours looks south across a 10-acre meadow to wooded hills and down the valley toward Brattleboro, Vermont, some 10 miles south (again, see figure 6.12). Our gazebo fulfills another purpose for a small building: to act as a destination, a sheltering place deep in the garden that invites people to explore our entire garden. When guests arrive at our garden, they can look out across the lawns and garden from the front door of the house and just see the peak of the roof of the gazebo. It is a civilized note, a shelter from light rain or hot sun; gazebo and garden shed act like bookends for our garden, anchoring foreground and background.

As guests walk into our garden, that bit of roof is in their minds. It acts as a hint of what's to come, and so a certain degree of anticipation is set up by those few square feet of cedar shingles visible from our driveway. When guests walk through many parts of our 1½-acre garden, they see part of the gazebo, but not all of it.

The entire south end of our garden is anchored by and focused on that gazebo. It also forms an implied extension of the architecture of the barn, the house, and the garden shed. To underpin the visual link between that gazebo and the house with attached barn 400 feet away, we stained the oak post and beams gray to echo the gray weathered boards of our old garden shed, as well as the gray stain on our 200-year-old farmhouse and barn.

A GAZEBO WITH FOUR VIEWS

Uprights and cross members of an open gazebo frame views. It's really quite magical how such a simple structure out in the garden can help you see your garden in a new way. Here are the four views we see from ours. After reading this, go out into your gazebo or to a spot where you might put one, to discover what you see from those four sides.

NORTH: One day I was sitting in the gazebo looking north up the 90-foot length of straight lawn path between two mixed shrub and perennial borders. I was astounded to see something I had not seen in five years of looking. There, in descending order, was the trian-

gular gable end of our house to the left and the gable end of our garden shed in the middle, and to the right of it and barely visible half a mile away, I could just barely make out the outline of the south gable end of our neighbor's barn across his cornfield. I realized that by pruning a couple of limbs from a maple tree in the middle ground and a few maple saplings by the dirt road behind the house, I would capture a clear view of that barn's gable end from the bench in our gazebo.

EAST: That discovery regarding the view north from the gazebo caused me to reassess the view in the other three directions. I sat on the east-facing chair in the gazebo and looked under the branches of a 100-year-old maple tree no more than 15 feet from where I sat. The gazebo uprights and cross members framed a Vermont still life: the arching branch of the maple, the low horizontal stone wall on the far side of the maple, the grouping of three pin oaks we had planted out in the meadow years ago, the teak bench sitting within the triangle of oaks, and the mowed path leading from the garden to that bench. I got my pruning saw and Felco #2s and, proceeding with great caution, pruned some of the lower branches of the maple to open up and more carefully compose the still life.

SOUTH: Then I stood in the gazebo and faced south. The gazebo framed a view of the stone wall, not 5 feet behind the gazebo, followed by a view of the west end of the 10-acre meadow, and from there, the dirt road, the wooded hills, and the view down the valley toward Brattleboro 10 miles south. How could I improve on that? Then it hit me. I turned around and faced north, and there was that 8-foot-wide, 90-foot-long panel of pure lawn geometry running straight to the gazebo entrance. Why not let that line leap right over the gazebo and stone wall and show up again

as a straight mowed path from the south side of the gazebo and continue to run some 300 feet down to the far edge of the meadow. It would be a path for the eye. I got on my John Deere riding mower with tape measure in hand and headed out into the meadow. I've mowed it weekly for the past six years.

WEST: This was exciting stuff. I then sat in the west-facing chair in the center of the gazebo, and I have to say that the west view in May is a knockout. Under a hedgerow of 10 or so high-pruned 100-year-old black cherries, black locusts, and maples, we have nur-

tured a carpet of white and blue *Phlox stolonifera*, *P. divaricata*, *Tiarella cordifolia*, and *Ajuga* 'Caitlin's Giant' some 40 feet wide and 100 feet long that have now all woven together. When they all bloom together, accented here and there with the acid green of *Euphorbia polychroma* and the pink of rhododendron 'Aglo,' it is extraordinary, especially when framed by the gazebo. But that day in August, I looked farther afield. I looked across the woodland garden and off into the distance. There, through a mass of maple limbs some 150 feet away, across the dirt road, I

FIGURE 6.12
We built the gazebo at the end of this long central lawn path to draw us and our visitors to the far end of our garden. Our house, garden shed, and gazebo provide three still points in an ever-changing garden.

SURPRISING USES FOR SMALL BUILDINGS

■ Fifteen years ago, a friend was sitting in the front room of her home east of Amherst, Massachusetts, looking out at the lawn and a few trees planted in it between her house and the busy road. Her barn, which doubled as a garage, was situated just off that busy road on the northeast corner of her front lawn, some 75 feet from her front door. Amherst was growing, traffic was increasing, and she didn't want to put up with the noise of visual pollution anymore. First she called up a carpenter to cut an 18-foot-wide, 12-foot-high opening in the back of her barn so that she could drive right through it. Then she hired a bulldozer operator to make a new driveway from the new opening in the back of the barn to a parking area closer to the house. All the excess topsoil, along with about 20 dump truck loads of more topsoil, got bermed up about 5 feet high out by the road in a big arcing curve from the barn to the other end of her property 100 feet from the barn. She then densely planted the berm with trees, shrubs, and perennials and now drives through the portal of her barn to a private front garden.

■ The late Bill Talbot, a sculptor and friend of mine from northwestern Connecticut, had a small one-story barn about 18 feet wide and 32 feet long attached to his home. Rather than continue storing his art supplies and lawn furniture in the barn, he built a new storage building on old lines well away from the house. Then he worked with a carpenter to take the metal roofing off the south-facing half of the roof and install sheets of glass instead. Then he hired a small front loader operator to excavate the gravel floor down 18 inches and backfill it with topsoil, leaving one area of existing gravel to support a table and chairs for eight. Over the next 20 years, he planted the most remarkable tropical garden within this 18-foot-high room. To eat dinner under a blooming acacia tree in mid-March is a wondrous experience.

■ John and Helen Daly asked me to help them site a 14-by-14-foot screened-in outbuilding they had just completed. I went along and discovered that what they had done was simply to remove the siding from a 100-year-old shed to expose all the uprights, bracing, and doorframe, leaving the roof intact. Their carpenter then replaced all that siding with screening and built a screened door from the old siding material. We decided to place the structure at the end of two rows of apple trees, which

could see our neighbor Harold Ranney's cows grazing on a hilltop half a mile away, their silhouettes outlined against the sky. I got my pruning saw and chainsaw and a 40-foot extension ladder, and following Mary's directions as she sat on the west-facing chair, I pruned a 20-foot-wide, 35-foot-high window between two maples. Now anyone who sits in the west-facing chair in the gazebo has this framed view of one of the most beautiful high meadows around, along with one of the last of the Jersey herds left in Vermont. All four of these views draw the agricultural past and present into our garden.

THE GAZEBO CAN BREAK DOWN VISUAL BARRIERS

Barry and Elsa Waxman had just moved from the suburbs of Boston into their new home in a high, expansive meadow in Vermont. Once the gardens and lawn I had designed were installed, I found that the mow line between lawn and meadow created a barrier, as it always does. There was no invitation to go from the house and surrounding gardens across the lawn and into the meadow. Elsa particularly loved the beauty of the meadow, and she agreed that she would love to walk in it. We hired Roger Kahle, who had built our framed a view of the meadows beyond and hills in the distance. We planted no gardens around it, just lawn.

You could do the same with any old shed or small outbuilding, but don't feel you need to remove the siding on all four sides of the building. Depending on wind, views, and privacy, you could remove it from one, two, or three sides only.

■ Fred Watson, a friend and avid gardener, had a small outbuilding at his farm in southern New Hampshire. He used it during the winter to store plants from his half-hardy collection but found that he needed to heat the building with electricity, something that irked him. Given that one of the primary crops of New Hampshire hill farms is rocks, he decided to employ their ability to collect and hold heat. He sheathed the south side of the shed up 8 feet to the roofline with copper and then laid topsoil against the copper sheathing, allowing it to assume its natural slope (its natural angle of repose). The slope started about 7 feet above grade and sloped down so that the bottom of the topsoil pile was about 10 feet away from the foundation of the shed. He then raked the ends of the soil down to form a clean slope (and shape) and then completely covered the soil with stones. In essence, he was following a very old New England tradition of stone mulching. Over time, moss took hold in the exposed soil between the irregularly shaped fieldstones; other diminutive perennials seeded themselves into the gaps as well. During the winter, the stones gathered heat all day, melting any snow that had fallen on them, and at night, they released that heat, thereby keeping the topsoil underneath – and the storage area within the shed – at a temperature above freezing.

■ Sonny Garcia and Tom Valva have a long, narrow garden at the back of their home in a suburb of San Francisco. They built a raised deck off the back of their kitchen so that they could sit outdoors and look down onto their garden. They then built a second freestanding raised deck at the very back of their garden. The underside of this 16-foot-square structure has become an enclosed utility and storage area, while a staircase on one side of the structure leads 8 feet up to a 16-foot-square garden viewing deck with handrails around it and table and chairs on it. From there, they can sit with friends and look down onto their intensely planted garden, one of the jewels of San Francisco gardening.

gazebo (see figure 6.4), to build one for the Waxmans on a point we had chosen after walking throughout their meadows looking for The View. Once the structure was completed, we planted a 75-foot-diameter circle of five sugar maple trees around the gazebo to make it feel cozy in their 50-acre meadow and then mowed a broadly curving 8-foot-wide, 200-foot-long path from lawn edge to gazebo. Because Roger had installed copper screens in the openings on each of the four sides of the gazebo, as well as on the door into it, grandchildren could sleep in the gazebo on a moonlit summer's night and not be bothered by mosquitoes.

Perhaps the most compelling change the gazebo, maples, and path effected was the assimilation of the meadow into a visual and physical relationship with the garden and, therefore, the house. Before, the mow line between meadow and lawn acted as a barrier, isolating the meadow from people in the house and garden. After, the lawn path broke down that isolating barrier, while the gazebo acted as the sheltering destination for the path. In one way or another, all outbuildings act in a similar way, drawing people to the shelter they provide and the gardens that surround them.

A GARDEN ALONG THE END OR SIDE OF A BARN

RAISED BEDS FOR VEGETABLES

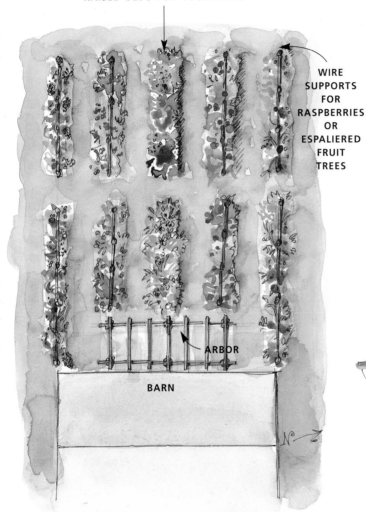

WIRE SUPPORTS FOR RASPBERRIES OR ESPALIERED FRUIT TREES

ARBOR

BARN

FIGURE 6.14 (BELOW)

The width of the building determines the width of the area. Align six raised beds for vegetable growing in line with the center of an arbor off one end of a building. Surround the area with a fence with gates for access.

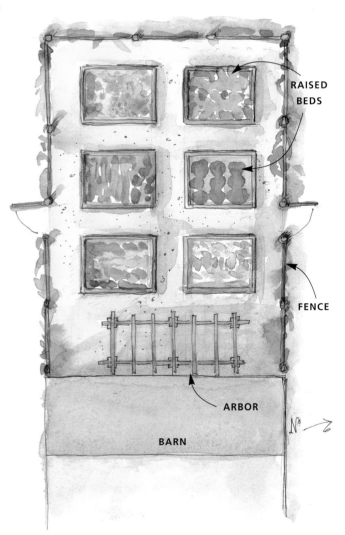

RAISED BEDS

FENCE

ARBOR

BARN

FIGURE 6.13 (ABOVE)

Center an arbor off one end of a large outbuilding. Run five pairs of long, narrow beds for soft fruits such as raspberries, blackberries, espaliered apples, or peaches. Central raised beds could be used to grow vegetables.

FIGURE 6.15

The side of this barn generates a line for a similarly painted picket fence some 16 feet from the barn. The fence not only captures the space between it and the barn but also provides a backdrop for the garden. Simplify paint color on sheds and barns to provide a quiet, unifying background for nearby gardens.

FIGURE 6.16

The ends of buildings generate the proportions and style of gardens adjacent to them. Here, a rustic barn provides the backdrop for an informal garden gathered around a circular brick sitting area. The gable ends of buildings don't shed ice and snow, so shrubs and trees near them won't be damaged in the winter.

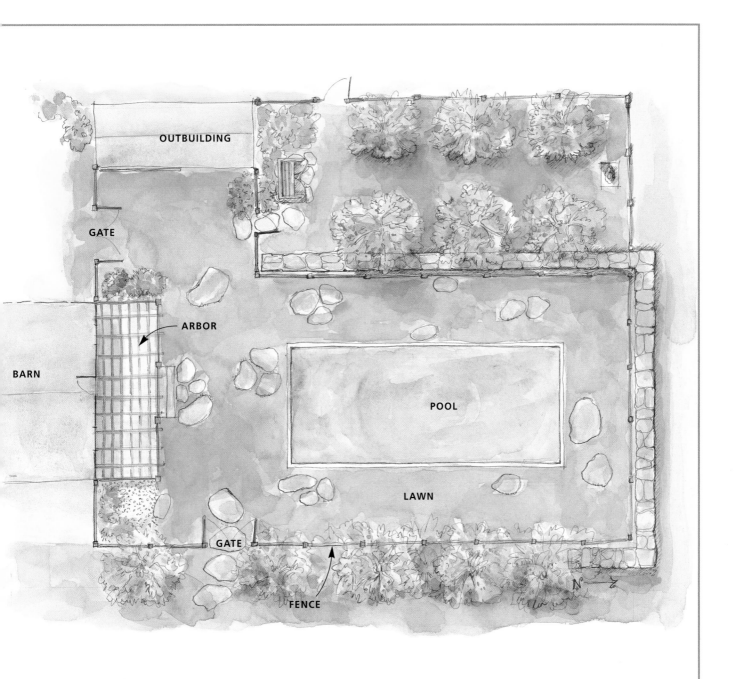

FIGURE 6.17

The side of a barn suggested the length of an arbor connected to it. The center of the arbor suggested the center for a swimming pool. A uniform lawn panel around three sides of the pool suggested fence and bed placement as well as the location of the retaining wall. The outbuilding near the barn helped me locate bench, fence, and crab apple allée for Barbara Ettinger and Sven Huseby.

PRACTICAL PROBLEMS SOLVED

1

ABOVEGROUND CASINGS FOR ARTESIAN WELLS

The top of a well casing is a black 6-inch-diameter steel pipe; only the top 18 to 36 inches of it is exposed above ground. If you have an artesian well, you will find this well casing close to your home and fitted with a blue cast-iron cap. Running up along one side of the casing and in under the cap is a 1-inch black plastic conduit. This conduit protects electrical wires that run down with your water line to the submersible pump suspended anywhere from 20 feet to hundreds of feet down in the water reservoir of your well. Because the role of the steel casing is to prevent soil, debris, and surface water from getting into your well, it runs from a minimum of 18 inches above grade through your topsoil, subsoil, and gravel or hardpan to about 12 inches into bedrock.

This discordant note in the garden can be hidden in a variety of ways, but keep in mind that if something goes wrong with your submersible pump, your plumber will have to pull it and the entire length of water and electrical lines out of the well. That line can either be coiled in a 30-foot-diameter circle on your lawn or pulled out into long looped lengths in nearby woodland or meadow. The point for gardeners, then, is to plant around three sides of the wellhead but leave a fourth side somewhat open so that service people

have an unencumbered space to which they can pull all that plastic line.

Here in the Northeast, a water line buried 4 to 5 feet deep, that is, the depth to which soil can freeze in the winter, runs from that casing usually in a straight line underground to a hole in your cellar wall and then to a pressure tank. When it comes to planting deeply rooted trees and shrubs, it is important to know exactly where that line is and at what depth. You don't want to plant important trees and large-scale shrubs above a water line that may have to be replaced at some point or where a backhoe might break the line as it digs a hole for a large-caliper tree.

You can use a number of simple solutions to hide this wellhead in such a way that it remains accessible, not the least of which is that you can paint it dark green, brown, or black to reduce its visual impact in your garden. For clients who live here in rural southern Vermont, I slipped a 36-inch-high hollow log over the 24-inch-high well cap, burying the bottom of the log 4 inches to make it look like the remaining trunk from a tree they had cut down. This solution will only look appropriate if your home is set in a wooded area where the cut-off trunk of a tree is something you would expect to see.

You can also design a garden around a well cap so that it is surrounded by shrubs and perennials on three sides, the fourth being within a flexibly branched *Pinus sylvestris* 'Nana' just at the lawn's edge. We dug a well 15 years ago, and plumbers have only had to gain access to the well cap once, caus-

ing only the slightest of damage to nearby plants. When it comes to hiding a well cap among shrubs and perennials, avoid planting only one or two shrubs near a wellhead and leaving it at that. Such a little island planting in a sea of lawn usually serves to draw attention to your attempt to screen a wellhead. Perhaps use the wellhead as an excuse to create a large new garden in that area. You can further screen the well cap from view by setting 24-to-36-inch-high boulders within the garden in such a way that they screen it.

If your home is over 100 years of age and was built at a time when dug wells were the only means of getting water for the house, then a little well house, the design for which could come from historic well houses, would look appropriate. Avoid setting a cute little pre-built well house over your well casing in the middle of the lawn.

The Main Points

- You only have a well cap if you have an artesian well; you don't have one if you are linked to a municipal water system.

- If you have a well cap at your woodland edge, set a hollow log over it.

- If it's in the middle of the lawn, plant a garden, not two evergreen shrubs, around it.

- Talk with your plumber to determine exactly where your water lines are from the well to your house. Record triangulation measurements and burial depth, which will enable you to locate the lines if any heavy equipment has to work near them.

2

DIGITAL SATELLITE RECEIVER DISHES

Television satellite dishes in North America, often discordant notes in our gardens, are focused on any one of around 300 satellites presently "parked" approximately 23,000 miles above the equator and roughly in line with the center of North America. Because they are in what is known as the Clarke Belt, a geosynchronous point in space first proposed by the science fiction writer Arthur C. Clarke that turns in sync with the Earth's rotation, they remain stationary relative to your dish or any other point on Earth. If you live in the central third of North America, your installer has to point your dish into the southern sky. Dishes located in the western third of North America must have an unimpeded view into the southeastern sky, while those in the eastern third of North America need an open view to the southwest.

Each satellite television provider has its satellite set at a slightly different angle relative to your home. For example, here in southern Vermont, a Direct TV dish needs to be set at 32 degrees above ground level to retrieve the signal; Dish Network's satellite is set at 22 degrees above ground level. The more acute, that is, the lower the angle, the more trees and shrubs will become a problem. The higher the dish is pointed into the sky, the less problem it will pose for the gardener who wants to screen his or her dish from sight. Talk to a variety of satellite providers to find out at what angle their dish will have

to be set if you want to position it on the ground and then screen it from view. Or visit a neighbor who has a system. Turn on their television, and then, with the remote, bring up the Install Menu onto the screen from the satellite receiver. Type in your zip code, and all the coordinates and angle for your dish with that provider will appear on the screen. Here are some solutions once you have chosen a provider.

You can solve the problem of the satellite dish in a number of ways. Site it as far away from the house as possible, thereby increasing the number of options you have regarding how you can hide it from view yet remain serviceable. You can install a dish 100 to 150 feet from the receiver atop your television without modifying the coaxial cable. If you want to place the dish

even farther away, there are many options. For example, your installer can insert an inexpensive 1-by-3-inch amplifier at around the 150- and 250-foot points in the coaxial cable. This will enable you to get the dish up to 350 feet from your television set. Another option is to increase the size of your dish from 18 inches to 24 inches. Work with a responsive installer, and you'll be able to position that little unsightly dish virtually anywhere on your property. Many installers who work for satellite dish companies here in the east want to install the dish close to your house with as little fuss as possible and leave. They won't bring up the options unless you ask for them.

If you don't have 200 to 300 feet of property to work with, if you don't want to pay to bury a long run of

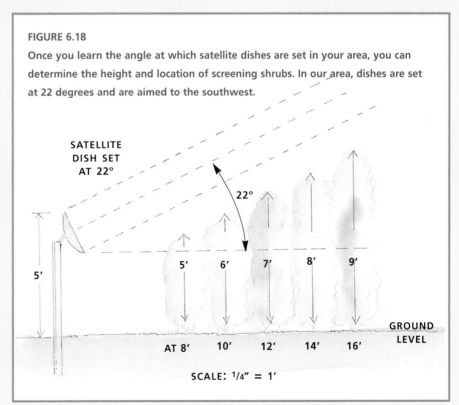

FIGURE 6.18
Once you learn the angle at which satellite dishes are set in your area, you can determine the height and location of screening shrubs. In our area, dishes are set at 22 degrees and are aimed to the southwest.

coaxial cable, or if distance doesn't help you find an unobtrusive place for the dish, try to find a place on the house, barn, or outbuilding that is out of sight from the most important parts of your garden. Some people have found good spots under a wooden raised deck, where it remains out of view from most parts of the garden. I have seen others set up under the soffit on the eave side or gable end of a barn, garage, or outbuilding.

Screening with plants is certainly an option, but the proximity of the shrubs to the dish will be a function of the angle at which the dish has to be set. You can determine this with a protractor once you know the angle at which your dish is set (see figure 6.18). Make a scaled drawing of your dish on a piece of graph paper, using a scale of $1/2$ inch = 1 foot. For example, draw a simple sketch of a 4-foot-high post with an 18-inch dish facing left and set at an angle that approximates your dish. Next draw a heavy horizontal line left from the base of the post to show approximate level ground. Now draw a dotted horizontal line from the bottom of the dish to the left and parallel with the line for the ground. Set the center of the base of your protractor where the dotted line meets the bottom of the dish, and then mark the 32-degree spot on your protractor. Draw a line with your pencil to connect the 32-degree mark with the center of the dish on your diagram. Now, using the $1/2$ inch = 1 foot scale, measure out 5 feet horizontally on the ground line and make a mark. Then measure vertically from that point on the ground line. You'll find that you can plant 4-to-5-foot-high shrubs 5 feet

away from the dish, just barely sufficient to screen the dish; go out 10 feet, and you can plant 6-to-7-foot shrubs, thereby screening the dish altogether. A dish set at 22 degrees, however, would drop those shrubs at each of those distances by about 12 to 18 inches. Keep in mind that these shrubs can't be allowed to grow higher.

The Main Points

- Dishes are getting smaller and smaller. Replace your older large dish with a modern small one.
- Before doing so, find a satellite dish installer who will work with you rather than tell you where your dish must go. There are many options.
- First work with the installer to find an inconspicuous place under the eave of the house or garage, keeping in mind the dish can be situated hundreds of feet from your home.
- If you can't find an out-of-the-way spot on a building, place it at the edge of your garden and then follow the mathematical guidelines in this entry to determine the maximum height of screening shrubs you'll need.
- Keep a record of where the dish line is buried so that you don't cut through it with a shovel.

3

ABOVEGROUND PROPANE AND NATURAL GAS TANKS

You may have one and possibly two unsightly 4-foot-high, 18-inch-diameter gray metal propane or natural

gas tanks resting upright and within inches of your home. Called "100 pounders" by propane suppliers here in the Northeast, they store liquified propane gas (LP) for a cooking stove and sometimes for home heating. On the other hand, you might well have a much larger and even more unpleasant-looking propane tank – as much as 4 feet high and 8 feet long – that holds a supply of propane gas for your furnace.

The 100 pounders are piped directly into your home, whereas the larger tanks are typically placed in a frame at least 10 feet from your house, with a copper or plastic line that runs from the tank underground and through the wall of your home to the appliance it feeds.

If you have two of either type, you know how unsightly they are. One very simple way to cut your visual problem in half is to check with your supplier to be certain that you, in fact, need both. I recently discovered that we have two only because for the last 40 years, well before we bought the place, there were always two here.

The reason there have been two here for years is true nationwide. Years ago, propane gas dealers did not have tanker trucks loaded with gas from which they could refill homeowners' tanks in situ. Instead, they would install two tanks. When one was empty, you called your supplier and he came along to replace the empty with a full tank. Today tanker trucks on regular refilling schedules are used throughout the industry, so you may well need only one tank. Once you have the minimum number necessary, you then want either to move them or to screen them from view, keeping in mind that the gas deliveryman will have to gain access to the top of both types of tanks with his 100-to-120-foot-long hose.

First, consider moving the tanks so that they are no longer in sight from important vantage points of your house or garden. You can locate your tanks at virtually any distance from the house as long as the deliveryman can park his truck in your driveway or on the road and reach the tanks. It's simply a question of the expense to which you are prepared to go to bury the copper or plastic tubing that will connect the tanks to your stove or heater without having to be set under existing or planned gardens.

For example, we have two 100-gallon tanks off the gable end of the barn to heat my office and two smaller, 4-foot-high tanks for our kitchen stove. I recently contacted my supplier to remove the two 100 pounders and bury a 50-foot copper line from one of the larger tanks heating my office directly to the kitchen stove linkup. In the meantime, I hired a fencing company to build a 6-foot-high fence around the two larger tanks with a 3-foot-wide hinged door in case the supplier has to remove or change one of the large tanks.

If, for some reason, you can't move yours and you have to resort to plants or fencing to screen them from sight, size up the situation. Is the tank under a dripline, where snow or excessive water will cascade down onto shrubs or fencing used for screening? Or is the tank located at the gable end of a building and thereby in a more protected, if not drier, spot? Is the tank located on the south side in full sun, on the east

or west sides in a half day of sun, or on the north side with no sun? Answers to these questions will help you select appropriate plants if they become part of your solution.

Choose shrubs that will mature or can easily be kept pruned to a height of between 5 and 8 feet. Also choose shrubs that are not brittle so that when the deliveryman fills the tank, he won't snap branches off in the process. Fothergilla, lilacs, forsythia, and *Arbor vitae* are all flexible plants; hydrangeas, mountain laurel, and rhododendrons are brittle.

To avoid drawing undue attention to the area of the tank and the isolated group of shrubs near it, integrate the shrubs within a larger garden idea along the whole side of the house. Repeat the shrubs you use to screen the tank at other points along that wall of your home. Underplant the shrubs with perennials to draw more attention to the plants and away from the tank.

You can also choose an architectural solution to the problem, either as a substitute to plants or in conjunction with them. Construct a 5-foot-high wooden fence with a 5-foot-high door around the tanks, and then plant vines on the fence or shrubs near it. Allow for 1/2-to-3/4-inch gaps between each vertical board to allow for good air circulation, paint it the same color as the adjacent wall of your home, and do not put a roof on it. The danger of poor air circulation surfaces in the highly unlikely possibility that a valve on a tank blows out and a large quantity of gas is released. If you provide good air circulation, gas will dissipate and not be a danger. Natural gas and propane suppli-

ers will not allow you to enclose tanks in buildings such as a garage, barn, or garden shed for this reason.

But whatever solution you choose – fencing and/or plantings – be certain that your solution fits into the larger scheme of things. Paint the fencing the same color as that of the house. Choose shrubs for screening that will appear elsewhere in the garden or along that same wall of the house. Set the fencing and adjacent plants into a larger garden, rather than just planting a few isolated shrubs to screen one or two small tanks. That is, try to make your planting and fencing decisions in light of other choices you have made nearby. Especially when it comes to plants, whenever in doubt, repeat.

The Main Points

- If you have more than one type of tank, ask your supplier whether you can consolidate in some way.
- If you find the tanks unsightly where they are, talk with your propane supplier about moving them to a location where they can be more easily screened.
- If they can't be readily moved, build a 5-to-6-foot-high solid board-and-batten or trellis fence around them. Plant clinging vines to integrate fence and garden, or plant shrubs that repeat those already in nearby gardens, leaving access for the deliveryman.
- Paint or stain the trellis or fence a color that echoes existing nearby colors to link new construction to old.

VISUAL INDEX TO THE PLANS

HERE YOU WILL FIND images of all forty-three garden and landscape plans used to illustrate the author's garden designs, ideas, and suggestions. Page references are included.

INTRODUCTION

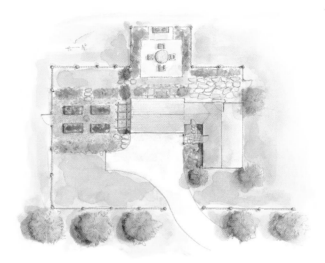

PAGE **14**

CHAPTER ONE: THE ENTRANCE GARDEN

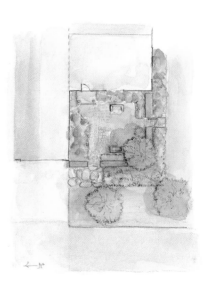

PAGE **22**   PAGE **30**   PAGE **31**

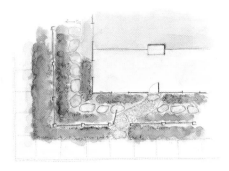

PAGE **35**

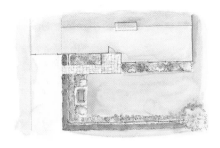

PAGE **38**

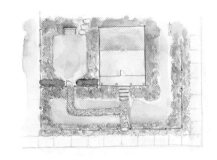

PAGE **40**

CHAPTER TWO: SIDE GARDENS

PAGE **56**

PAGE **59**

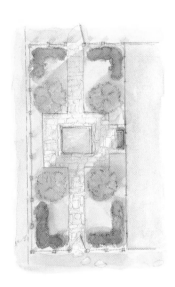

PAGE **61**

PAGE **64**

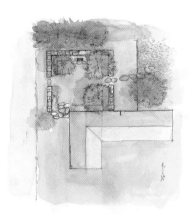

PAGE **66**

CHAPTER THREE: BACK GARDENS, PATIOS, AND TERRACES

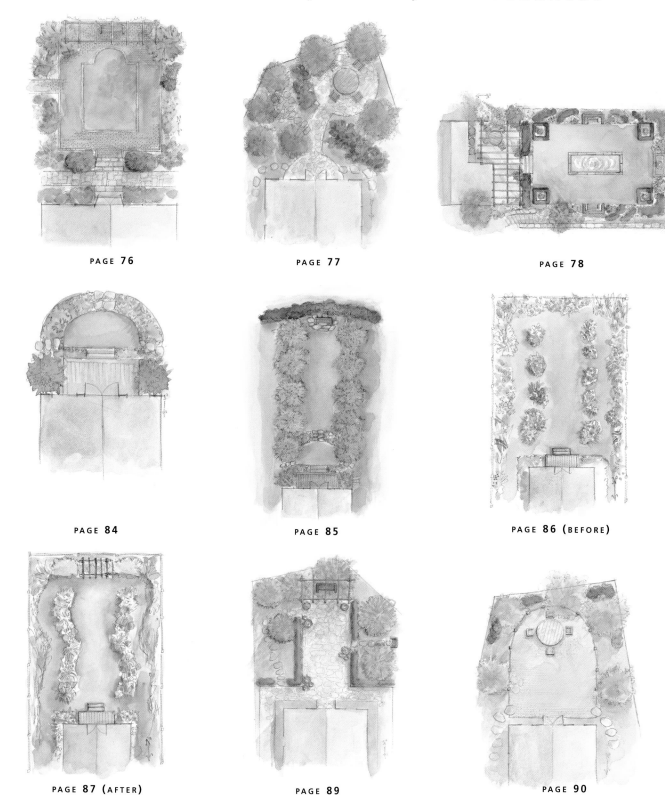

PAGE **76**

PAGE **77**

PAGE **78**

PAGE **84**

PAGE **85**

PAGE **86** (BEFORE)

PAGE **87** (AFTER)

PAGE **89**

PAGE **90**

CHAPTER FOUR: GARDENS IN AN ELL OR COURTYARD

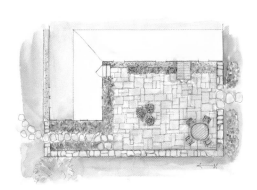

PAGE **107**

PAGE **108**

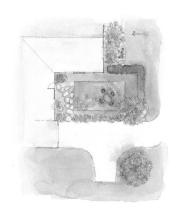

PAGE **109**

PAGE **110**

PAGE **112**

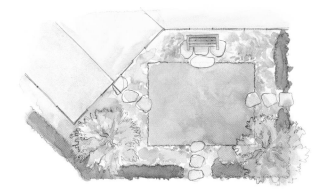

PAGE **113**

PAGE **115**

181

CHAPTER FIVE: GARDENS BETWEEN BUILDINGS

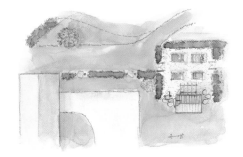

PAGE 131

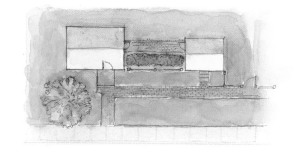

PAGE 132

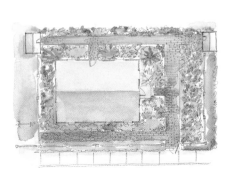

PAGE 133

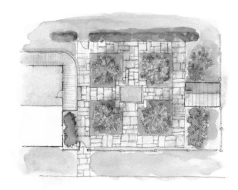

PAGE 133

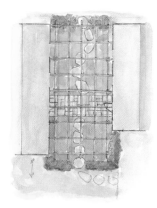

PAGE 134

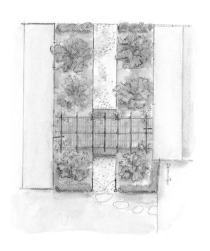

PAGE 134

PAGE 135

PAGE 135

PAGE **138**

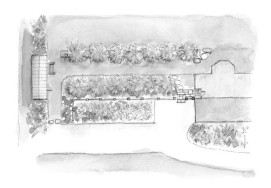

PAGE **143**

CHAPTER SIX: OUTBUILDINGS AND GARDENS

PAGE **160**

PAGE **170**

PAGE **170**

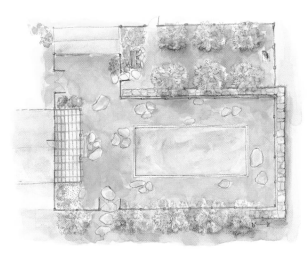

PAGE **173**

GLOSSARY

Allée – a walk with trees on either side

Arbor – a garden structure, often wooden, that supports vines or shrubs trained to the trelliswork under which people sit

Avenue – an approach to a home or property lined with trees on either side

Balusters – short upright posts in a series supporting a handrail that together form a balustrade

Casement window – a window with hinges on one of its vertical sides that swings open like a door

Clapboard – overlapping horizontal boards that cover the timber-framed wall of a house

Deck – an open, unroofed extension of the inside floor, often attached to the back or side of a house

Dormer – a roof gable, usually with a window set into it, which is usually located at right angles to the main roof structure. It is used to increase headroom and to allow light into rooms directly under the roof.

Dripline – that line below the length of an eave of a house onto which rainwater drips

Eave – the part of the roof that projects beyond the wall that supports it; the dripline is on the eave side of a house

Elevation – a drafting term indicating the perspective of a house or garden plan as seen when standing on the ground

Ell – a wing of a building that meets the main building at a right angle

Fascia – the flat, vertical surface immediately below the eave of a house; the fascia is a board nailed vertically along the ends of the roof rafters to cover them

Finish grade – the surface of leveled and smooth topsoil in final position for landscaping

Frost line – the depth to which frost penetrates the earth in your region

Gable end – the triangular end wall of a house that comes to a peak

Gazebo – a small roofed but usually open-sided building in a garden where one can sit

Geotextiles – any of the synthetic landscaping cloths that, once laid on the surface of the garden and covered with mulch, act as a weed barrier or to prevent erosion

Hip roof – a roof that rises from all four sides of the house

Hortus conclusus – a small enclosed garden

Loggia – a gallery open to the air on one side and set into the side of a home

Mullions – a vertical piece of stone, metal, or wood that divides panes of a window

Outbuilding – a barn, shed, or other structure that is situated away from the main building

Patio – a paved area adjoining a house that is used for outdoor living

Pavilion – an outdoor structure, often formal, acting as a summerhouse or other ornamental building in a garden

Paving – a stone or brick surface in a garden on which people walk or set furniture

Peastone – rounded stone the size of a pea

Pergola – a framed garden structure consisting of vertical posts and horizontal crosspieces under which people walk

Pitch – the incline or rise of a roof, typically expressed in feet of rise per feet of run of 12 feet. If a roof rises 10 feet over a horizontal distance of 12 feet, it has a pitch of 10/12.

Plan view – a drafting term indicating the

perspective of a structure or garden one would get if looking down on it from above.

Plot plan – a drawing which shows the location of a home relative to its building lot boundaries; it often includes lines to indicate elevation changes, as well as major trees, features such as stone walls, and sometimes major utility lines

Porte cochère – a roofed structure extending from the side or front entrance of a home over an adjacent driveway to shelter those getting in or out of vehicles

Portico – a porch or covered entrance to a building; a roof supported by pillars, posts, or columns

Riser – the upright (vertical) section of a step or stair

Sash – the frame that holds the glass in a window, often the movable part of the window

Scupper – the drain in a downspout or flat roof, usually connected to the downspout

Soffit – the underside of an eave; the underside of a roof overhang

Splash block – a pad of concrete or fiberglass which is placed under the lower end of the downspout from roof gutters to divert water away from the house

Tapis-vert – an expanse of usually rectangular lawn

Terrace – a paved outdoor area that is raised above adjacent ground by a retaining wall

Trelliage – trellis or latticework; sometimes decorative and not necessarily supporting vines

Trellis – a lattice for supporting a plant

Trim – the framing or edging of openings and other features on the façade of a home. Trim is usually a different color or material from that of the adjacent wall.

Also go to construction glossaries on the Internet:
Homeglossary.com
HomeownerForums.com
Homebuildingmanual.com
Soundhome.com

SELECTED BIBLIOGRAPHY

Alexander, Christopher, et al., *A Pattern Language*. New York: Oxford University Press, 1977.

Dickey, Page, *Inside Out: Relating Garden to House*. New York: Stewart, Tabouri and Chang, 2000.

Guinness, Bunny, *Creating a Family Garden: Magical Outdoor Spaces for All Ages*. New York: Abbeville Press, 1996.

Hayward, Gordon, *Garden Paths: Inspiring Designs and Practical Projects*. Ontario, Canada: Firefly Books, 1997.

Hayward, Gordon, *Garden Paths: A New Way to Solve Practical Problems in the Garden*. Boston: Houghton Mifflin, 1998.

Hayward, Gordon, *Stone in the Garden: Inspiring Designs and Practical Projects*. New York: W. W. Norton & Co., 2001.

Key, Richard, *Outdoor Living: Designing a Garden for Relaxation, Entertaining and Play*. London: Conran Octopus, 2000.

Moyer, Janet Lennox, *The Landscape Lighting Book*. New York: John Wiley and Sons, 1992.

Smith, Linda Joan, *Garden Structures*. New York: Workman Publishing, 2000.

PHOTOGRAPHY CREDITS

Richard Brown: Cover, pages 7, 91, 145, 164, 167, 188.

Patrick Chassé: pages 24, 25.

Richard Felber: pages 4, 8, 12, 21, 28, 33, 34, 42, 49, 51, 75, 80 (top), 80-81 (bottom), 81 (top), 82, 88, 105, 106, 111, 116, 117, 118, 127, 136, 140, 141 (right and left), 154, 155, 163, 171, 172.

Gordon Hayward: pages 26, 63, 103, 123, 130, 142.

Saxon Holt/Photo Botanic: pages 53 (top), 62, 65.

Andrew Lawson: pages 29, 79, 150.

Jerry Pavia: pages 52 (top), 52-53 (bottom), 54, 104, 137, 149.

INDEX

Page numbers in *italics* refer to illustrations.

acid rain, 69
air-conditioning condensers, 16, 124–25
Alexander, Christopher, 23–24, 57, 63, 139, 144
allees, 83, 85, 92, *143, 173*
   see also arbors; trees
annuals, for screening raised decks, 95
arbors, 81, *81,* 84, 85, *87, 89,* 102–3, *130, 134,*
   145, 170, 173
   see also allees; trees
artesian wells, 174
Austin, Alfred, 13
axial arrangement, axis, 81, 83, 145, *145*

back doors, *see* back gardens
back gardens, 74–101, *75, 76, 77, 78, 79*
   curved beds and paths in, 91, *91*
   from existing decks or patios, 80–86, *81, 82, 83,*
      84, 85, 86
   new designs for, 86–92, *87, 89, 90*
barbecues, 99–101, *100, 101*
barns, 160, *160,* 168, *170, 171, 172, 172, 173*
bedrock, designing around, 117–78
Belser garden, 59–60
Benedek, Armand, 27
Benjamin Powell House, *129*
boardwalks, *83*
Borges, Jorge Luis, 74
Boswell garden, 13–16
boundary lines, of gardens, *56, 77,* 86–87, *110,* 157
Bowles garden, 41
breezeways, *141*
Brett and Hearne garden, 100
Brine garden, 142, 143–44
Brookes, John, 79
bubblers, 109, *109*
buildings, outbuildings, 148–77, *149, 150, 153,*
   154, 155
   design and materials of, 156–57
   moving of, 132, *133*
   spaces between, 126–47, *127, 128, 129, 130,*
      131, 132, 133, 134, 135, 136, 137, 138,
      140, 141, 142, 143
   see also barns; garages; gazebos; sheds
bulkheads, 120–24, *121*
   painting of, 122, *122*
Byers garden, 122, 138

cars:
   blocking views of, 47–48, *47–48*
   see also garages; parking
Carver, George Washington, 20

ceilings, of gardens, 130
cellar doors, *see* bulkheads
Charleston, S.C., 129
Chasse, Patrick, 24, 27, 165
Church, Thomas, 20, 27, 50, 102
Clarke, Arthur C., 175
Clarke Belt, 175
climbing plants and vines, 93, *93,* 94, 95
clothes dryer vents, 146–47
clotheslines, 146
CLRR Associates, 76
Colonial Williamsburg, 121, 129, *129, 132,* 133,
   133
color:
   of painted bulkheads, 121, 122, *122*
   of painted outbuildings, 153–54, 171
condensers, air-conditioning, 16, 124–25
Cooke garden, 107–8, 109
courtyards:
   gardens in, 32–34, 102–5, *104, 105,* 114–17,
      114, 115, 116, *116, 117,* 119–24, *140*
   trees in, 113
   windows and, 116
Cowles garden, 60–62
Crespo garden, 114–15
curtain drains, 70, 119–20, *119*

Daly garden, 168
Dash garden, 153
Davidson garden, 29–30
decks:
   back gardens and, 80–86
   in ells, *108*
   railings on, 93, *93*
   raised, 93–95, *93*
deer, motion-sensing lights and, 46, 47
Dig Safe, 27
Dodge garden, 25, 94
drainage systems, *30,* 69–71, *70,* 119–20, *119*
driplines, 69–72, *70, 103*
   and ells, 119–20, *119*
driveways, 20, 22, 29, 47–49, *47*
drought-tolerant plants, 73
dry conditions, 71–72
drying, of laundry, 146–47
Dunbar garden, 63

east-facing gardens, 57–58
eaves, rainwater and, 69
edges, of gardens, *110*
   see also boundary lines, of gardens; property lines

edging stones, in erosion control, 119, *119*
electrical meter boxes, 43–45, *43*
elliptical gardens, 92
ells:
   drainage systems in, 119–20, *119*
   garden designs in, 31–32, *31,* 102–25, *106, 107,*
      108, 109, 110, 112
   naturally occurring features in, 117–18, *118*
   trees in, 113
   windows and, 116, *118*
entrance gardens, 20–49, *22, 24, 25, 26, 28, 29,* 30,
   42
   between buildings, *131*
   in courtyards, 32–34, 114–15, *115*
   in ells, 31–32, *31,* 110, *110, 112*
   and front doors, 27–28, *30, 31,* 32, *42*
   paths in, 20, 22, 23, 24, *25,* 27–28, 40–41, *40, 42*
   for "secret" entrances, 34–36
   trees in, *24, 25, 25*
erosion, *see* soil erosion
Ettinger/Huseby garden, *173*
excavation, 27

fastigiate deciduous trees, 113
fences, *34, 35,* 40, *40, 49, 61, 171*
   around air-conditioning condensers, 124–25
   in back gardens, *90*
   between buildings, *131,* 132, *132*
   between houses and streets, 37–38, *38,* 39
   in side gardens, *53,* 54, *54, 55, 56*
   around swimming pools, 95–96
   see also privacy; screening; trelliswork
Fisher garden, 116, *116*
floodlights, 46–47
"footprint," in scaled drawings, 36
Foundation Planting (Waugh), 39
foundation plantings, 27, 37, 38–39, 114, *114*
foundations, driplines and, 70, *70*
French doors, *75, 80*
front doors, entrance gardens and, 27–28, *30, 31,*
   32, 42
fruit trees, *170*
Fry garden, 77–78, *158,* 160–61

garages, 47–48, *47–48, 128, 134,* 142, *142,* 148,
   158, 160–61, 163
Garcia/Valva garden, 169
Gardens Are For People (Church), 20
gas tanks:
   aboveground, 176–77
   underground, 72–73, *73*

gazebos, 148, *150, 152,* 153, 154, 159, 165–69, *167*
Gee garden, 91–92
Geller, Keith, 35–36
Gothic arches, 153, *153*
grates, for barbecues, 100–101, *101*
gravel, around barbecues, 99–100, 101
Greek Revival style, 154, *154*
grills, *see* barbecues
guesthouses, *149,* 151
Guyer garden, 41
guy wires, 45–46

Hall garden, 124, 153–54
Harrison, Peter Joel, 148
Hartwell Perry's Ordinary, 121
hedges, *113*
    between buildings, *131,* 132, *132*
high-pruning, of trees, 68–69
Hobhouse, Penelope, 165
house siting, around natural features, 117–18
houses, gardens completely surrounding, 41
Huntington garden, 108–9

ice, driplines and, 71
Ingmire garden, *136*
irrigation systems, 71–72

Jelich garden, 132–33, *133*
Jenner garden, 143
Jesup, Jonathan, 156

Kahle, Roger, 168–69
Kheel garden, *107,* 120–21
Kieley garden, 120, 124
Kugle garden, 114

lampposts, 46
Lapham garden, 161, 163
laundry rooms, clotheslines and, 146
lawns, *40,* 91, *91,* 92
    in back gardens, 79, 83, *84, 85, 86, 87*
leachfields, 96, 97–98, 98–99
Lear garden, *63,* 102–4
Leys garden, 146
light fixtures, 46–47
liquefied propane (LP), 99
Longwood Gardens, 83
LP, *see* liquefied propane
Lyman garden, *154*

ma, 132
McCabe garden, 153, 163–65, *164*
McCanna garden, 163
McGrath garden, 64, 66
Marandino garden, 117–18
Matweecha garden, 139
meter boxes, 43–45, *43*
meterless technology, 44
meter pedestals, 44, *44*
Miller garden, *151*
module, 23, 54

motion-sensing detectors, 46, 47
mow line, 169

naturally occurring features, designing around, 117–78
negative space, 139
New Orleans, La., Garden District of, 40–41
nonparallel buildings, 143–44, *143*
north-facing gardens, 63–67, *63, 65, 66*
    see also shade, shade gardens

Oehme and Van Sweden, 28, 29
Olmsted Brothers, 39
outbuildings, *see* buildings, outbuildings
Owen garden, *153*

painting, *see* color
parking, 20, 22, 23, 47–49, *52, 53*
paths, path systems, 141–42, *142, 143*
    in back gardens, *80–81, 81, 83, 84, 87,* 91
    in entrance gardens, 20, 22, *22,* 23, 24, *24,* 25, *25, 26,* 27–28, *28, 28, 30,* 40–41, *40, 42, 83,* 137, *137*
    in side gardens, *53,* 67, *76*
    trelliswork and, 144
patios, 74–101
    back gardens and, 80–86
Pattern Language, A (Alexander), 23–24, 57, 63, 139, 144
Patterson, Bill, 83
Patterson garden, 104–5
paving, 90, *90,* 105, *105*
perennials, for leachfield plantings, 98–99
pergolas, *130, 134, 142,* 143
Peterson garden, *131*
phototropic instinct, 60, 65
planting, near septic tanks, 98–99
plants, trailing, *93,* 95
pools, *see* reflecting pools; swimming pools
porches, *63,* 110
positive space, 139
power lines, 43–45, *44*
primary paths, 28
privacy, 34–36, *35,* 37–39, *42,* 54–55, 68, 85, 89, *90,* 96, *132*
    see also fences; screening; trelliswork
propane tanks, *see* gas tanks
property lines, 56, *56, 61,* 77, 89, *89*
    see also boundary lines, of gardens
proportion, 23
Prozzo, Gerry, 68
Prozzo garden, 90–91, 112, 137, *137*
pump chambers, on septic tanks, 96, 97, 98
Punderson garden, 118

Quinn garden, 37–39

railings, on decks, 93, *93*
rainwater, soil erosion and, 69–71
raised beds, *170*
raised decks, 93–95, *93*

reflecting pools, 78, *78*
retaining walls, 20, 22, 23, 24, 30, *79, 80,* 90, 91, 107, *107*
risers, on buried gas tanks, 72–73
river rocks, *119,* 120
Robinson, Rodney, 76
roofs:
    overhangs of, 71–72
    valleys of, *30,* 71, 119, *119,* 120
Rose, James, 34–35

Saladino, John, 126, 139–40
satellite dishes, 175–76, *175*
scaled drawings, 36–37, *37,* 86, 142
Scott Arboretum, *76*
screening:
    of aboveground gas tanks, 177
    of air-conditioning condensers, 124–25
    on raised decks, 93–95, *93*
    of satellite dishes, 176
    of septic tank vents, 98
    see also fences; privacy; trelliswork
sculpture, 33–34
secondary paths, 28
"secret" entrances, garden design for, 34–36
septic tanks, 96–97, 98, 99
setback regulations, 157
Severinus Durfey House, 130, *130,* 133, *133*
Seymour garden, 53–57, 60, 65
shade, shade gardens, 63–67, *65, 66,* 68, 115, *115*
shaping, of trees, 68–69
sheds, 148, *149,* 151, *151,* 153, 154, 159, 163–65, *163, 164*
shingle-style home, 22, *22*
shrubs:
    under driplines, 70, 71
    for privacy, 35, *35*
side gardens, 42, *42,* 50–73, *51, 55, 61, 62, 63*
    fences and, *53,* 54, *54, 55, 56*
    paths in, *53,* 67, *76*
    shade and, *65, 66*
    west-facing, *59, 64*
Siegal garden, 23
siting, of outbuildings, 154, 159
sitting areas, *64, 79,* 89, *89,* 91, *104, 107,* 108–9, *113, 172*
sliding doors, *112*
Smith, Tim, 63
snow, driplines and, 70, 71
soil erosion, 69–72, 119–20, *119*
south-facing gardens, 60–63, *61,* 65, 90–91
space, positive vs. negative, 139
spaces between buildings, 126–47, *127, 128, 129, 133, 134, 135, 138, 142*
    breezeways and, *141*
    fences and, *131, 132*
    framed views and, *136*
    paths in, *137, 143*
    pergolas and, *142*
    urban, *130*
    walls and, *140, 141*

Stan Hywet Gardens, 116
stones, under driplines, 69, 70, *70,* 71, 119, *119*
streets:
    separation between houses and, 37–39, *38*
    see also privacy
sunlight, 57, 58, 59, 63
Sunrise Garden, 58
Sunset Garden, 60
swimming pools, 95–96, *173*

Talbot garden, 168
Taylor House, 129, *132*
telephone poles, 45
terraces, 74–101, *79*
Terry Shane Teaching Garden, 76
tertiary paths, 28
thinning, of trees, 68–69
trailing plants and vines, *93,* 95
transition spaces, 23–24, 67
trees:
    near barns, *170*
    for courtyard gardens, 113
    for ell gardens, 113
    in entrance gardens, *24, 25*

high-pruning of, 68–69
lighting fixtures and, 46, 47
near septic tanks and leachfields, 99
shaping of, 68–69
solving problems with, 68–69
thinning of, 68–69
    see also allees; arbors
trelliswork, *62, 81,* 93, 94–95, 124–25, 140, 144
    see also fences; privacy; screening
trenches, under driplines, 69, 70
triangulation, 36–37, 86

urban gardens, 130, *130*
utility lines:
    digging near, 27
    in scaled drawings, 36
utility poles, 45–46

valleys, of rooflines, 119, *119*
vegetables, raised beds for, *170*
vent pipes, of septic tanks, 96, 97, 98
vertical gardening, 30–31
vines, *93,* 94, 95, 140
Vitzthum garden, 108, 109

walls, in gardens, 20, 22, 23, 24, 30, *79, 80,* 90, 91, 107, *107,* 140, *140, 141*
Waterhouse garden, 20, 22–23
Watson garden, 169
Waugh, Frank, 39
Waxman garden, 57–58, 66–67, 168–69
Weather Service, U.S., 71
weeds, under decks, 94
wells, artesian, 174
Wells garden, 33–34
west-facing gardens, 58–60, *59, 64*
Wharton, Edith, 13
White garden, 154
windows, garden design and, *61,* 105, *105,* 112, 116, *118*
wires, guy, 45–46
Wirtz and Roossine garden, 35

Y-shape path, 109–10

zoning, 157